PROGRESSIVE POLITICS IN THE GLOBAL AGE

PROGRESSIVE POLITICS IN THE GLOBAL AGE

EDITED BY **HENRY TAM**

Polity

First published in 2001 by Polity Press in association with Blackwell
Publishers Ltd.

Editorial office:
Polity Press
65 Bridge Street
Cambridge CB2 1UR, UK

Marketing and production:
Blackwell Publishers Ltd
108 Cowley Road
Oxford OX4 1JF, UK

Published in the USA by
Blackwell Publishers Inc.
350 Main Street
Malden, MA 02148, USA

A catalogue record for this book is available from the British Library.

Library of Congress Cataloging-in-Publication Data
Progressive politics in the global age / edited by Henry Tam.
      p. cm.
   Includes bibliographical references and index.
   ISBN 0-7456-2578-9 — ISBN 0-7456-2579-7 (pbk.)
   1. Social justice. 2. Social policy. 3. Family policy. 4. Democracy. 5. Free enterprise. 6.
   Globalization. I. Tam, Henry Benedict.
   HM671 .P76 2001
   361.6'1—dc21
                                                                          2001032938
Typeset in 10.5 on 12 pt Sabon
by SetSystems Ltd, Saffron Walden, Essex
Printed in Great Britain by MPG Books Ltd, Bodmin, Cornwall

This book is printed on acid-free paper.

Contents

PART I   Progressive Ideals

Preface

This book grew out of a series of discussions on the future of progressive politics, which I held with European and American colleagues in 1999. We were concerned with the development of Anglo-American market ideology and its role in driving forward a neo-liberal agenda for globalization. Despite the emergence of 'Third Way' political strategies to counter the ascendancy of the New Right, the need to articulate progressive ideals and translate them fully into a global reform philosophy was yet to be met.

Whilst the contributors to this book have been variously described as 'civic republican', 'progressive communitarian', 'radical democrat' and 'federalist', there are important common strands in our social and political writings. Above all, we want to advance the progressive cause of greater democracy and social justice in the face of the rapidly growing global corporate powers. Market forces, cutting across all national and cultural boundaries, are undermining family stability, community spirit and political solidarity. Increasingly, the ability of nation-states to protect and enhance the well-being of their citizens is curtailed by worldwide business interests which shape financial policies, media priorities and the funding resources for political campaigns themselves.

I hope the reader will find this book both useful in bringing together the views of a wide range of progressive thinkers and stimulating in the challenges it poses to politicians and public policy advisers. Globalization is transforming the way we live our lives. Far from being a reason to submit to the rise of plutocratic rule, it makes it more urgent than ever to improve the tools for democratic action. In the global age, we need a global vision for progressive reforms.

I am grateful to the many colleagues who have either contributed directly to this book, or have given me much encouragement to take this project forward. The support given by David Held, Lynn Dunlop, Louise Knight, Sandra Byatt and Sarah Dancy at Polity is also much appreciated. Finally, my thanks as ever to Celia, Jessica and Antonia for being so positive about the time I had to set aside for writing and editing. The weekends, alas, are never long enough.

Henry Tam

Notes on Contributors

David M. Anderson is Director of the Democracy Online Project's National Task Force (www.democracyonline.org), Associate Research Professor at The George Washington University's Graduate School of Political Management in Washington, DC, and Senior Research Associate at the Institute for Communitarian Policy Studies, USA. He has published articles and columns on communitarian Third Way public philosophy, feminism, family policy and various aspects of online politics. (davidand@gwu.edu)

Benjamin R. Barber is Professor of Political Science, and Director of the Walt Whitman Center for the Culture and Politics of Democracy, Rutgers University, USA. He is the author of *The Conquest of Politics*, *Strong Democracy*, *Jihad vs McWorld*, *A Place for Us* and *A Passion for Democracy*. (bbarber@rci.rutgers.edu)

Robert N. Bellah is Elliot Professor of Sociology, Emeritus, University of California, Berkeley, USA. He is the author of *The Broken Covenant* and co-author of *Habits of the Heart* and *The Good Society*.

Mark S. Cladis is Associate Professor and Chair, Vassar College, NY, USA. He is the author of *A Communitarian Defense of Liberalism: Emile Durkheim and Contemporary Social Theory*. (macladis@vassar.edu)

Charles Derber is Professor of Sociology, Boston College, USA. He is the author of *The Wilding of America* and *Corporation Nation: How Corporations are Taking over our Lives and What We Can Do*

About It and co-author of *What's Left* and *Power in the Highest Degree*. He is currently working on a new book, *Awakening In Seattle*. (derber@bc.edu)

David Donnison is Emeritus Professor, Department of Urban Studies, University of Glasgow, Scotland. He is the author of *The Politics of Poverty*, *A Radical Agenda* and *Policies for a Just Society*. (carmichael@easynet.co.uk)

Aneta Gawkowska teaches sociology at the Collegium Civitas in Warsaw, Poland and is a researcher at the Graduate School for Social Research of the Institute of Philosophy and Sociology at the Polish Academy of Sciences. She has published many articles, including 'Free to Serve: Communitarian Attitudes in the Modern United States of America' and 'Walzer's Utopia of a Just Disharmony'. (s032@staszic.sns.waw.pl)

Ernst Hirsch Ballin is a member of the Dutch Council of State. Formerly, he was Minister of Justice of The Netherlands, Minister for The Netherlands' Antillean and Aruban Affairs and a Senator. He is also Professor of International Law, Tilburg University, The Netherlands. (ballin@kub.nl)

Bill Jordan is Professor of Social Policy at Exeter and Huddersfield Universities, UK, and Reader in Social Policy at North London University. He has held Visiting Chairs in Amsterdam, Aalborg, Bremen, Bratislava and Budapest. He is the author of some twenty books in political thought, social policy and social work, including, most recently, *The New Politics of Welfare* and (with Charlie Jordan) *Social Work and The Third Way: Tough Love as Social Policy*. (G.M.Watson@exeter.ac.uk)

David Dyssegaard Kallick is a regular contributor to the US progressive press, including the *Utne Reader*, *The Nation* and *In These Times*. He has written for *Fabian Review* in Britain and *Social Kritik* and *Information* in Denmark. He has been editor of *Social Policy* magazine, and senior fellow of the Preamble Center. He is a co-founder of the New York Progressive Network. (ddkallick@tuna.net)

Ferdinand Kinsky is Director of CIFE (International Centre for European Studies), Professor at the Institut européen des hautes études internationales, Nice, France, and Director of the quarterly review, *L'Europe en formation*. He is the author of *The Future of the European Union*. (kinsky.cife@wanadoo.fr)

Kevin Mattson is Professor of American Intellectual History at Ohio

University. He is the author of *Creating a Democratic Public: The Struggle for Urban Participatory Democracy During the Progressive Era* and, more recently, *When Intellectuals and Politics Mattered: The New Left as an Idea, Democratic Thought and the Possibilities of Radical Liberalism 1945–1970*. (mattson@rci.rutgers.edu)

Linda C. McClain is Professor of Law, School of Law, Hofstra University, USA, and former Faculty Fellow, Center for Ethics and the Professions, Harvard University, USA. She has published a number of articles on feminist jurisprudence, on prominent civic republican, communitarian and feminist critiques of liberalism, on matters of family and welfare policy and on reproductive rights and responsibilities. (lawlcm@hofstra.edu)

José Pérez Adán is Professor of Sociology, University of Valencia, Spain, President of the Inter-American Foundation for Science and Life and Head of the Spanish Association of Socioeconomics. He is the author of *La Salud Social* (Social Health). (jose.perez@uv.es)

Joseph Romance is in the Department of Political Science, Drew University, USA. He is a co-author of *A Republic of Parties: Debating the Two-party System*. (jromance@drew.edu)

Philip Selznick is Professor Emeritus of Law and Sociology, Jurisprudence and Social Policy Program, School of Law, University of California, Berkeley, USA, and founding Chairman of the Center for the Study of Law and Society and of the Jurisprudence and Social Policy Program in the School of Law at UC, Berkeley. He is the author of *The Moral Commonwealth*. His chapter in this volume is adapted from a work in progress, *The Communitarian Persuasion*, to be published by the Woodrow Wilson Center Press. (selznick@uclink4.berkeley.edu)

Marc Stears is a Fellow of Emmanuel College, Cambridge, UK, and teaches in the Faculty of Social and Political Sciences, University of Cambridge. He has written widely on Anglo-American ideologies and his book comparing American progressivism and British socialism in the early twentieth century is forthcoming with Oxford University Press. (mds49@hermes.cam.ac.uk)

Richard Steenvoorde is an Associate Researcher at the Faculty of Law, Globus Institute for Globalization and Sustainable Development, University of Tilburg, The Netherlands. He is also a Visiting Scholar at Sarum College, Salisbury, UK. (r.a.j.steenvoorde@kub.nl)

John Stewart is Emeritus Professor of Local Government, School of

Public Policy, University of Birmingham, UK. He is the author of numerous guides to local democracy and community government and co-author of *Management for the Public Domain*. (williaaa@spp2.bham.ac.uk)

William M. Sullivan is a Fellow at the Carnegie Foundation for the Advancement of Teaching, USA, and Professor of Philosophy, La Salle University, USA. He is the author of *Reconstructing Public Philosophy* and *Work and Integrity* and co-author of *Habits of the Heart* and *The Good Society*. (sullivan@carnegiefoundation.org)

Henry Tam is a public policy adviser in the UK and a Fellow of the Globus Institute for Globalization and Sustainable Development, University of Tilburg, The Netherlands. He has also been a guest lecturer at the University of Cambridge, UK, and other academic institutions. He is the author of *Communitarianism: A New Agenda for Politics and Citizenship*, *Serving the Public* and *Responsibility and Personal Interactions*, and editor of *Punishment, Excuses and Moral Development*. (htam.global@talk21.com)

Wim B. H. J. van de Donk is Professor of Public Administration at the University of Tilburg, in the Centre for Law, Public Administration and Informatization of the Schoordijk Institute, The Netherlands. He has published widely about the meaning of informatization for politics, democracy, law, policy-making and public administration. He is currently involved in research into the role of third-sector organizations in public governance. (wim.b.h.j.vddonk@kub.nl)

Wlodzimierz Wesolowski is Professor of Sociology at the Institute of Philosophy and Sociology, Polish Academy of Sciences and Collegium Civitas, Warsaw, Poland. His fields of interests are social stratification and political sociology. He has written extensively on political elites, political parties, parliament and transformations of post-communist societies. His recent works include *Polityka i Sejm: formowanie sie elity politycznej* (Politics and Seym: The Formation of the Political Elite, co-edited by Barbara Post) and *Partie: nieustanne klopoty* (Political Parties: Unending Troubles). (wwesolow@ifispan.waw.pl)

Stuart White is a Tutorial Fellow in Politics, Jesus College, University of Oxford, UK, and formerly Assistant Professor in the Department of Political Science at the Massachusetts Institute of Technology, USA. (stuart.white@jesus.ox.ac.uk)

Introduction

Henry Tam

Progressive politics has always been about dispelling prejudices, improving democratic accountabilities and, above all, promoting the common good. For over a century, its proponents have pressed for reforms against injustice and oppression of all forms. Why is it, then, that so many contemporary theorists as well as politicians are calling for a new way to take progressive ideas forward? Is it because globalization, the scourge of so many established standards and traditions, is derailing progressive politics from its conventional track? Could it be that the contentment of the rich, combined with the apathy of the poor, is draining away the democratic energy needed to fuel any major reform programme? Or has it got something to do with the belief that in order to gain power, politicians must be prepared to use any vehicle capable of winning the electoral race, even if it is not going to deliver many of the political changes that progressive advocates have always championed?

To understand the call for a major reorientation of progressive thinking, we need to turn back to the 1990s, by which time the New Right formula of market deregulation, public service cutbacks and invocation of traditional values had already dominated the political landscape in Britain and America for nearly two decades. Buoyed up by the collapse of Soviet communism, it was poised to take over the world as the definitive ideology for humankind (Fukuyama, 1992). Even in countries where social democratic regimes had managed previously to pursue progressive ideals without obstacles comparable to a Thatcherite or Reaganite policy agenda, the emergence of global financial and trading arrangements in line with the distinctly Anglo-

American laissez-faire market model began to set unprecedented limits on what nation-states could do for the welfare of their own citizens.

Both Sweden and Germany, for example, have found that their progressive achievements were being eroded by transnational market forces. In 1994, Sweden discovered that international purchasers were rejecting its bonds. Faced with higher borrowing costs than all other advanced industrial nations, with the exception of Italy, Sweden was forced to tighten credit and cut public expenditure (Greider, 1996). The high inclusiveness that Swedish society once took pride in sustaining was further undermined when trade unions declared that their relatively strike-free, cooperative approach to moderating wage demands might not be able to continue as top Swedish executives began to award themselves increases of more than 100 per cent of their salaries. In response, the representative of Swedish employers claimed that 'Swedish companies are only adapting to a global market where top dogs at American and British companies, for instance, get much bigger salaries than their Swedish counterparts – and lose much less than the 60% that high earning Swedes pay in income tax' (Tunhammar, 2000). Similar problems have besieged Germany, where even a government headed by the Social Democratic Party was pressurized by global financiers into cutting its borrowing requirements by driving public sector pay increases to well below those obtained by private sector workers.

At the same time, the existence of tax havens has enabled corporations to exploit the human and environmental resources of an area and not have to pay anything in return. Furthermore, with the help of the Internet, businesses can have their nominal bases in countries with the lowest corporation tax rates and use computer-links rather than physical contacts to legitimize transactions. As businesses, and the opinion-forming media outlets they control, become more and more powerful, many of those with progressive aspirations fear that any attempt to revive the state-focused left-of-centre politics – once sustained by the postwar consensus – would only lead to more electoral defeats. Against this backdrop, a new approach was sought. For party political opponents of the New Right, it was to be found in a deliberate positioning of progressive politics as beyond both the New Right and the Old Left. Relaunching themselves as 'New Democrats' and 'New Labour' in the USA and UK respectively, they claimed to represent a new way – a Third Way – which brings with it a renewal of progressive politics for the global age. On such a platform, the Democratic governor, Bill Clinton, was elected American President in 1992 and the Labour leader, Tony Blair, became the

British Prime Minister in 1997. They, together with allied think tanks and sympathetic academics (Etzioni, 1995; Giddens, 1998), mapped out a new agenda designed to win over the support of the electorate as well as command the allegiance of progressive reformists. However, even before the new-style Democrats failed to retain the American presidency in the highly controversial 2000 elections, many had already expressed concerns that the challenge to revive progressive politics had not so much been met as bypassed.

The purpose of this book is to bring together thinkers who have been at the forefront of demanding a deeper examination of the direction that progressive politics should take in the new century. Unlike some of the 'Third Way' proponents who prefer to project themselves as uniquely 'new', the contributors to this book regard their writings as flowing from long-established currents of progressive thought, connecting not with any single 'guru', but with a diverse range of theorists united by a commitment to promote more inclusive and democratic communities (see, e.g., Barber, 1984; Bellah et al., 1996; Boswell, 1994; Derber, 1998; Donnison, 1991; Etzioni, 1997; Marquand, 1988; Phillips, 1991; Ranson and Stewart, 1994; Selznick, 1992; Sullivan, 1986; Tam, 1998; and Walzer, 1992).

Four aspects of progressive politics in particular are looked at in this book. First of all, we revisit the ideals which have underpinned progressive reforms. Whilst pragmatic compromises should never be ruled out in politics, it is important to have a clear overall vision, lest electoral vicissitudes lead to irrecoverable shifts away from the abiding goal of improving democracy and social justice. Secondly, we will consider why progressives should engage much more with how families of equals need to function in contemporary society, and what help they require in bringing up new generations of citizens. Instead of a false dichotomy of either relying totally on the state or leaving everything to individual families, we will explore the kind of mutual support that should exist between citizens' families and their state. Thirdly, the growth of corporate power and the alienation of citizens from political discourse have made it more urgent than ever to focus on issues of power and democracy. Again, the emphasis on encouraging communities and citizen groups to become more active in tackling the problems they face is not to be taken as a substitute for wider examinations of prevailing power structures. Governments, as the depository of the collective sovereign power of all citizens, must act to remove barriers which prevent the fair and open engagement of the public in shaping decisions by state or private bodies which affect their well-being. Finally, we will look at why globalization, far from making progressive reforms less appropriate, is creating new forms of instability and injustice which can only be rectified by political action. Precisely because the capacity of nation-states to act is increasingly restricted by the expansion of global corporate forces, we need to consider how new forms of governance can be developed. 'New' politics would be of little value if it does not deliver genuine solutions to the perennial problems of injustice and exclusion.

Let us begin with the issue of progressive ideals. The manner in which Third Way exponents on both sides of the Atlantic have tried to relaunch progressive politics as something significantly distinct not just from the New Right but also from the Old Left leaves many pondering just what aspects of traditional left-of-centre ideals were being jettisoned. In Anthony Giddens's characterization, for example, the Old Left had special features, such as 'pervasive' state involvement and domination, collectivism, Keynesian demand management, full employment, strong egalitarianism, a comprehensive welfare state and internationalism (Giddens, 1998). The problem with this characterization is that, on the one hand, it includes elements which few who sincerely embrace progressive politics can turn away from – the pursuit of full employment, commitment to reducing inequalities, a dependable state-backed system of welfare for all and belief in internationalist ideals. On the other hand, it points to areas which many within the progressive tradition have, long before the Third Way brand was conceived, devoted considerable energy to revising and adapting to changing circumstances – displacement of the 'pervasive' state model with partnership working, rejection of nationalization as a necessary political tool, supplementing Keynesian economics with supply-side management, and moving from a union-led collectivism to a participatory model of collective democracy.

Already, back in 1981, the statement, 'The road that was pursued by state socialism and, for other reasons, the road that is being pursued now by the new conservatism lead to societies we do not want to live in. Therefore, what we ought to consider is whether we should follow another road, and where it might lead us', was made by one of the founding members of the British SDP – Social Democratic Party (Williams, 1981). Significantly, the SDP did not see itself as establishing a new political tradition but as preserving one which social democrats across Europe and progressive liberals in North America had been successful in taking forward since the end of the Second World War. For the SDP, the danger was not that the postwar progressive politics was becoming obsolete, but that leading politicians on the left and some of their supporters were moving towards a state-centred model which, for progressives at any rate, was already long discredited. To understand this perspective, we have to move further back to the ideas of thinkers such as John Dewey, L. T. Hobhouse and other key figures of the American Progressives and British New Liberals, who shaped reform outlook from the end of the nineteenth century through to the 1930s and 1940s, laying the foundations for the American New Deal and the British welfare state.

It was, crucially, towards the last quarter of the nineteenth century that Anglo-American-style laissez-faire capitalism began to overtake both state and church in most English-speaking countries in being the most powerful force to impact on individual well-being and social cohesion. The people who knew best how to make money through business transactions started to reshape economic and political power structures in their own exclusive favour. Diametrically opposed to the new privileged classes, who stood to gain most from the commercial freedom to exploit human and natural resources, were those attracted to Marxist ideas which advocated the complete replacement of the market regime. However, not all those dissatisfied with the growing market ideology embraced Marxism. The 'progressives' – a term explicitly adopted by British Labour and Liberal politicians who shared a common agenda as well as by American reformists amongst Republicans, Democrats and Populists – rejected radical socialist ideas for three main reasons. To begin with, they could not accept the anti-democratic concentration of power in any single state institution or vanguard party as a reliable lever for change. Secondly, they regarded as dangerously naive the call to replace competitive processes and private ownership in every sphere by either comprehensive state planning or some form of idealized anarchy. Last but not least, they were firmly opposed to the violent overthrow of prevailing arrangements in favour of the untried and untested wisdom of a few revolutionary leaders.

The progressives preferred to introduce gradual reforms for the common good, building on steady improvements to the democratic infrastructure and to citizens' own capacity to participate in civic deliberations. In many ways, the threat of Marxist radicalism, especially with the rise of Soviet Communism in the early twentieth century, helped to challenge the complacency of capitalist societies and made them more ready to consider progressive reforms. Yet the visible decline of communist politics, culminating in the collapse of the Soviet regime, combined with the spread of the Anglo-American laissez-faire market system on a global scale, fuelled the triumphalism of the New Right. By the early 1990s, the prospects for progressive politics looked bleak. It was, therefore, significant that at that juncture Bill Clinton and Tony Blair reignited the progressive bid for political power with a common set of themes: securing equal opportunity for all; enhancing the responsibility of citizens *and* the government; and promoting a genuine sense of community. These themes appear to point to a continuation of the century-old progressive tradition. However, in seeking to avoid alienating the corporate sector in their quest for electoral success, both Clinton and Blair tried to project their politics as radically different from previous progressive governments in their respective country. Consequently, many people wondered whether progressive politics had found a new platform to deliver its reform objectives, or whether it was being watered down so much that it was becoming virtually indistinguishable from moderate, or, as some have called it, 'compassionate', conservatism.

In Part I of this book, the core ideals of progressive politics are considered by a group of theorists who bring a strong historical perspective to the debate. Robert Bellah and William Sullivan, in chapter 1 of this volume, expose the weaknesses of the Third Way attempt to renew progressive politics and argue instead for an approach which draws on richer cultural resources to sustain the drive for reforms. They maintain that no political movement can rely on shifting tactical alliances and compromises to succeed if the public at large cannot be motivated to engage in its realization. They illustrate their analysis with the examples of John Maynard Keynes and William Beveridge, who located their specific reform proposals within a much broader and deeper social vision of mutual responsibility and the common good. Bellah and Sullivan trace the underlying philosophy which inspired Keynes and Beveridge in Britain and progressive reformists such as Herbert Croly, John Dewey and Jane Addams in America to New Liberals of the late nineteenth and early twentieth century such as T. H. Green, L. T. Hobhouse and J. Hobson. The significance of the New Liberals is picked up and elaborated by Marc Stears and Stuart White in chapter 2. For Stears and White, the contemporary tendency amongst commentators like John Gray to view Third Way politics in terms of a revival of a centrist form of New Liberalism distorts not just what New Liberalism stood for, but overlooks the true path progressive reformists today should follow. They distinguish those liberals who embraced humanized competition as a key political objective from leading New Liberals who were committed to pursue the ideal of a cooperative commonwealth. Whilst the former drifted towards the Conservative Party, the latter became influential thinkers who contributed greatly to the founding of the progressive welfare state by the Labour Party.

In the remaining chapters of Part I, other perspectives on progressive ideals are examined. Ferdinand Kinsky describes in chapter 3 how personalist thinking on federalist distribution of power and the inclusion of all citizens as members of shared communities has been a major progressive force in Western Europe. From Eastern Europe, Wlodzimierz Wesolowski and Aneta Gawkowska reflect in chapter 4 on the ideal of solidarity and how it has in practice helped to drive forward a reform movement which steers clear of laissez-faire capitalism and state communism in Poland. Focusing on a central concept which has run through the entire history of progressive thought, Philip Selznick considers in chapter 5 why the quest for community is so important in giving purpose to progressive reforms. Importantly, Selznick explains that suspicions about ambivalence of what community life consists of in practice can only be overcome by a critical understanding of what kind of community we ought to promote.

In Part II of the book, we turn our attention to the interrelationships between families, citizens and the state. The postwar generations of left-of-centre politicians have on the whole neglected the importance of families and their role in socializing children into the responsible citizens of the future. Their oversight has meant that the issue has been seized by politicians on the right who advocate the retention of traditional family structures, irrespective of the inherent injustice they embodied for women, not to mention the potential abuse of paternal authority against children if the latter were not adequately protected by state-instituted systems. Furthermore, families cannot be expected to carry out their civic duties in bringing up good citizens if they are placed at such a social and economic disadvantage that they simply cannot function with any degree of stability or self-belief. It is no coincidence that in America and Britain, where the New Right philosophy has been dominant in making the state and society more and more subservient to market freedom, the rates for family breakdown, teenage pregnancies, school exclusion and youth offending are far higher than countries across continental Europe. The more that market forces are allowed to cut through human relationships within families and communities, the less able are parents to bring up their children in a secure and stable environment, and the bigger the challenge becomes for society – through its political processes – to rectify the problematic consequences.

Linda McClain tackles this subject in chapter 6, with reference to the New Democrat attempts in America to establish a new 'social contract' in support of working families. Such a contract is premised on the idea that good parenting and moral education are important in so far as they contribute to the development of democratic citizenship. However, as McClain points out, care work not paid for in commercial terms is nonetheless a vital component in sustaining healthy family life. An exclusive concern with improving access to employment can run the risk of undermining the value, and hence the practice, of care given by family members. Instead of compartmentalizing the needs of families into social and economic ones, a holistic approach is required. One proposal for developing a progressive family policy is put forward by David Anderson in chapter 7. Anderson's 'Family Unity Act' sets out how the new focus on helping families discharge their civic as well as their economic responsibilities can be taken forward with a specific package of support. His Family Unity Act is designed to appeal to progressive-minded members of the Republican as well as Democrat parties. He argues that democratically agreed policies and funding, implemented by state agencies, are far more likely to deliver the help needed by families than if it is left to individuals to cope on their own or corporations to choose whether or not to assist.

One of the dominant themes in New Right mythology is that traditional family values can work together with increasingly deregulated markets to produce more individuals who will look after themselves without reference to the state. In reality, market forces disrupt traditional care patterns in families and make it more pressing for the state to assist families in looking after their members effectively. As José Pérez Adán explains in chapter 8, even in a country such as Spain, where family and community ties have been considerably stronger than in America or Britain, the rapid spread of the anglophone consumerist culture means that nothing can be taken for granted any more in terms of family policy. Pérez Adán considers recent electoral battles in Spain to show that politicians who have been on the whole progressive in wanting to combat injustice and poverty have nonetheless not yet registered the need to respond to the impact that globalization has on family and community life.

The call to parents to give better care to their children is hollow, if not downright hypocritical, when it is made by people who are demanding that workers should be prepared to work longer and more irregular hours, accept low wages and move long distances to find new jobs even though that would involve uprooting children and elderly parents, leaving them without any community-based care network to call on. The affront to people's dignity in denying what they ought to be able to rely on as citizens of a civilized community is an issue addressed by Joseph Romance in chapter 9. Romance explains why a progressive notion of citizenship should engage both the responsible participation of individual citizens and the commitment of the state to meet their needs. He praises the intention of welfare reform to return a sense of self-belief to those who have not been able to make an adequate living for themselves and their families, but warns that the rhetoric of reform must not be used as a front to cut public expenditure when the reform programme can only work with a higher level of governmental support. Progressive politics needs to shift welfare policies from being subsidies for the poor to serving as investment in the development of inclusive communities for all.

One of the most difficult obstacles for progressive reforms has always been the unequal distribution of political power. The drive towards greater enfranchisement for citizens in the developed countries from around the mid-nineteenth to mid-twentieth century moved the political systems in those countries towards much more equitable power structures. However, since the 1970s corporate power, helped by an expanding global laissez-faire market system, has been in the ascendancy. Corporate power controls the financial markets, which can virtually dictate the economic policies of most countries in the world, the media where public opinions are shaped and, not least, the level of electoral campaign funds available to competing political parties. It is understandable that both New Democrats and New Labour position themselves as business-friendly parties. But this approach is accompanied by the constant danger of losing sight of policy objectives which many businesses simply reject. In Part III of the book, we turn to the dilemma of how unjust power structures can be reformed in the midst of corporate hegemony.

Many politicians and their advisers now assume that the only effective means to change the corporate sector is to speak its language, share its perspective and grant it concessions in return for specific reform support. This has been well exemplified by Giddens's defence of Third Way thinking (Giddens, 2000): emphasizing the importance of consumer choices with no corresponding reference to the plight of workers; equating private sector downsizing as a model for increasing customer responsiveness; accepting higher inequalities of outcome so long as they are created by equality of opportunity; justifying low tax policies on the basis that 'the better-off sections of the electorate have become resistant to paying very high taxes' (pp. 97–8); and declaring that welfare spending has reached its limit. If this outlook goes beyond electoral rhetoric and actually guides government policies, then it amounts to a radical departure from the progressive ideals of community and solidarity. Far from viewing taxation as a civic virtue which good citizens take pride in paying for their collective well-being, it denigrates it as a cost on private individuals which should in principle be kept to a minimum. Indeed, the negative portrayal of taxation is contrasted with the positive 'wealth creation' of commercial transactions. In other words, when a government seeks to raise more tax revenue from its citizens according to their abilities to pay in order to improve public health, reduce crime and protect the environment for all, that is somehow undesirable in itself. But when a private business raises its revenue from its customers – because it sells fast cars that pollute their environment, perfume that appeals to their vanity or cigarettes that damage their hearts and lungs – then it must be praised as a contribution to the country's wealth.

Of course, tax money could be misspent, the management of public services abused. But in most Western countries, the record of the vast majority of government bodies is undoubtedly better than that of many private organizations. The perfectly legitimate request that public money be handled wisely and efficiently is quite different from the untenable proposition that tax revenue is something to be reduced for its own sake. The real challenge is to engage citizens more in taking an active interest in the development of public policies and the channelling of collective resources to implement them. In chapter 10, Kevin Mattson examines the call for active citizenship and distinguishes between voluntary action which leaves the public domain untouched, and civic action which lies at the heart of a vibrant polity. For Mattson, democratic participation should be nurtured and protected at every level of community life. How decisions are made by neighbourhood associations, school governors, local authorities, business organizations, national governments or global institutions should be shaped by the deliberative involvement of those who will be affected by such decisions. The practical barriers are wide-ranging, but that is precisely why government bodies must be prepared to legislate if persuasion does not lead to effective reforms of decision-making structures in the private or public sector. Government institutions themselves must change and enable citizens to learn about and guide public policies.

The attempts to 'modernize' or 'reinvent' government are critically considered by John Stewart in chapter 11. Wider citizen involvement in public policy development cannot be reduced to the gathering of the unreflective views of individuals through opinion surveys, simply indicating which government policies would or would not gain popular support. The promotion of deliberative discussions of complex issues is an essential feature of a true learning society. Stewart points out that the New Right has distorted the function of management in the public domain by insisting that it should follow the example of commercial enterprise. Although Third Way exponents have recognized that this is a flawed approach, they have not mapped out a clear alternative consistent with progressive political thinking. By contrast, Stewart's vision of the public domain brings citizens and government bodies together to assess common problems and consider how best to respond to them. Neither a political elite nor an idealized market is invoked for resolving public dilemmas. Ordinary citizens, learning to co-operate in shared deliberations, hold the key.

In parallel with citizens being more effectively engaged in the shaping of public policies, the corporate powers which dominate not just national, but also global, policies need to be brought more under democratic controls. In chapter 12, Charles Derber criticizes the Third Way mindset, which all too readily concedes to businesses their demands for lower taxation, less regulation and greater labour flexibility. Ralph Nader, who stood against the broadly pro-business Gore and the unreservedly pro-business Bush in the hotly disputed 2000 American presidential election, had praised Derber's writings as a 'luminous contribution' to the 'awakening and heightened sensitivity about the concentration of too much power and wealth in too few hands' (Derber, 1998: x). The media consensus, itself shaped by the corporate interests of their multinational owners, has tried to marginalize any political views that are deeply critical of the business sector. Derber shows that unless there is the political courage to take action to make private corporations serve the public, and not vice versa, democracy will continue to be seriously undermined.

One of the reasons why politicians, even those who are sympathetic to progressive ideas, hesitate to take on corporate power is because they fear they would not be able to rally public support. The vicious circle begins with compromises with the business sector in order to secure political power and ends with a power that is no use in launching any serious reforms of unjust corporate practices. The public witnesses this and concludes that democratic politics is futile; voter turnout and civic participation decline further. In chapter 13, Benjamin Barber argues that the only remedy is to press for more democracy. With government, business institutions and civil society in general, Barber maintains that progressives need to keep faith with democratic engagement. If people are becoming seduced by commercial offers, reluctant to pay taxes, distrustful of the efficacy of public policy solutions, then the only democratic means to transform the situation is to reach out to them, explain the dangers of prevailing arrangements and persuade them to lend their support to an effective reform agenda. To pander to the selfish instincts of individuals as opposed to cultivating their civic virtues leads inexorably to pluto-cratic polarization and social fragmentation.

The degeneration of the civic-minded Roman Republic into the crass materialism of the Roman Empire could foreshadow the col-lapse of democratic nation-states into an all-embracing commercial imperialism. Already, the Anglo-American-inspired global market is sweeping aside social ties, civic loyalty – not to mention the ethos of public service. Instead, individuals are encouraged to view education as primarily about enhancing their earning capacity to satisfy their cravings for branded products. In an increasing number of schools, commercial sponsors are invited to have a direct presence to get their message across to successive generations of new consumers. In Part IV of our book, we turn our attention to the force of globalization. It is not surprising that one of the most prominent reasons cited by Third Way theorists and politicians for rethinking traditional social democratic and progressive liberal politics is that globalization has changed the rules of the game. Corporations can increasingly fix up transnational arrangements and individual states are left more and more powerless to regulate or tax business activities. Such activities, in turn, as Mark Cladis explains in chapter 14, threaten not only our system of democracy, but the sustainability of our living environment itself. Assumptions regarding the acceptability of globalization can-not be left unchallenged. In many cases, it is not so much the inevitability of a supranational process which drives the destructive consequences of global commercialization, but the choices made by individuals in their daily lives which shape the process. Such choices reflect preferences derived from personal conceptions of how our respective lives may be lived. Where conventional politics has been disengaging from such concerns, progressive politics in the global age should reconnect political strategies to the life experiences of citizens in their everyday communities.

The need to work with and support local communities in dealing with the large-scale transformation brought about by globalization is poignantly demonstrated in chapter 15, in which David Donnison contrasts the fates of two Scottish communities. Donnison argues that where globalization has damaged the economic infrastructure and social fabric of a community, there can be no substitute for public policies to rebuild the employment, education and housing opportunities required. He rejects Third Way rhetoric, which attempts to project support for the corporate sector as the key to regeneration. For him, any form of 'new' politics which does not enable those in a relatively powerless position to rebuild their own community strengths is unlikely to succeed in achieving long-term progressive objectives.

In chapter 16, David Dyssegaard Kallick outlines a range of economic development ideas from what he terms a 'New Progressive' perspective. Echoing Benjamin Barber's concern with pressing for more democracy across the political realm, the private sector and civil society in general, Kallick points to examples of action that can be taken forward in each of these domains. He highlights the problem of growing inequalities in countries like America, Britain and others, which follow their market-led model of deregulated growth, and suggests that civil society agencies, including labour unions, must be supported not only in democratizing themselves, but also in challenging pre-tax income differentials which undermine social cohesion.

The theme of new economic thinking is further developed by Bill Jordan in chapter 17. Jordan argues that far from globalization making it impossible to combat social and economic exclusion, it is disrupting the balance of power between established economic powers to such an extent that it may be possible for progressive economic reforms to come into play. Contrary to the prevalent view that globalization inevitably takes key economic decisions out of the hands of government bodies, he points to the degree to which political agencies and labour movements can work together to establish effective controls over commercial organizations. For this to happen, cultural resources on engendering a true sense of solidarity across classes divided by social mobility would need to be drawn upon.

Some Third Way exponents have suggested that progressive politicians can only win power if they refrain from challenging global corporations. In return, economic prosperity would continue to grow and, even with lower tax rates, there would be more tax revenue to be spent on improving health, education and other urgent social programmes. In reality, this is untenable for two reasons. First, it ignores the fact that the more dependent governments become in relation to businesses, the less able are they to reform the iniquitous practices that businesses have no wish to alter by themselves. That is why politicians should mobilize public opinion to support the progressive cause and build up a democratic base for reforms that may not entirely suit the corporate giants. Secondly, economic growth, premised on even the most addictive form of consumerism, cannot last forever. There will be recessions. When they happen, businesses will almost certainly argue that tax rates should go even lower and regulations reduced even further, so that they, above all else, can make a good recovery. Advocates for a progressive alliance with businesses would then face a dilemma: cut public support when the public most needs it, or rally business backing for enhanced public support which, further down the line, might help business to recover. A progressive political force would only contemplate the latter option. If businesses were to refuse to back it, the argument could be won by taking the issue directly to the people.

Of course, some would say that such an approach is a one-way ticket to the political wilderness. It is understandable that with the increasing corporate encroachment on state powers it may appear that nothing can stand any realistic chance of reining in global business powers. However, that is precisely why new political institutions need to be urgently developed. In chapter 18, Wim van de Donk, Ernst Hirsch Ballin and Richard Steenvoorde draw from the more progressive Third Way tradition in The Netherlands in outlining what could be done to help us navigate through the 'uncharted waters' of global power development. They refer in particular to the evolving institutions of the European Union, and it is instructive to note that those who are the most fervent advocates of laissez-faire markets are also prominent opponents of the European Union becoming a stronger political force, capable of dealing with corporate powers which operate across the nation-states of Europe.

Ultimately, all progressive-minded citizens and politicians have to face up to an inescapable dilemma. Moving forward too hastily, progressive politics could fall into reckless radicalism, wrecking all that is in place for the sake of an imaginary 'promised land'. Holding back too cautiously, it could slide into reactionary compromises, preserving prevailing power structures in spite of all the iniquities they contain. The task of progressive thinkers is to maintain a clear focus on the underlying ideals of inclusive community life and to check the effectiveness of current and alternative policies against them. The global age is bringing with it an unprecedented array of communication channels. These should be used to engage as many citizens as possible in sharpening their critical awareness of what political and corporate powers mean for their lives. Only by discovering how things could change for the better through collective democratic action would they be ready to mobilize and support progressive political reforms.

References

Barber, B. (1984) *Strong Democracy: Participatory Politics for a New Age* (Berkeley: University of California Press).

Bellah, R. N., Madsen, R., Sullivan, W. M., Swidler, A. and Tipton, S. M. (1996) *Habits of the Heart: Individualism and Commitment in American Life* (London: University of California Press).

Boswell, J. (1994) *Community and the Economy: The Theory of Public Co-operation* (London: Routledge).

Derber, C. (1998) *Corporation Nation* (New York: St Martin's Press).

Donnison, D. (1991) *A Radical Agenda: After the New Right and the Old Left* (London: Rivers Oram Press).

Etzioni, A. (1995) *The Spirit of Community* (London: Fontana Press).

Etzioni, A. (1997) *The New Golden Rule: Community and Morality in a Democratic Society* (New York: Basic Books).

Fukuyama, F. (1992) *The End of History and the Last Man* (London: Hamish Hamilton).

Giddens, A. (1998) *The Third Way* (Cambridge: Polity).

Giddens, A. (2000) *The Third Way and its Critics* (Cambridge: Polity).

Greider, W. (1996) *One World, Ready or Not: The Manic Logic of Global Capitalism* (New York: Simon Schuster).

Marquand, D. (1988) *The Unprincipled Society* (London: Fontana).

Phillips, A. (1991) *Engendering Democracy* (Cambridge: Polity).

Ranson, S. and Stewart, J. (1994) *Management for the Public Domain* (Basingstoke: Macmillan).

Selznick, P. (1992) *The Moral Commonwealth: Social Theory and the Promise of Community* (London: University of California Press).

Sullivan, W. M. (1986) *Reconstructing Public Philosophy* (London: University of California Press).

Tam, H. (1998) *Communitarianism: A New Agenda for Politics and Citizenship* (Basingstoke: Macmillan).

Tunhammar, G. (2000) *The Economist*, 'Those Egalitarian Swedes', 3 June.

Walzer, M. (1992) 'The Civil Society Argument', in C. Mouffe (ed.), *Dimensions of Radical Democracy: Pluralism, Citizenship and Community* (London: Verso).

Williams, S. (1981) *Politics is for People* (Harmondsworth: Penguin Books).

Further Reading

Barber, B. (1995) *Jihad versus McWorld* (New York: Times Books).

Bellah, R. N. (1995/96) 'Community Properly Understood', *The Responsive Community*, 6(1), Winter.

Cladis, M. S. (1992) *A Communitarian Defense of Liberalism: Emile Durkheim and Contemporary Social Theory* (Stanford: Stanford University Press).

Collini, S. (1979) *Liberalism and Sociology: L. T. Hobhouse and Political Argument in England 1880–1914* (Cambridge: Cambridge University Press).

Crouch, C. and Marquand, D. (1995) *Reinventing Collective Action* (Oxford: Blackwell).

Dennis, N. and Halsey, A. H. (1988) *English Ethical Socialism* (Oxford: Clarendon Press).

Derber, C. (1994) 'Communitarian Economics', *The Responsive Community*, 4(4), Fall.

Dewey, J. (1930) *The Quest for Certainty* (London: George Allen and Unwin).

Dewey, J. (1939) *Liberalism and Social Action*, reprinted in J. Ratner (ed.), *Intelligence in the Modern World: John Dewey's Philosophy* (New York: Random House).

Dewey, J. (1966) *Democracy and Education* (New York: Free Press).

Dewey, J. (1991) *The Public and its Problems* (Athens, OH: Ohio University Press).

Douglass, R. B. (1994) 'The Renewal of Democracy and the Communitarian Prospect', *The Responsive Community*, 4(3), Summer.

Freeden, M. (1986) *The New Liberalism: An Ideology of Social Reform* (Oxford: Clarendon Press).

Galston, W. (1991) *Liberal Purposes: Goods, Virtues, and Diversity in the Liberal State* (Cambridge: Cambridge University Press).

Giddens, A. (1994) *Beyond Left and Right: The Future of Radical Politics* (Cambridge: Polity).

Gray, J. (1993) *Beyond the New Right* (London: Routledge).

Gutmann, A. (1987) *Democratic Education* (Princeton: Princeton University Press).

Hall, J. A. (ed.) (1995) *Civil Society* (Cambridge: Polity).

Hirst, P. (1994) *Associative Democracy: New Forms of Social and Economic Governance* (Cambridge: Polity).

Hobhouse, L. T. (1921) *The Rational Good* (London: George Allen and Unwin).

Hobhouse, L. T. (1966) *Social Development* (London: George Allen and Unwin).

Hobhouse, L. T. (1994) *Liberalism and Other Writings*, ed. J. Meadowcroft (Cambridge: Cambridge University Press).

King, D. (1987) *The New Right: Politics, Markets, and Citizenship* (Basingstoke: Macmillan Education).

Kinsky, F. (1995) *Federalism: A Global Theory* (Nice: Centre international de formation Européenne).

Kloppenberg, J. T. (1986) *Uncertain Victory: Social Democracy and Progressivism in European and American Thought, 1870–1920* (Oxford: Oxford University Press).

Marquand, D. (1999) *The Progressive Dilemma* (London: Phoenix).

Mill, J. S. (1987) *On Socialism* (Buffalo, NY: Prometheus Books).

Mill, J. S. (1994) *Principles of Political Economy* (Oxford: Oxford University Press).

Miller, D. (1990) *Market, State and Community* (Oxford: Clarendon Press).

Mouffe, C. (ed.) (1992) *Dimensions of Radical Democracy: Pluralism, Citizenship and Community* (London: Verso).

Mounier, E. (1952) *Personalism* (London: Routledge).

Pateman, C. (1970) *Participation and Democratic Theory* (Cambridge: Cambridge University Press).

Ryan, A. (1995) *John Dewey and the High Tide of American Liberalism* (New York: W. W. Norton).

Sandel, M. (1982) *Liberalism and the Limits of Justice* (Cambridge: Cambridge University Press).

Sandel, M. (1996) *Democracy's Discontent* (London: Belknap Press of Harvard University Press).

Stewart, J. (1995) *Innovation in Democratic Practice* (Birmingham: INLOGOV).

Stewart, J. and Tam, H. (1997) *Putting Citizens First* (London: MJ/SOLACE).

Tam, H. (1993) 'How We Should Live', *The Philosopher*, October.

Tam, H. (ed.) (1994) *Marketing, Competition and the Public Sector* (Harlow: Longman).

Tam, H. (ed.) (1995) *The Citizens' Agenda* (Cambridge: White Horse Press).

Tam, H. (ed.) (1996) *Punishment, Excuses and Moral Development* (Aldershot: Avebury Press).

Tam, H. (1999) 'Time to take a Stand: Communitarian Ideas and Third Way Politics', *Local Government Voice*, July.

Walzer, M. (1983) *Spheres of Justice* (New York: Basic Books).

Walzer, M. (1987) *Interpretation and Social Criticism* (Cambridge, MA: Harvard University Press).

Walzer, M. (1994) *Thick and Thin* (Notre Dame, IN: University of Notre Dame Press).

Wesolowski, W. (1995) 'The Nature of Social Ties and the Future of Postcommunist Society', in J. A. Hall (ed.), *Civil Society* (Cambridge: Polity).

Young, M. and Halsey, A. H. (1995) *Family and Community Socialism* (London: IPPR).

PART I

PROGRESSIVE IDEALS

1

Cultural Resources for a Progressive Alternative

Robert N. Bellah and William M. Sullivan

The aim of steering a path between over-reliance on the market and excessive dependence on the state has always been at the heart of progressive politics. Recent attempts by so-called 'Third Way' thinkers and politicians to renew progressivism, however, have failed to deliver an agenda worthy of the progressive cause in the new century. According to Robert B. Reich (1999), the essence of the Third Way is to liberate market forces while easing the transition for those who would otherwise fall behind. In practice, it has turned out that the economic winners have been fewer than Reich would like, while the losers or those barely advancing have proven distressingly many. The Third Way has given the winners pretty much what they want. It has been far less successful in fulfilling the other part of its implicit bargain.

In the USA and the UK, even left-of-centre governments have built on a neo-liberal (or conservative, in US parlance) legacy to advance deregulation, privatization, free trade, more flexible labour markets and reduced social supports. While recent economic growth has aided those at the bottom of the ladder, it has done little to reduce inequalities significantly. Even less has it reduced economic insecurity for the majority. To succeed, claims Reich, 'the Third Way will need to be turned into a political movement all its own'. But that will demand a moral vision, an explicit 'social contract' in which the winners, in return for getting all they need to prosper and generate wealth, would agree to 'apply a portion of their added booty to equipping the losers' so that they can 'move into the fast-moving global economy together ... [as a] people who, because they are linked by culture and belief, are willing to pool certain of their resources so that all of their members have a fair chance of succeeding' (1999: 46–51). By appealing to patriotism and the sense of participating in a national historical project as the Third Way's missing moral fulcrum, Reich has identified more than a massive challenge to political leadership. He is underlining the often overlooked fact that culture, publicly shared symbolic meaning, matters decisively in politics. Without a political message with strong cultural resonance, no collective public action to reshape the 'social contract' in a truly progressive direction will be forthcoming.

Third Way attempts to renew progressive politics have frequently been confused in their own self-understanding and weak in their cultural appeal. Partly as a consequence, the 'new' politics of Clinton (and, indeed, Blair) has remained fragile despite popular leadership and some impressive accomplishments. Gore's narrow defeat in the 2000 presidential election, despite eight years of economic prosperity, may be regarded as strong evidence of this situation. So far, the cultural basis for the aspirations of Third Way thinking, importantly different in its several national articulations, continental European as well as British and American, has remained mostly inchoate. It is time we turned our attention to developing the symbolic resources which can enable citizens to interpret their concerns in ways that connect to the vision of human betterment with equity and solidarity that is the moral heart of progressive politics.

We believe that there are rich cultural resources for a progressive alternative and that they can be found in a strong conception of a good form of life shared in several variations in many overlapping communities. Much of this chapter will be devoted to describing those resources, but we want to clarify what we mean by cultural resources and how they function in different national societies to enable political advance through an historical illustration. Progressive politics has a history which dates from the nineteenth century, and as a body of ideas it has a distinct lineage. Its horizon and its goals have always been universal, reflecting and at the same time developing ideas of human betterment that resonate widely in Western culture and beyond. At the same time, as a political tradition, the strength of progressive politics has lain in its variety of local manifestations, as specific individuals and groups have tried to formulate their collective aspirations in ways that made sense and excited loyalty within specific national contexts.

To illustrate what this means, consider the two figures most identified with the idea of the mixed economy and the welfare state, the twin pillars of twentieth-century progressivism. Both were British:

John Maynard Keynes and William Beveridge. Keynes has become synonymous with the economic regime of those decades of prosperity, especially in the Anglo-American world, while Beveridge's idea of a 'welfare state' to provide social cohesion through institutions of civic membership has come virtually to define the political ideals of that era. If Keynes and Beveridge exemplify a kind of leadership that for a period promised to actualize the ideals of social democracy, it is important to notice the cultural and institutional bases of their role. Culturally, Keynes and Beveridge were the heirs and beneficiaries of a militant tradition in British intellectual life, centred around thinkers known as 'New Liberals' such as T. H. Green, L. T. Hobhouse and J. Hobson (see Stears and White, ch. 2 this volume). Similar intellectual developments were taking place in the United States from around the turn of the century in the broad 'Progressive' movement, including figures such as Herbert Croly, John Dewey and Jane Addams, often directly influenced by British thinking of the New Liberal stripe. All these developments were parts of a larger, transatlantic current of debate and discussion which succeeded in establishing a new perspective on long-lamented social ills such as poverty, urban disorder and disease (see Rodgers, 1998).

What was new, and shared by these groups, was the belief that social problems were the results of failures in social organization rather than of individual incompetence or vice. As the historian Harold Perkin notes: 'Problems thus defined as institutional and societal, rather than moral and individual, cried out for collective, professional solutions rather than moral discipline or exhortation' (1989: 357). The effect on politics, and ultimately on the shape of Britain and the United States as the twentieth century unfolded, was vast and dramatic. It is striking that Keynes's recent biographer, Robert Skidelsky, characterizes Keynes as consistently speaking 'in the name of culture rather than expertise'. In claiming a right to direct affairs, Skidelsky notes, Keynes 'addressed the world as a priest, not as a technician. And though he rearranged its theology, economics spoke through him, as a church, not as a branch of the differential calculus' (1992: 407). What Keynes relied upon were 'those larger frameworks of thought which had proportioned knowledge to the purposes of human life', frameworks closely connected to the sense of larger purpose that Skidelsky terms 'religion' (ibid. 408).

'We misunderstand Keynes', Skidelsky argues, 'if we see him simply as an academic economist and fail to recognize his self-understanding as a member of the British "clerisy" – a secular priesthood setting standards of value and behavior, practicing the arts of leadership and mutual accommodation' (ibid. 8). The same applies to William Beveridge, the author of the famous wartime reports on social insurance and full-employment policies which provided the architecture of the postwar social contract in the UK. Beveridge, like Keynes, came from a professional family, was educated at a public (that is, private boarding) school and then at Oxford. Like many idealistic Oxford undergraduates in the late nineteenth and early twentieth centuries, Beveridge was drawn into social service at Toynbee Hall in the slums of London's East End, putting his philosophical and social scientific training to work in studying unemployment. While Keynes pursued an academic career in economics at Cambridge, Beveridge worked in the high civil service, developing a widening system of social insurance which provided the practical basis for the postwar order. Along with many other, lesser known figures, Keynes and Beveridge exemplified the combination of intellectual and practical energies in the public service which the ideal of the clerisy was meant to evoke.

The term was coined in the nineteenth century by Samuel Taylor Coleridge to describe his hopes for a new kind of intellectual to help guide and improve a society reeling from the joint dislocations of industrial capitalism and revolutionary democracy. Well before Keynes and Beveridge, figures such as Thomas and Matthew Arnold, John Stuart Mill and T. H. Green created a cultural climate that allowed for important changes in the nation's educational system, shaped its first true civil service and helped inspire the social responsibility state of the mid-twentieth century. Keynes drew on this cultural heritage but also took it in a more inclusively democratic direction in his more speculative writings on economics, moral philosophy and the future of civilization. These were typically essays designed not for specialists or officials but for general public enlightenment and discussion. He insisted that economic growth was never an end in itself and that capitalism could never by itself produce a decent or humane civilization.

The point, Keynes liked to insist, was to maximize not material abundance but 'goodness' in the sense of a general ideal of cultivated humanity. It was the role of the economist, and especially the economist-statesman, to use governmental economic policy to make possible a swifter advance from an obsession with security and accumulation to what today are sometimes called 'post-materialist values'. Thus Keynes consistently looked not to business or the markets – even though he made and lost large sums on the London stock market – but to government and cultural institutions as the important agents of social progress. Since wealth was only a means rather than an end, Keynes advocated not only state regulation of the national economy, as is well known, but also the involvement of the state in shaping and altering the 'preferences' of individuals.

As nations become more affluent, argued Keynes, the state should invest and work to lead people to expand their preferences beyond material consumption towards the 'higher pleasures'. To confront the deflationary crisis of the Great Depression of the 1930s, Keynes famously advocated deficit spending and public investment. However, quite apart from economic emergency, as early as the 1920s he advocated extensive public investments in culture, education, grand civic architecture and 'protecting the countryside', not to improve economic performance but to enhance the quality of national life. Even higher education, access to which Keynes thought should be expanded and made less class-dependent, should, he thought, be seen less as a kind of economic investment in a skilled workforce than as a way to enhance civilization by spreading enjoyment of the higher pleasures.[1] It is not clear that these ideas flow from the discipline of economics. But they are consistent with his sense of calling as member of the national clerisy: counselling and persuading his fellow-citizens to consider the ethical dimension of the collective life, how they could best use their growing national wealth to 'live wisely and agreeably and well'.

As Anthony Giddens (1998) reminds us in *The Third Way: The Renewal of Social Democracy*, there is considerable evidence that we are today in a new cycle of modernity. In this current era, many of the solutions which Keynes, Beveridge and other earlier progressives developed need to be rethought and radically reformed. Yet, there is an evident continuity in moral aspiration and political purpose between their concerns and those that agitate us today. What we can learn from them, however, is not only the moral inspiration of their lives – though in today's cynical climate that is no small thing – but also the need to think reflexively about our problems within a progressive vision of politics as contributing to human betterment.

When one speaks of a progressive alternative, the question that naturally follows is: alternative to what? The obvious answer is alternative to both state domination and market domination. And what is that alternative? Again, the obvious but rather vague answer would be society. If we understand society as something close to what Jürgen Habermas calls the lifeworld – that is, the sphere of life governed by linguistic communication, which includes family, neighbourhood and the realm of public will formation – then we will begin to be a little more specific. From this point of view, state and market are parts of society and extend their capacities through the use of the non-linguistic media of power and money. They are essentially means through which society more effectively seeks to realize its intrinsic ends. But, as we have seen nowhere more clearly than in the twentieth century, the means may become ends in themselves, may invade and colonize the lifeworld, subordinating its intrinsic ends to the means turned ends of power and money. In the middle of the twentieth century this danger was clearest in the form of state totalitarianism. At the turn of the twenty-first century the danger is clearest from what might be called market totalitarianism. State power is still abused in many parts of the world and such abuse is not absent anywhere, but today the greater danger is from the marketization and commodification of every part of the lifeworld, which globalization in its primary meaning seems to signify.

If we ask what cultural resources might be alternative to these dangers, we might begin by asking what today is the progressive alternative to these ideological polar opposites? Here, terminology becomes problematic. There is something to be said for terms such as social democracy, democratic socialism, social liberalism or the new liberalism, and communitarianism, but they are all in some way or other problematic. Communitarianism has enjoyed a vogue of late – many of the contributors to this volume have used the term – and has the virtue of insisting on the social basis of personhood, but in the eyes of many of the proponents of individualism it is easily identified with totalitarianism or fundamentalism. After all, weren't the Nazis interested in promoting community (*Gemeinschaft*)? Those of us who have been labelled communitarians have become rather tired of explaining that we do not mean *that* kind of community. So, along with others in this volume, we are ready to use the term 'progressivism',[2] though that term too is quite vague until we know what the person who uses it means by progress. We hope to make our views on that issue clear by the end of the chapter.

As foils to our argument we will use Henry Tam's *Communitarianism: A New Agenda for Politics and Citizenship* (1998), which supplies the basis for what we mean by progressivism, but which we want to extend in some respects and qualify in others, and Anthony Giddens's *The Third Way* (1998) as representative of the Third Way approach that we think needs bolstering through a more vigorous and substantive progressivism. To make our own position clear, we believe that modernity and how to deal with it is the central problem for progressives. Our task is to recover modernity's genuine achievements from the deep pathologies which it has created. There is some affinity between our view and that of Habermas when he affirms the Enlightenment but wishes to save it from what he calls its distorted forms.

In *Communitarianism* Tam offers three central principles to define what we are now calling progressivism: cooperative enquiry, shared values and participation. Cooperative enquiry is a central principle because it is the process through which society gains its guiding knowledge. Although Tam recognizes Aristotle as an important predecessor in the development of cooperative enquiry, and, as we shall see, owes him a great deal in his thinking about the three principles generally, in speaking of cooperative enquiry he draws mainly from modern thinkers, beginning with Francis Bacon. We would argue that Aristotle is not the only premodern predecessor of cooperative enquiry but that, on the contrary, all the great religions and philosophies of the first millennium BC can be seen as important predecessors. If progressivism is not to be simply the ideology of modern Western secularists, we must examine its roots in all the great traditions and the potential these roots allow for an overlapping consensus on a global basis. In premodern societies, political power and economic necessity frequently limited the scope and application of cooperative enquiry, but we cannot afford to overlook the resources with which it provides us from long before modern times.

It would also be a mistake to make the Greek example and its direct successors our only model of cooperative enquiry. The prophetic movement in ancient Israel and the rabbinic movement in Judaism were also movements of cooperative enquiry, seeking to relate received traditions to current realities. Parallels can be found in Islam, Hinduism and Buddhism. In China cooperative enquiry enjoyed an efflorescence in the late first millennium BC and Confucianism and Taoism have had continuous traditions of cooperative enquiry ever since. Though the application of non-Western traditions to social reality suffered the same limitations as the Western ones in premodern times, they provide valuable sources for reflection for us today.

While cooperative enquiry covered many fields in all the premodern civilizations, it is safe to say that there was a focus on the ethical, usually, though varyingly, seen in a religious perspective. Here, it is Tam's second central principle of progressivism – shared values – that provides the context for useful dialogue with the ethical resources of the great traditions. Tam makes a surprising, though we think defensible, move when he spells out what the four shared values are and justifies his choice not with deductive argument but empirically, as being the common beliefs of mankind. We are not happy with Tam's term 'values', because in the contemporary scene it is used to describe whatever subjective and arbitrary beliefs any individual or group may have (as in 'you have your values, I have my values, and we'll just have to leave it at that'), which is just the opposite of how Tam wants to use the term, that is, as beliefs that have objective reality. To meet this terminological difficulty, we prefer to speak of 'virtues' or 'conceptions of the good' rather than values.

Let us consider the four conceptions that Tam takes as critical to characterize a good society: love, wisdom, justice and fulfilment. There is a strong Aristotelian feeling about this list. Wisdom and justice are cardinal virtues for Aristotle (as they were for Plato). Love, as Tam uses it, seems to have some other roots, but Aristotle's term for friendship, one of his most important virtues, is *philia*, which can be translated as 'love' in some contexts. Tam's notion of fulfilment has no equivalent Aristotelian virtue, but it approximates Aristotle's idea of happiness, by which he does not mean the modern notion of subjective pleasure, but a condition in which all one's capacities, especially the capacities for virtuous action, have been actualized or realized.

Looking at the first of Tam's ethical conceptions, love, let us note that he derives it from 'experiences of loving and being loved, caring for others, passion, tenderness, friendship, sympathy, kindness, compassion and devotion' (1998: 15). Although 'friendship' is part of this picture, the ideas of 'caring for others' and 'compassion and devotion' would appear to draw on more than Aristotle and to be influenced by the New Testament idea of love (*agape* in Greek, not *philia*), which is natural in a culture long saturated with Christian teachings. There are of course biblical equivalents for Tam's other virtues, notably justice and wisdom. But it would take no great effort to discover, as Tam's idea that these are the common ethical ideals of mankind would imply, that we can find overlapping equivalents in all the great traditions. Here we may just note the Confucian parallels of *jen*, variously translated as benevolence, humanity, human-heartedness, etc., to love, and *i* or *yi*, sometimes translated as righteousness, to justice.

We would argue that the primary virtues are not only shared throughout the human species – that is, present even in tribal societies that may not have a philosophical concept of them but understand them in practice – but even incipiently among some of the higher non-human mammals. Frans de Waal (1996) has convincingly described behaviour that can only be characterized as evidence for love and justice among the chimpanzees. Thus, if these virtues are not part of the genetic code, a potentiality for them must be genetic, and they are part of the cultural code in human beings.

Before we get too cheered by the evidence for morality among humans and higher mammals, we should remember what Aristotle and other classical thinkers did not forget: that for every virtue there is a corresponding vice – for Aristotle *two* corresponding vices, since he saw virtue as a mean between two contrasting vices (courage as the mean between cowardice and foolhardiness, for example). The vices are just as 'natural' as the virtues, indeed from some perspectives more natural, since the virtues must be learned. The capacity of the human psyche, amplified enormously by vicious institutions, to counter the life of the virtues with the most appalling behaviour is something to which any serious progressive needs to give attention. It is an issue to which we will return.

Linked to the fact that the virtues always exist in precarious relation to the vices is the fact that even when we have a sense of the right thing to do, and we must remember that virtue is more a matter of practice, even habit, than theory, we may not know how to relate our moral intuitions to new circumstances. It is here especially that we will depend on cooperative enquiry in clarifying what is required of us as individuals and communities.

Tam's third principle is participation in the process of decision-making by those affected by it. In modern times we have come increasingly to accept the idea of the inclusion of all members of a community in its decision-making process, although even where it is accepted in principle it is nowhere fully realized in practice. With respect to the third principle as well, we would argue that in premodern societies, though full participation was sharply limited, the idea was nevertheless present. When Saint Paul said that in Christ there is 'neither Jew nor Greek, slave nor free, male nor female', he was expressing an ideal that could be realized in the church if at all but was not then possible in political society. The Confucians argued that moral virtue knew no bounds of blood or class and that even a peasant could be a sage and thus in principle a ruler. The Buddhists had a saying that 'a monk does not bow down before a king', meaning that a serious pursuit of the religious life transcended the power relations of this world. It was the Greeks who came closest to our ideal of democratic participation – Aristotle spoke of the *polis* as a society in which citizens ruled and are ruled in turn – but there were sharp limits to their notion of citizenship, even in Athens: not only were women and slaves excluded, but so were resident aliens. Only adult males of Athenian descent were full members of the political community. Nevertheless, our modern idea of full inclusion owes much to these premodern precursors.

This might be a good point to allude to an issue that has plagued the discussion of communitarianism: that is, what kind of community for which full inclusion is the ideal are we talking about? Part of the problem arises from the scope of a community in which we can imagine an effective consensus about conceptions of the good. Alasdair MacIntyre (1999), for example, from whom we have learned much, nonetheless believes that a genuine political community must necessarily be a small one – he gives the examples of New England fishing towns, Welsh mining villages and the ancient *polis* – because only in such small communities could a really substantive consensus exist. We believe, however, that in the modern world this would amount to a counsel of despair, because so few people can live in such small bounded communities. Rather, we conceive of the relevant communities as involving multiple overlapping memberships and as ranging from neighbourhoods to churches to work groups to nations to the entire species. The richness of the shared conceptions of the good will certainly vary according to the several groups to which one belongs, but we believe that, though it requires much work to specify them, common beliefs can be found at every level and that people can be actively included in many different kinds of community.

In a sense, the progressive movement is part of the general trend of modernity, for modernity has been in many ways a movement to generalize and actualize the moral heritage of traditional societies. Modernity has been associated with the encouragement of cooperative enquiry at many levels; it has spawned efforts to create a more just and loving society in which wisdom is used to make possible greater human fulfilment; and it has seen significant advances towards greater social inclusion, extending full citizenship to those without property, to former slaves, to women and to minorities of various kinds, including racial and sexual minorities. We can never forget that advances derived from the cooperative enquiry of science, medicine and public health have exterminated many diseases, extended longevity and improved the quality of life, at least for significant portions of the human race.

At the same time modernity has been associated with some of the greatest horrors in human history: terrible wars, unrelenting persecutions, genocide and the creation of millions of refugees – in short, organized hatred that it would be hard to equal in any previous period. It has also been accompanied by unprecedented environmental devastation with, as yet, uncalculated consequences, economic collapses and, even in periods of relative prosperity, economic inequalities and uncertainties that have left many people in poverty and many others anxious and insecure. The technological achievements have been enormous, but every one of them has had its cost. The automobile, for example, is a great convenience but profoundly destructive both of city life and of the environment. It would be comforting to think that the good and the bad sides of modernity could be surgically separated and that we could have one without the other. But only a profound analysis of modernity will allow us to begin to see what are the deep causes of these pathologies and how our whole way of life may need to be reordered if we are not to face continuing catastrophes.

Most of the pathologies of modernity can be traced to the political and economic totalitarianisms to which it has given rise. The ultra-nationalism associated with political totalitarianism has spawned wars, persecutions, genocide and the mass expulsion of populations. Unrestrained markets have led to massive inequalities, not only within but between nations, grave instabilities associated with boom and bust, enormous population shifts as the market has rendered traditional agriculture unsustainable, forcing millions into the shanty-towns of enormous and under-serviced cities, and technological advance made subservient to corporate profit rather than human service. These aberrations have become possible when power and money have overwhelmed the operation of Tam's three central principles of progressivism: cooperative enquiry, shared values and participation.

The strength of the progressive perspective is that it understands that these aberrations have become possible in part because, in different ways, both power and money have operated to isolate the individual and weaken the communities in which individuals are embedded. Today, for example, the capitalist economy seeks to make it possible for the individual to satisfy all needs through market transactions. Its logical end is the individual alone with a computer (such an individual might not just consume but work alone with a computer) through which the purchase of everything is now available. Progressives through cooperative enquiry, the life of the virtues and political participation need to attempt to create numerous over-lapping communities that would reduce the power of the market and the state and make them the servants of the people and not their masters.

We should not forget that the influence of the bureaucratic state and the free market can be and have been, when exercised with moderation, a source of the liberation of the individual from oppressive and authoritarian group control. The modern state and market have made possible the creation of public space, particularly urban public space, within which progressive principles could be advanced. The institutionalization of rights, first civil, then political and social, became possible in societies that were increasingly differentiated and flexible politically and economically. Communitarians are sometimes accused of rejecting these achievements of modernity, but, as progressives, we wish to make it clear that we wish to preserve and extend them.

We do, nonetheless, see that the concept of the freedom of the individual and the institutional complex that made it sociologically possible contained the seeds of pathology when they led to reifying the individual consciousness and weakening the nexus of social solidarity. Robert Putnam (2000) has demonstrated the extent to which these processes have eroded the social and cultural bases of democratic collective action in the United States. This is very much in the tradition of progressive social thought, which has, since the nineteenth century, been concerned with combating these pathologies. It was Hegel who famously saw that the moralistic absolutizing of freedom in the case of Robespierre could turn into the absolutely destructive negativity of the reign of terror in the French Revolution. For Hegel, even the sublimity of Kant's ethical universalism would be only a moment of abstract morality (*Moralität*) unless it could be institutionalized in the actual ethical life (*Sittlichkeit*) of a people. Hegel worried that the increasing dominance of economic relations could undermine the very possibility of ethical life, either by atomizing society or, in reaction, by leading to an authoritarian state. These concerns with respect to major tendencies of modernity need to guide Third Way political understanding.

The job that we 'organic intellectuals' of the progressive movement inherit from Hegel, Mill, Green, Durkheim, Dewey, Beveridge and Keynes is to devise a political programme appropriate to the societies in which we live. If we are off the mark in our understanding of society, all the 'musts' and 'shoulds' in the world will not help us in the face of the reality we are up against. Our first task, if we are to combine moral seriousness with social scientific insight, is to consider how far we are from the kind of society that would embody Tam's three central principles, and how we might possibly get from here to there.

From this perspective, Anthony Giddens's *The Third Way* can provide a point of reference as well as critique. On the whole, Giddens avoids a critique of ontological individualism, its origin in the insecurities inherent in modern societies and its anti-civic consequences. His is a practical political programme, designed to meet the needs and fulfil the desires of contemporary citizens. It is to be preferred to the existing practical alternatives, but it is not clear that it can meet Robert Reich's challenge to provide an alternative to state-centred social democratic politics, on the one hand, or the market-enthusiasm of neo-liberalism, on the other. Giddens's presentation of the Third Way often seems to come close to splitting the difference between currently attractive alternatives – neo-liberal and social democratic – without offering either a new analysis or the prospect of deep institutional reform.

What might be done here? Consider for a moment one of Giddens's best encompassing policy ideas, his notion of the 'positive welfare society'. Giddens contrasts the principles he advocates with the list of problems to which William Beveridge addressed his pivotal 1942 *Report on Social Insurance and Allied Services*. As Giddens puts it, 'positive welfare would replace each of Beveridge's negatives with a positive: in place of Want, autonomy; not Disease but active health; instead of Ignorance, education, as a continuing part of life; rather than Squalor, well-being; and in place of Idleness, initiative' (1998: 128). Autonomy, health, education, well-being and initiative: these are the goods that Giddens wishes public policy at every level to foster. He emphasizes that they cannot be realized without considerable public provision and organization, for which the modern state, even transnational institutions, are essential. Giddens sums up the institutional meaning of the Third Way in the 'social investment state' which exists to serve the 'positive welfare society' in order to realize freedom for all its citizens, within a developing, interdependent global society. All this resonates with Keynes's advocacy of a broader cultural understanding of human freedom and fulfilment as the necessary justification, but even more the real purpose, of market economies.

How, concretely, might this make a difference in the current situation? Giddens's proposals would seem to imply that Third Way politics take up the earlier progressive assertion that economic imperatives must be evaluated, balanced against and, if necessary, subordinated to, ethical and cultural ends. Yet, the Third Way, as described by Reich, and by Giddens himself, has shied away from any formulation so sweeping or decisive, lest it be portrayed by its opponents as backward-looking or less than optimistic about the future of our market-driven societies. If, however, the only cultural resources we can call upon derive from the matrix of market fundamentalism (a position that Giddens would hardly defend), then we have little leverage over today's one-sided global order.

Giddens's notion of 'positive welfare' rightly focuses on the enhancement of individual life. To effectively criticize and challenge the hegemony of the reigning neo-liberalism, however, any Third Way political vision must spell out a richer and, finally, quite different understanding of individual flourishing. Here, Henry Tam's progressive communitarianism is a surer guide. What is crucial is to highlight, in policy as well as principle, what Tam calls 'Durkheim's "moral individualism"', according to which 'individuals are encouraged to fulfill their potential while recognizing that being able to contribute to the fulfillment of others is an integral (and *not* an instrumental) part of their own fulfillment' (1998: 224). In fact, only an understanding of freedom and human possibility considerably broader than – and therefore explicitly critical of – this reigning instrumental individualism, with its focus on the market, can provide a reasoned basis for an alternative political and social vision.

One of the focal points of such an alternative has to be the organization of the economy so that work can become more public in its focus and import. This would entail public support for the effort of citizens to contribute to the larger goals of the 'active welfare society' as well as private economic advancement. Here, the ability to draw upon a fuller understanding of freedom and the good life is crucial for imagining alternatives. Progressive thinkers have long emphasized the need for public action and institutions to uphold conditions for 'positive freedom', so that citizens have realistic options to fulfil themselves through taking part in significant collective purposes. Ulrich Beck, for example, has cited many studies across Europe which show that 'more and more people are looking both for meaningful work and opportunities for commitment outside of work. If society can upgrade and reward such commitment and put it on a level with gainful employment', he argues, 'it can create both individual identity and social cohesion' (quoted in Giddens, 1998: 127). This kind of culturally imaginative political vision, however, is exactly what the Third Way, at least in its American and British forms, has generally lacked or seemed too timid to develop.

We live in a world where persuasion, not coercion, is the only road to a progressive future. For this reason, the task of a genuinely progressive movement at the present time may be to develop, ideologically and organizationally, capacities for long-term influence. This will involve not only understanding better where we are and how we got here, but how the whole moral heritage of the human species might help us out of our present predicaments. Yet, at a time when the idea of democracy has attained perhaps its broadest appeal ever, there is special urgency in putting forward the moral nucleus of the progressive vision. This, we argue, is the idea that freedom is made secure and given content through solidarity, and that it is in the broadest civic membership possible that freedom finds significance and fulfilment.

Notes

1 The quotations are from 'Economic Possibilities For Our Grandchildren', cited in Skidelsky (1998).
2 'Progressivism' and 'progressive communitarianism' are the most frequently used terms by the contributors to this book. It is not so much a question of which specific term is being used as of the common strands that run through the different contributions, which point to a shared approach to renewing progressive politics.

References

de Waal, F. (1996) *Good Natured: The Origins of Right and Wrong in Humans and Other Animals* (Cambridge, MA: Harvard University Press).

Giddens, A. (1998) *The Third Way: The Renewal of Social Democracy* (Cambridge: Polity).

MacIntyre, A. (1999) *Dependent Rational Animals* (Chicago: Open Court).

Perkin, H. (1989) *The Rise of Professional Society: England Since 1880* (London and New York: Routledge).

Putnam, R. D. (2000) *Bowling Alone: The Collapse and Revival of American Community* (New York: Simon and Schuster).

Reich, R. C. (1999) 'We Are All Third Wayers Now', *The American Prospect*, March–April: 46–51.

Rodgers, D. T. (1998) *Atlantic Crossings: Social Politics in a Progressive Age* (Cambridge, MA: Belknap Press of Harvard University Press).

Skidelsky, R. (1992) *John Maynard Keynes: The Economist As Saviour, 1920–1937* (London: Macmillan).

Skidelsky, R. (1998) 'Two Cheers For Consumerism', *New York Times*, 14 August.

Tam, H. (1998) *Communitarianism: A New Agenda for Politics and Citizenship* (New York: New York University Press).

2

New Liberalism Revisited

Marc Stears and Stuart White

Looking Back to the Liberals

In contemporary discussions of the future of progressive politics there is a pronounced tendency for commentators to look back to the past for inspiration. The familiar perspectives of the Left – Marxist or Fabian socialist – are widely (though not necessarily correctly) thought to be exhausted. The best way forward, it is often claimed, is to retrieve a theoretical perspective which, though once displaced by these more familiar perspectives, now has more relevance to our times. In this vein, for example, Paul Hirst (1994; 1997) asks us to look back to the Guild Socialism of G. D. H. Cole and the mutualism of Pierre-Joseph Proudhon as inspiration for a new non-statist, 'associationist' model of economic democracy (see also Stears, 1998; Kinsky, ch. 3 this volume). The New Democrats in the USA claim to be looking back beyond 'big government' New Deal liberalism to the small-business-friendly New Freedom progressivism of Woodrow Wilson and Louis Brandeis.[1] Others refer us back to social republican ideology as variously expressed in later Chartist platforms, in the writings of Thomas Paine, Thomas Spence and, not least, Jean-Jacques Rousseau.[2] This tendency to look back for inspiration has been intensified in Britain by the Labour Party leadership's effective strategy of rebranding the party as 'New Labour' in stark contrast to 'Old Labour', and by its attempt to articulate a distinctive Third Way philosophy to clarify what New Labour is about. In response to the frequently asked questions, 'What does New Labour stand for?', and 'What is the Third Way?', commentators, and Tony Blair himself, have repeatedly appealed back to the 'New Liberalism', which is associated at the political level with the Liberal governments of 1906–14 (for Blair's view, see Blair, 1996).

A particularly cogent expression of this viewpoint is provided by John Gray. According to Gray, there is consensus in Britain in support of a 'post-social democratic conception of social justice'. The political philosophy which 'best expresses' this alleged consensus is 'liberalism – not the egalitarian liberalism of Rawls, but the New Liberalism advocated in Britain by L. T. Hobhouse, T. H. Green and John Maynard Keynes in the early decades of this century'. This was, according to Gray, 'a liberalism concerned with reconciling the demands of individual choice with the needs of social cohesion; but it was not . . . egalitarian'. Gray continues: 'Like John Stuart Mill before them, the New Liberals wanted a society in which all careers were open to talent, in which inequalities were neither fixed nor impermeable, and in which no one's basic needs went unmet. They rejected a stratified society but they saw nothing inherently unfair in economic inequalities.' In contemporary circumstances this New Liberal conception of social justice can be best met by targeting public spending on the most disadvantaged. Tax policies, Gray claims, 'need not be more than very moderately progressive' (1997: 8–9).

We believe that the New Liberals do indeed provide important lessons on the way forward for progressive politics. But these are not necessarily the lessons which Gray seeks here to draw out. Journalistic commentary on this subject typically overlooks the internal diversity of New Liberalism, the fact that, as a political movement, it brought people together with rather different philosophical perspectives. Attending to that diversity is, however, important in understanding New Liberalism and in considering the lessons it might have for contemporary progressivism.[3]

We shall proceed in this chapter as follows. We begin by presenting a brief historical account of the huge transformation which British liberalism underwent in the years prior to the First World War. Innovation in social policy was a key feature of liberalism in this period and the challenge of meeting the 'Social Question' forced Liberals to innovate ideologically. We then take a closer look at the ideology of New Liberalism, focusing on the writings of three leading lights of the period: John A. Hobson, Leonard T. Hobhouse and Winston S. Churchill. We distinguish between a centrist ideology of humanized competition, ably articulated by Churchill, and a more radical ideology of the cooperative commonwealth which we find in the works of Hobson and Hobhouse and which looks forward to the frankly socialist conception of society presented in the work of R. H. Tawney. Though both currents could converge in support of the Liberal government's struggle for social reform, the latter looked forward to a much deeper transformation of capitalist society than the former. John Gray picks up only on the former, relatively conservative current within New Liberalism, a current that readily supports his argument for a progressive politics that has minimized its egalitarian ambition. But we argue, finally, that it is in fact the latter, more radical current of New Liberalism which holds the real lessons for progressives today. This current offers, we think, the right model of how progressives should engage in politics: supporting struggles for immediate and partial reform, while embedding the case for immediate reform in an understanding of social justice which ultimately points to further and deeper social change.

The Transformation of Liberalism

The political rise of the New Liberals in the early twentieth century presents many striking parallels to that of New Labour at the century's end. In 1906, the Liberal Party returned to government in a landslide election victory after many years in the electoral wilderness. They had torn themselves apart for the previous two decades over the leading issue of the day – Irish Home Rule. Their electoral prospects had been resurrected only by Conservative administrative incompetence. Although their election victory itself was not much of a shock, the enormous scale of their victory did raise a few electoral eyebrows. Furthermore, like Tony Blair's late twentieth-century party, the victorious Liberals attempted to distance themselves from their predecessors by adopting the epithet 'New'.

Closer analysis, however, reveals that these analogies quickly break down. To begin with, the New Liberals were much bolder with their new-found power. Moreover, their transformation was far more dramatic. The last time that the Liberals had enjoyed parliamentary authority, under the leadership of William Ewart Gladstone, they had been the party of fiscal moderation, of balanced budgets, of laissez-faire, of keeping the government out of the economy and society and of rolling back the frontiers of the state. The self-styled New Liberal government of 1906, however, introduced a vast sweep of dramatic new social welfare reform: reform that often placed the government in the very heart of society and economy. Indeed, in many ways, this was the first of what were to become known as the 'tax and spend' governments.

On the spending side, the government introduced measures that covered the entirety of the life-cycle. The New Liberals aimed to secure free school meals and medical checks for needy children, administer a national system of Labour Exchanges for those looking for work, guarantee national health and unemployment insurance for the most vulnerable of the working population, oversee minimum wage boards for those in 'sweated industries' and directly provide old age pensions for those unable to work any longer. On the taxing side, all of this expansion was to be paid for by an increase in income tax on the rich, death duties and levies on the sale of land. In a few short years, Britain went from possessing one of the smallest systems of state poor relief in the industrialized world to possessing one of the, if not the, largest (Freeden, 1978). Progressive politicians and policy experts from Europe and from the United States looked on at the New Liberal government's activities with awe. These experts knew, even if most of the British public did not, that they were witnessing the beginning of the redistributive welfare state (see Rodgers, 1998).

The introduction of all these reforms did not go without opposition. Powerful press interests, the owners of large businesses and, most of all, the Conservative Party were enraged by the proposals. But the Liberals refused to compromise. The conflict between the parties came to an especially dramatic head when the Liberal Chancellor of the Exchequer, David Lloyd George, proposed to introduce a super tax on incomes of over £5,000 a year, death duties and a duty that would tax 20 per cent of the value of land use. Even though these proposals all look fairly modest from a post-Second World War standpoint, the budget so angered Conservative critics that they were willing to threaten a constitutional crisis. Using their in-built majority in the House of Lords, they threw the budget out. The elected chamber was thus defeated by the unelected one on the question that was most central to the whole business of government: the distribution of public resources. It prompted, in 1910, two of the most tightly and viciously fought general elections of British political history. Both were contested on the issue of 'Peers versus the People' and although neither really offered a decisive verdict, the Conservatives eventually gave in just before the British system of parliamentary democracy dissolved before them.

The question of what led to such a dramatic transformation of liberalism has puzzled historians and political scientists for generations. It was once thought that, however paradoxical it may seem, the best explanation lay with electoral calculation. On this view, although the New Liberals appeared to be bold, they were actually only acting expediently; they were desperately trying to survive in a rapidly evolving political environment. The case for such an interpretation begins with a glance at the immediate past. Throughout the late nineteenth century, Liberal politics was dominated by just one issue: Home Rule for Ireland. Driven on by the determination of Gladstone, this had blocked out almost every other concern. Following a series of staggering electoral defeats, however, and with Gladstone's retirement and death behind them, the Liberals needed to find an alternative issue with which to identify. The desire to do so was then joined by the demands of the ever-growing manual working class and by the apparent need to see off the challenge of the newly established Labour Party. With the Conservative Party attracting the support of the new middle class of professionals and businessmen, the Liberals needed to halt the rise of Labour, and to steal their working-class voters in order to survive. It was as such, the argument goes, that in 1906 the Liberals turned *en masse* to social reform.[4]

There is no doubt some truth in all of this, but there are also substantial weaknesses in such an explanation. Most notably, to contemporaries the Labour Party was not as great a threat as it appears with the benefit of hindsight. Labour won only two seats in the 1900 election, and polled little more than 1.5 per cent of the national vote. Furthermore, those Labour politicians who were elected, or who enjoyed some national prominence, were not fire-breathing radicals, demanding ever more expansive systems of welfare. Rather, they were, on the whole, trade-union officials interested in the day-to-day issues of union life. Indeed, as the leading Labour historian Duncan Tanner (1990) has revealed, on many issues of social policy the Labour Party's position was more moderate than that of the Liberal Party of 1906. The reason for this moderation is even more striking. Labour politicians were cautious on the question of state-based social reform because there was (and remains) very little evidence that the working class itself, or at least certain sections of it, was particularly interested in state social welfare at this time. Workers had their own institutions – trade unions, friendly societies, cooperatives, churches and chapels – which tried to cope with the welfare demands of their members. And even if these organizations were not always successful, they were at least independent; they were the workers' own organizations, where members made the rules and administered the funds. This was all the more important because many of them were sceptical, indeed even scared, of state intervention. The only experience most workers had of state social welfare

before 1906 was the workhouse of the New Poor Law – that institution so clearly portrayed in the works of Charles Dickens – where
poor relief was made available only in truly awful conditions. This
was a working-class population that knew nothing of old age pensions
or national insurance, let alone a functioning National Health Service
(Orloff and Skocpol, 1984; Pelling, 1979; Vincent, 1967).

The old argument about electoral expediency, then, does not
provide much of an explanation for the transformation of liberalism.
But that is not to say that the election results were not important in
shaping the process of change. The pattern of electoral devastation
in the 1890s and 1900, followed by dramatic electoral triumph in
1906, allowed a new generation of Liberal MPs to emerge. Unfettered by the interests and factional allegiances of the old liberal
order, the years in the wilderness brought in a new generation. In
1906, of the 401 Liberal MPs returned to Parliament, more than 200
had never sat there before. The pattern of innovation was reinforced
by a renewal amongst the civil service and the pressure groups that
advised the government. Experts in the quantitative study of social
policy and in the direction of large-scale social experiments, led by
the likes of B. S. Rowntree and the young William Beveridge, began
to infuse the policy-making machine in the early years of the twentieth century (Schweber, 1996). Shocked by the economic destitution
that their large-scale social surveys had revealed, and by the desperate
state of the volunteers for the British armed services in the Boer War,
these new experts had begun to shape both ideological and practical
responses to the old form of industrial capitalism (Rowntree, 1901).
As they entered the policy-making process for the first time, they
brought with them a series of new attitudes and new ideological
commitments to the centre of British government. It was those
commitments that shaped New Liberalism and those commitments
that created a new form of politics.

The Ideology of New Liberalism

Let us now take a closer look at the ideology which surrounded the
transformation of liberalism in these years. One of the new generation of up-and-coming politicians of the day, and at this time a
stalwart ally of the Chancellor Lloyd George, was Winston Churchill.
In 1909, in the course of the developing conflict with the Lords over
the 'People's Budget', Churchill published *Liberalism and the Social
Problem*, a collection of speeches and newspaper articles, which set

forth, as he saw it, the philosophy underpinning the government's programme of social reform. Of particular note, we think, is Churchill's essay, 'Liberalism and Socialism', in which he attempts to explain how the liberal conception of social reform differs from, while incorporating the valid insights of, socialism (1909: 67–84). For Churchill, the challenge for enlightened reformers is to find the right balance between 'collective organization' and 'individual incentive' (ibid. 80). On the one hand, he argues, the socialists are right to think that there must be, in modern society, a large sphere of 'collectivism'. The state must tax away the unearned increment to land value and use this to provide public services for all; it must regulate natural monopolies, perhaps even take these industries into public ownership; and it should become a 'reserve employer of labour' and undertake to care for 'the sick and aged, and, above all . . . the children' (ibid. 81). First and foremost, the state must seek the 'universal establishment of minimum standards of life and labour, and their progressive elevation as the increasing energies of production may permit' (ibid.). It must, as Churchill put it in another essay, ensure 'tolerable basic conditions for our fellow countrymen' (ibid. 224); it must protect its citizens against misfortunes 'that can happen to a man without his being in fault in any way, and without his being able to guard against them in any way' (ibid. 237). In this way, the state can ensure that the 'left-out millions', the 'shut out millions of the weak and poor', are able to achieve a basic standard of civilized existence (ibid. 78, 223).

The ambition, however, is clearly to set a floor beneath which no one shall be allowed to fall (through no fault of their own) and not to seek equality beyond that. As Churchill puts it, in a passage which expresses almost perfectly the predominant attitude towards inequality in today's New Labour circles:

> I do not want to see impaired the vigour of competition, but we can do much to mitigate the consequences of failure. We want to draw a line below which we will not allow persons to live and labour, yet above which they may compete with all the strength of their manhood. We want to have free competition upwards; we decline to allow free competition to run downwards. (ibid. 82)

The picture that emerges from Churchill's book is, then, remarkably similar to the version of New Liberal philosophy described by John Gray. The good, just society is a competitive, meritocratic society with (presumably) differential reward for the more talented. But it is a floor-constrained meritocracy, and public spending, targeted at the needy, is essential in fixing the floor. For short, we may refer to this conception of the good society as humanized competition. The end of progressive politics, on this Churchillian view, is to replace unfettered, laissez-faire competition with humanized competition. Of course, many liberal policies, such as the super tax, death duties and the raft of new land-based taxes which Lloyd George was cooking up, would have the effect of hitting those at the top of the income and/or wealth distribution ladder, and it is perhaps a telling comment on the aspirations of today's centre-left that Gray finds this particular aspect of liberal policy 'politically unfeasible' in contemporary circumstances. (Given the hostility of the House of Lords, such tax policies were not easy to implement then.) But the clear emphasis is on ensuring a universal basic floor of income, not on imposing some kind of universal ceiling to the acquisition of income and wealth.

Let us now turn to a second theorist of New Liberalism, the journalist and philosopher, L. T. Hobhouse. Hobhouse approaches the question of social reform in terms of a theory of distributive justice, what we may call his functionalist theory of distributive justice. He summarizes this theory as follows:

> The central point of Liberal economics . . . is the equation of social service and reward. This is the principle that every function of social value requires such remuneration as serves to stimulate and maintain its effective performance; that every one who performs such a function has a right . . . to such remuneration and no more; that the residue of existing wealth should be at the disposal of the community for social purposes. Further, it is the right . . . of every person capable of performing some useful social function that he should have the opportunity of doing so. (1994[1911]: 100)

A Liberal fiscal policy would, consistent with this conception of distributive justice, identify non-functional incomes, tax them, and use the funds to help ensure adequate opportunities for all to perform a useful social function. Targets for taxation thus included not only the usual liberal target of unearned increments in land values, but all ground rent, inherited wealth, income from speculation and all returns to labour above those necessary to bring forth productive effort at the socially required level and quality. Churchill, too, was ready to tax the unearned increment. But theorists such as Hobhouse looked to the deeper principle underlying that policy and arguably drew out the full policy implications of that principle with more consistency and with more extensive redistributive implication.

But the differences do not stop there. In the third edition of his book, *The Labour Movement*, Hobhouse makes clear that what is needed is a new ethos within production: 'We want a new spirit in economics – the spirit of mutual help, the sense of a common good. We want each man to feel that his daily work is a service to his kind, and that idleness or anti-social work are a disgrace' (1912: 75).[5] People should be rewarded according to function, and they should work not only from a concern for personal gain, but, in part, from a sense of social service. This addition is important because it impacts back on the issue of what kind of pay differentials are necessary to bring forth adequate productive efforts, and thus of how much inequality can be justified on functionalist grounds. If those with scarce talents view their work primarily in terms of the good it provides for them as individuals, then society may have to agree to pay them substantial differentials. But if the talented work primarily from a sense of social service, their efforts might be brought forth with less special pecuniary incentive. At the limit, in which all, as John Stuart Mill put it, have learned to dig and weave (as well as fight) for their country, there need be no differentials at all. All bring forth their best productive efforts from a sense of social duty (and/or intrinsic pleasure in the work) and receive the same social wage in return. This conception of the good society, society as a cooperative commonwealth, is less meritocratic and more egalitarian than that which we find expressed in Churchill's essays.

At least two things, however, kept Hobhouse firmly in the Liberal fold. One was his democratic gradualism. The cooperative commonwealth could not be built by destroying the existing social order and starting from scratch. It had to be built incrementally from within the existing social order and, moreover, in a manner consistent with democratic (parliamentary democratic) principles. The reforms of the 1906–14 government could be seen, in this light, as the first major steps in the right direction. The other was his refusal to see the state as the sole agency of coordination in the cooperative commonwealth. Though leftist New Liberals such as Hobhouse differed from Guild Socialists such as Cole in according a primary coordinating role to the state, the central thesis of *The Labour Movement* is that the cooperative commonwealth will gradually be built through an interactive, mutually supportive partnership between the state, at central and municipal levels, and movements within what we now call 'civil society'. Trade unions would always retain a key role in protecting producer interests, enforcing payment of a fair, functionally appropriate pre-tax wage. And production itself would be increasingly coordinated and controlled, not only by the state, but by the cooperative movement. Growth in the public and cooperative sectors would help diffuse the new spirit of mutual service through society.

A very similar conception of the good society, as egalitarian cooperative commonwealth, can be seen in the writings of the other leading New Liberal theorist, John A. Hobson, who considers the 'right limits on individual property' and comes up with a version of the functional wage standard described in Hobhouse's writings: 'Whatever portion of his product is necessary as an incentive to an individual to work is his rightful property' (Hobson, 1996 [1902]: 173). The word 'incentive' here may mislead. As Hobson immediately goes on to explain, this 'incentive' payment in fact consists of two things: '(1) That which is necessary to maintain, from the material physical standpoint, the energy required for work; (2) that which, in addition, *may be required* to operate as an inducement upon the will of the individual' (ibid. 173, italics added). The first component of the incentive payment is relatively fixed. But the second will vary with: '(a) The satisfaction which accrues to the individual from the functional activity involved in working. (b) The selfishness of the individual' (ibid.). These are not fixed, but can change. As society succeeds in making work more intrinsically rewarding, and in cultivating the ethos of mutual service to which Hobhouse looks forward, the more incentive payments for productive services will converge on the first 'material physical' component. Primary wages will (probably) become more equal, and a growing proportion of the national product will become part of the 'surplus', over and above the functional fair wage, which can be taxed without impairment of productive effort and spent for the good of all citizens. The vision is not at all unlike the sketchy account given by Karl Marx (1976) of how pay differentials which are essential on efficiency grounds in the early stages of communism will gradually give way to a distribution based on the principle, 'From each according to his ability, to each according to his needs.'[6]

This brief discussion does not, of course, in any way cover the full range and diversity of New Liberal opinion. But we have, perhaps, managed to draw out two distinct social ideals which informed New Liberalism: an ideal of humanized competition, and an ideal of the cooperative commonwealth. The former is meritocratic; the latter is more substantially egalitarian and even, at the limit, convergent in its distributive aims with the Marxist conception of the good society. The significance of this difference should not be exaggerated, of course. 'Centrist' and 'leftist' New Liberals could agree on many points of immediate policy in the years before World War I. The differences became much more significant, however, after that war had devastated British liberalism.[7] In the radically changed political context of the postwar years, as liberalism waned and the Labour Party rose, a centrist New Liberal like Churchill felt compelled to retreat from the Liberal to the Conservative Party, while leftist New Liberals such as Hobson and Charles Trevelyan moved into the Labour Party. Leftist New Liberalism exercised a powerful influence over the ideas of the rising generation of Labour-inclined theorists such as Harold Laski and R. H. Tawney. Tawney's *The Acquisitive Society*, published in 1921, reworks the functionalist theory of property rights developed by Hobson and Hobhouse and argues explicitly for a new social order in which productive functions are performed from an ethos of professional service rather than self-interested profit maximization (see also Laski, 1925: esp. 185). As an ideological force, leftist New Liberalism thus merged into, and helped form, the ethical socialism of the newly ascendant Labour Party. It is not too much of an exaggeration to say that by 1950, though the Liberals had almost disappeared as an independent political force, New Liberalism had won the day through its permeation and conversion of the other two political parties: centrist New Liberalism had become part of the common sense of the postwar Conservative Party and leftist New Liberalism a large part of the common sense of the Labour Party (though other ideological traditions continued to inform each of these parties).

Lessons for Contemporary Progressives

When contemporary politicians and commentators hark back to New Liberalism, holding it forth as a model for the future of progressive politics, we need, therefore, to ask which of the creeds they mean to refer to, centrist or leftist. In general, like Gray, they mean to refer to the centrist, Churchillian tendency, to the conception of the good society as a society of humanized competition, a floor-constrained meritocracy. This is the 'Third Way' between a Conservative Party, which, purging itself of paternalist and New Liberal inheritances, increasingly sees the Churchillian humanization of capitalism as antithetical to healthy capitalist competition, and a traditional Left, committed to a supposedly anachronistic conception of society as a cooperative commonwealth. Is the virtue of this Third Way the lesson that the New Liberals have, then, for contemporary progressives?

Humanized competition is undoubtedly in some respects an attractive vision of the good society. The concern to ensure that the 'left-out millions' get an adequate income and basic opportunities certainly captures one of the most important demands of social justice. Some of the implications of meritocracy are quite radical when the ideal is properly understood. And, in its specifically Chur-chillian version, the ideal of humanized competition contains an appreciation of the state's role in welfare provision which progres-sives perhaps need to remind themselves of at a time when some on the centre-left are inclined to exaggerate the possible gains from handing over sundry welfare functions to independent associations within civil society.[8]

We are not convinced, however, that the ideal of humanized competition ought to define the limits of progressive aspiration. We do not think, firstly, that floor-constrained meritocracy exhausts the demands of social justice. Meritocracy rightly attacks unequal advan-tage attributable to differences in social background. But it does nothing to address inequalities in access to income, wealth and other requisites of the good life, attributable to differences in natural endowments. And, as John Rawls (1972) famously points out, if it is unfair for people to be disadvantaged in their access to income and wealth by bad luck in the social lottery, it is hard to see why it is no less unfair for them to be disadvantaged in their access to income and wealth by bad luck in the genetic lottery. John Gray may well be right when he says that there is no consensus in British society at present in favour of this view. But we do not see that as a reason why progressives should abandon the view. A democratic progressive politics must work to build a consensus in support of its values, deploying arguments, as Rawls does, to show how radical ideas which currently lack widespread support follow from other, more widely accepted ideas. Moreover, it is possible that as our under-standing of the genetic determinants of life-chances increases, and concern grows about the possible uses to which employers and insurance companies might put genetic testing and screening, there will be increased support for using the state to pool risks and moderate the inequalities produced by meritocratic competition. To this extent, we think the egalitarian ideal of the cooperative common-wealth retains its importance.

It might be argued that even if this robust egalitarianism remains desirable, it is simply unfeasible in a context of economic globaliza-tion. In response we would, first, caution against an exaggerated estimation of the pressures of globalization (Vandenbroucke, 1998) and, secondly, point to the possible benefits of what Philippe Van Parijs has called 'democratic scale lifting' – development of transnational regulations and rights of economic citizenship – to cope with these pressures (1995: 226–32). Thirdly, we would look to another distinctive feature of the ideal of the cooperative common-wealth to counter these pressures: the ethos of social service, of active commitment to the common good. We believe it is vitally important that progressives continue to espouse this social ethos and to cele-brate it as an alternative to the individualistic ethos that has recently made such inroads into the thinking of the centre-left.

They ought to do so, in part, because this ethos is instrumental in promoting social justice, perhaps especially in the present context of economic globalization. Such an ethos is important not only to the distant realization of utopian levels of equality ('From each according to her ability, to each according to her needs') but even for the achievement of more modest, incremental advance in the near future. There has been an exciting upsurge of work in the last few years on 'asset-based' strategies for increasing equality. Work in this vein includes Bruce Ackerman and Anne Alstott (1999) on stakeholding, Samuel Bowles and Herbert Gintis (1989) on 'asset-based redistribu-tion', as well as James Meade's (1989) pioneering work on the subject. Assuming they can be reconciled with tightening ecological constraints, these strategies offer the Left a possible way forward, beyond the reactive politics of defending the existing, highly imper-fect welfare state. An ecologically sustainable asset-based egalitari-anism will, however, require substantial solidarity amongst individual citizens to enact and make effective the relevant policies. Even if enough citizens can be persuaded to vote for such policies, a particular worry is that the talented might undermine them by seeking more remunerative employment in less egalitarian countries (see Van Parijs, 1995: 226–32). An ethos of social service, and an attendant willingness to work for the communal good as much as for personal gain, would seem necessary to prevent such subversion of local asset-based egalitarian strategies.

In addition, the development of a stronger ethos of the common good arguably has an important role to play in enhancing our quality of life. The sociologist Richard Wilkinson (1996) has drawn together compelling evidence of a relative income effect on health outcomes: that is, controlling for average income and absolute poverty, higher levels of economic inequality within a given country correlate with poorer health outcomes. Though the causal nexus behind this corre-lation is hard to sort out, there is suggestive evidence that one connection between inequality and poor health lies in what Wilkin-son calls the 'psychosocial features' of inegalitarian societies: in the widespread feelings of indifference to others, insecurity and stress, and the low self-esteem that inequality engenders or which is engendered by the same market ethos which allows inequality to flourish. One of the many suggestive statistics Wilkinson draws attention to is the international correlation between income inequality and road accidents. He comments: 'In many ways driving behaviour is likely to be a sensitive reflection of how people see themselves as related to unknown members of the public in society at large. Do people see other members of the public as fellow citizens with whom their welfare is interdependent, or do they merely see each other as obstacles in each other's way?' (1996: 155). A society organized around a stronger ethos of the common good, one that reminds us of our interdependency, might be expected to temper this psychosocial malaise and thereby increase health and quality of life.

So we believe that the Hobson/Hobhouse/Tawney conception of the good society, society as cooperative commonwealth, egalitarian in economics and, relatedly, animated by an ethos of mutual service and commitment to the common good, retains its relevance to progressives today. But what also retains its relevance, in our view, is the particular way in which progressive thinkers such as Hobson, Hobhouse and Tawney attempted to connect their conception of the good society with practical politics. All subscribed to what we referred to above, in connection with Hobhouse, as democratic gradualism: progressive politics is about the struggle for incremental reform against a background of stable democratic institutions. But for these thinkers and activists, reformism is embedded in and inspired by a larger background picture of the good society, one that points beyond the immediate agenda of reform, whatever the immediate importance of this agenda and however fierce the struggle over its implementation might be. This might seem an utterly commonsensical view of progressive politics. But when we compare it with some alternative views we can perhaps appreciate the importance of reminding ourselves of it.

One alternative, which G. A. Cohen, in an important essay on the state of the Left, calls 'Adaptive Preferences', throws out the long-term vision precisely because it is not immediately attainable (see Cohen, 1996: 245–65). The vision is chopped down to conform to what seems more politically feasible within a relatively short timespan. In our view, much of the recent interest on the Left in the ideology of centrist New Liberalism and the ideal of humanized competition has the quality of adaptive preferences. Adaptive preferences has the virtue of political realism, but it buys its realism at the price of core progressive values. A second alternative – what Cohen calls 'Vanity of Vanities' – reacts to political difficulty in the opposite way. It retains ethical commitment to the long-term vision, the cooperative commonwealth, and airily repudiates politics because politics cannot feasibly accommodate this vision in full any time soon, because the immediate agenda for change falls short, perhaps a long way short, of this vision. In place of philosophically light-weight political realism, we have politically marginalized, self-right-eous carping. Or perhaps it is not politics per se that is the problem, but democratic politics. That thought points towards the third – and utterly discredited – alternative: authoritarian vanguardism. Perhaps the most important lesson that New Liberals such as Hobson and Hobhouse have to teach progressives today is that they need not choose between these three unattractive alternatives. Progressivism, rightly understood, is democratic gradualism embedded in the ambition to rebuild society as an egalitarian cooperative common-wealth. It might well take longer, much longer, to realize this ambition than even such gradualists as Hobson and Hobhouse thought, and, to some extent, different policy instruments to those they envisaged; but this *is* the proper progressive ambition.

Notes

1   See the website of the Democratic Leadership Council (www.dlcppi.org).
2   See Bowles and Gintis (1998) on 'neo-Jeffersonian' egalitarianism; Nissan and Le Grand (2000), referring back to Paine; and, on Rousseau in particular, see White (2000).
3   John Gray's argument is quite different from that advanced in Alan Ryan's 1999 essay on new Labour and New Liberalism. Ryan believes that the New Liberalism of Hobhouse and his associates does represent a genuine third way which progressives should explore, but he also thinks that New Labour has a very imperfect grasp of this New Liberal third way. For Gray, New Liberalism is the missing theory of extant New Labour practice; for Ryan, New Liberalism offers a critique of that practice. Some (though not necessarily all) of this disagreement might be explained by the fact that Gray and Ryan focus on different currents of thought within New Liberalism, Gray tending to what we will call the centrist tendency, Ryan more towards the leftist tendency.
4   On the Conservatives, see Green (1995). This argument is frequently advanced in theoretical descriptions of the rise of welfare. See, for example, Miller (1999: 5–7).
5   It might be argued that this book is a poor guide to Hobhouse's views in his mature, New Liberal period because the first edition was published in the early 1890s when he was more closely identified with the socialist left. But Hobhouse had the book republished periodically and the third

edition, from which we quote here, advertised as 'completely revised', was published in 1912, a point at which there can be no doubt of his Liberal affiliations.

6 This is not to say that there are not some differences. Hobson, at least, believed when he wrote *The Social Problem* that 'brain workers' tend objectively to need more income to maintain functional efficiency than manual workers (1996[1902]: 164–5). This questionable, and somewhat self-serving view, seems to have been commonplace amongst British middle-class radicals around this time. It finds an echo, for example, in Russell, 1989[1916]: 92. There is no warrant (that we know of) for ascribing such a view to Marx.

7 The significance of these differences within interwar Liberalism is studied in depth in Freeden (1987), an analysis to which we are much indebted.

8 Speaking of the Old Age Pensions Act, Churchill says: 'Without a hitch, perfectly smoothly, punctual to the minute, regular as clockwork, nearly 600,000 aged persons are being paid their pensions every week. That is a wonderful and beneficent achievement, a good job well worth some risk and sweat to finish. Nearly eight millions of money are being sent circulating through unusual channels, long frozen by poverty, circulating in the homes of the poor, flowing through the little shops which cater to their needs, cementing again family unions which harsh fate was tearing asunder, uniting the wife to the husband, and the parent to the child' (1909: 235–6). For a critique of associationalist welfare, see Stears, 1999: 570–89.

References

Ackerman, B. and Alstott, A. (1999) *The Stakeholder Society* (New Haven, CT: Yale University Press).

Blair, T. (1996), 'The Radical Coalition', in Blair, *New Britain: My Vision of a Young Country* (London: Fourth Estate), pp. 4–21.

Bowles, S. and Gintis, H. (1998) *Recasting Egalitarianism* (London: Verso).

Churchill, W. S. (1909) *Liberalism and the Social Problem* (London: Hodder and Stoughton).

Cohen, G. A. (1996) 'The Future of a Disillusion', in Cohen, *Self-Ownership, Freedom and Equality* (Cambridge: Cambridge University Press), pp. 245–65.

Freeden, M. (1978) *The New Liberalism: An Ideology of Social Reform* (Oxford: Oxford University Press).

Freeden, M. (1987) *Liberalism Divided* (Oxford: Oxford University Press).

Gray, J. (1997) 'Goodbye to Rawls', *Prospect*, 24, November: 8–9.

Green, E. H. H. (1995) *The Crisis of Conservatism: The Politics, Economics and Ideology of the British Conservative Party, 1880–1918* (London: Routledge).

Hirst, P. (1994) *Associative Democracy* (Cambridge: Polity).

Hirst, P. (1997) *From Statism to Pluralism* (London: University College London Press).

Hobhouse, L. T. (1912) *The Labour Movement*, 3rd edn (New York: Macmillan).

Hobhouse, L. T. (1994[1911]) *Liberalism and Other Writings*, ed. James Meadowcroft (Cambridge: Cambridge University Press).

Hobson, J. A. (1996[1902]) *The Social Problem* (Bristol: Thoemmes Press).

Laski, H. (1925) *The Grammar of Politics* (London: Allen and Unwin).

Marx, K. (1976[1875]) *Critique of the Gotha Programme* (Peking: Foreign Languages Press).

Meade, J. (1989) *Agathatopia: The Economics of Partnership* (Aberdeen: University of Aberdeen).

Miller, D. (1999) *The Principles of Social Justice* (Cambridge, MA: Harvard University Press).

Nissan, D. and Le Grand, J. (2000) *A Capital Idea: Start-Up Grants for Young People* (London: Fabian Society).

Orloff, A. S. and Skocpol, T. (1984) 'Why Not Equal Protection? Explaining the Politics of Public Social Spending in Britain, 1900–1991 and the United States, 1880s–1920', *American Sociological Review*, 49: 726–50.

Pelling, H. (1979) *Popular Politics and Society in Late Victorian Britain* (London: Macmillan).

Rawls, J. (1972) *A Theory of Justice* (Oxford: Oxford University Press).

Rodgers, D. (1998) *Atlantic Crossings: Social Politics in a Progressive Age* (Cambridge, MA: Harvard University Press).

Rowntree, B. S. (1901) *Poverty: A Study of Town Life* (London: MacMillan).

Russell, B. (1989[1916]) *Principles of Social Reconstruction* (London: Unwin).

Ryan, A. (1999) 'Britain: Recycling the Third Way', *Dissent*, 46(2), Spring: 77–80.

Schweber, L. (1996) 'Progressive Reformers, Unemployment, and the Transformation of Social Inquiry in Britain and the United States, 1880s–1920s', in D. Ruschemeyer and T. Skocpol (eds), *States, Social Knowledge, and the Origins of Modern Social Policies* (Princeton: Russell Sage Foundation), pp. 163–200.

Stears, M. (1998) 'Guild Socialism and Ideological Diversity on the British Left, 1914–1926', *Journal of Political Ideologies*, 3: 289–306.

Stears, M. (1999) 'Needs, Welfare and the Limits of Associationalism', *Economy and Society*, 28: 570–89.

Tanner, D. (1990) *Political Change and the Labour Party 1900–1918* (Cambridge: Cambridge University Press).

Tawney, R. H. (1945[1921]) *The Acquisitive Society* (London: Harcourt, Brace, Jovanovich).

Van Parijs, P. (1995) *Real Freedom for All* (Oxford: Oxford University Press).

Vandenbroucke, F. (1998) *Globalisation, Inequality and Social Democracy* (London: Institute for Public Policy Research).

Vincent, J. (1967) 'The Political Feelings of the People' in Vincent (ed.), *Pollbooks: How Victorians Voted* (Cambridge: Cambridge University Press), pp. 43–50.

White, S. (2000) 'Rediscovering Republican Political Economy', *Imprints*, 4(3): 213–34

Wilkinson, R. G. (1996) *Unhealthy Societies: The Afflictions of Inequality* (London, Routledge).

3

Federalism and the Personalist Tradition

Ferdinand Kinsky

Introduction

'Neither individualist nor collectivist, we are Personalist' was the title of a paper given by Alexandre Marc to Denis de Rougemont, when the two future leading thinkers of the Personalist Movement first met in the early 1930s. This title already echoed the progressive orientation of the New Liberals in Britain in the early twentieth century and looked forward to contemporary 'Third Way' attempts to renew progressive politics in Europe and America. It was the expression of their concern about the growing individualism in Western democracies and the market economy, as well as about totalitarian ideologies and systems such as communism and Nazism.

Reflection on the question of how to organize the cultural, economic, political and social structures of our world led personalists to propose federalism as a model. But the meaning of personalist federalism went far beyond the organization of a federal state, which is what is usually meant by this term. Federalism is generally known as a method of power-sharing between federal institutions and member states, sometimes also as a model for transnational integration, especially within the European Union, or for devolution and regionalism within our states. But the implementation of federalist principles also appears in the power-sharing structures of multinationals or even smaller corporations, unions and all kinds of economic and social associations. The first thinker to develop such a global concept of federalism was Pierre-Joseph Proudhon. In the early 1930s his theory of a federalist society was taken up by the Personalist Movement and, after World War II, the school of thought founded by Alexandre Marc and inspired by Denis de Rougemont. Some of their major concepts are shared today by British communitarians such as Jonathan Boswell and Henry Tam, and American communitarians such as Amitai Etzioni and Michael Walzer.

The Principles of Personalist Federalism

Each individual person belongs to various private communities and groups but also to a number of different public structures, such as a municipality, a region, a nation, a transnational continental community and, finally, to humanity. This pluralist state of affairs is often insufficiently recognized and usually rejected by ideologists, who tend to put the emphasis on one exclusive or privileged identity. Thus, nationalism tries to claim that citizens belonging to a nation-state or an ethnic community trying to secure its own statehood are the factors that should count more than anything else. All other forms of solidarity – such as being attached to a family, a neighbourhood community, a village or town, a region or a community beyond the nation-state (such as the European Union or the UN), a church or any other religious community, or to any number of transnational NGOs – should be treated as less important than national identity. In the case of a conflict of interests, everything should be sacrificed to the nation. This is very similar to Marxist-Leninist ideology, which advocated that belonging to a particular social class was more important than any other identity.

Personal federalism rejects this way of privileging one exclusive identity and tries to recognize the existing variety and pluralism by the general accreditation of freedom and self-government for all groups as well as the necessity of a global federal organization. This objective could be reached by the implementation of the following principles:

1. Individual liberty and social responsibility for each human being, each community and each group: conditioned by legal and financial guarantees of autonomy and self-government at various levels.
2. Conflicts between autonomous communities, organizations or public levels should be solved neither by mere competition

without rules, nor by arbitrary decisions of an omnipotent centre, but by mutually accepted solutions, rules or covenants between partners. This is the principle of cooperative federalism.

3. The federal division of power assures that each level – the global institutions as well as those of the member-organizations or sub-groups – possesses adequate means to solve its own problems. The principle of subsidiarity intends to protect not only autonomy and self-government at the grass-root level, but also greater efficiency and a higher degree of transparency.

4. Checks and balances, a principle introduced into the American constitutional system by the Founding Fathers, should be generalized according to the school of personalist federalism. Just as each person's individuality only makes sense within a community, or at least within a framework of human relations, so no political, social, economic or cultural entity should exist without at least the counterpower of another group or institution.

5. The model of personalist federalism tends to increase the democratic principle of participation. Not only individuals but also member-organizations or sub-groups should participate in common decision-making procedures or institutions. Participation becomes precisely effective through the other principles mentioned above. Individual members of autonomous grass-root communities have a better knowledge of their local problems and of the other members and therefore are more likely to be able to participate in decision-making than those who govern from far away in highly centralized mass organizations. The solution of conflicts by mutual agreements, covenants or generally accepted rules is to be preferred to any decision imposed by a powerful centre.

The above-mentioned principles may be observed as the basic rules of most federal state systems, in particular for the power-sharing between the federal institutions and those of the member states. But, as previously mentioned, those principles can be implemented in any complex organization composed of sub-groups. A bank or an industrial firm, a trade union or a farmers' association, a political party or an association of sports clubs may be too centralized and therefore lacking in democracy or too diversified and therefore facing a problem of anarchy or separatism. Federalism guarantees unity as well as the recognition and protection of diversity. But this is often misunderstood.

In Britain and France, two countries where devolution was introduced very recently and where there is no historical experience of federalism, this term is often confused with centralism. Hence, the concept of a federal Europe is frequently seen with horror as heralding the end of a national identity. Incidentally, the same confusion with centralism exists in Canada and, for historical reasons, also in the United States, where the federalists are generally those who support the strengthening of the central government. On the contrary, federalism in Germany and Switzerland is, above all, considered as the protection of regional autonomy. Mr Stoiber, Prime Minister of Bavaria, often expressed his opposition to a common European currency in the name of federalism. And since 1949 Bavaria has always refused to ratify the Federal Republic of Germany's constitution, which it considers to be too centralized.

The Personalist Movement has always interpreted federalism as an attempt to reach a necessary degree of unity without destroying diversity or to reach an institutional recognition and guarantee of greater diversity without destroying unity by devolution.

Minimum Social Income

Beyond the federalist effort to increase the chances of democracy, a number of proposals were developed by the Personalist Movement in order to allow each individual to be a free and responsible person. This objective can only be reached on condition that a minimum social income is guaranteed to everyone.

This concept of a minimum social income for all was first developed by the French personalist thinkers Alexandre Marc and Arnaud Dandieu in the early 1930s. It was supposed to replace the then existing social security system. Each person should be given, at birth, a special bank account to be used for basic needs only (food, lodging, clothing, education, health). The objective was to give each individual a certain degree of independence. Hence, there would be no need for a guaranteed minimum wage level, and individuals could earn varying degrees of extra income from their labour. Of course, expenditure on anything not connected to basic needs was not supposed to be covered by the minimum social income bank account.

The minimum social income for all was meant to be financed both by former welfare state expenditures and by a citizen service that everyone would carry out during one or two years of his or her life. In the early 1930s, personalist thinkers were of course influenced by the consequences of the 1929 financial crisis and the emerging totalitarian systems. They considered that the macro-economic system should be divided into two separate parts:

- in the area concerning basic needs, production and consumption should be planned, not like the Soviet system but in a participatory and federalist way, based on the participation of employers, unions, consumer associations, etc.;
- beyond basic needs, production and consumption should be entirely left to the market.

In the decades following World War II, both the market and the welfare state reached a remarkable level of success. But more recently they have been challenged by the effects of globalization and of neo-capitalist shareholder values. Welfare expenditures are being reduced everywhere in Europe. Conservative politicians and ideologists praise the US model, but no European politician could afford to transfer the American welfare system to their own country because such a move would certainly damage their election prospects. Thus, the German post-World War II label of 'social market economy' still describes the general system applied in Europe, even if there are important differences between the various national approaches. An example was given by the Blair–Schröder attempt to introduce Third Way/New Centre thinking in the late 1990s, which was heavily criticized by French socialists as being too market-orientated.

To some extent, aspects of what some left-of-centre politicians in Britain and America termed the 'Third Way' can be compared with the personalist positioning of federalism as a path for steering clear of neo-liberal individualism and collectivism controlled by the omnipotent state. Amitai Etzioni (1995) adds to the critical analysis of massification as formulated by the Personalist Movement both in the early 1930s and after World War II. He does not neglect the necessity of a certain institutionalization even though his proposals appear to take into account the American tradition of mutual neighbourhood assistance and associative life that has already been admiringly observed by Tocqueville (1968). Like the personalist federalists before him, Etzioni defends both the autonomy of grass-root communities and their participation in 'a community of communities' (1995: 147). He speaks of 'pluralism within unity' and he expresses his hope of seeing the emergence of a global community capable of dealing with general questions concerning the whole of humanity. It is important to note that Etzioni was a leading member of the World Federalist Movement before founding the American Communitarian Movement.

Nevertheless, the institutional arrangements proposed by Etzioni remain relatively modest compared to those of the personalist federalists. This is probably due to the difference between the Anglo-Saxon tradition and the continental European, in particular French, habits.

The Origins of Personalist Federalism

Often quoted as the father of anarchism and 'libertarian' socialism, Pierre-Joseph Proudhon was also an important forerunner of personalist federalism. In his model of society, mainly but not only presented in his last work *Du principe fédératif*, Proudhon proposes a structure made up of autonomous communities which federate on the basis of contracts freely negotiated and entered into. Alexandre Marc's interpretation of Proudhon's federalist theory was: 'power should be everywhere, even at the centre'. Proudhonian grass roots consisted of local communities such as villages, organized neighbourhoods in large cities as well as workshops and small factories. They should all be autonomous and democratically self-governed, and should federate in larger regions as well as in common units of production, which, in turn, were supposed to form federated nations and, finally, a global transnational federation.[1] Proudhon proposed a kind of 'social contract', but, unlike Rousseau, the application of this principle was not meant to lead to the oppression of atomized individuals in a collectivist system. The underlying principles of Proudhon's social contract finds its expression in 'mutualism'. Conflicts should be limited and regulated by balanced contracts between the different autonomous communities. Proudhon's interpretation of anarchy was not negative. He admitted the necessity of political organizations as long as they were based on mutualism or contractualism.

Alexandre Marc used to describe Proudhon's methodology as an 'open dialectic'. Tensions and conflicts should neither be solved by the rule of the strongest – as happens in the anarchy of pure market competition without controlled rules, or in the non-structured international society – nor should the polarity disappear in a centralized nation-state where conflicts are solved by the uncontrolled peacemaking of persons or institutions. The 'open dialectic' of personalist federalism refuses the 'either/or' approach to thinking and proposes the 'as well as' method (Marc, 1970). Proudhon's dialectic thinking is based on his observations of antinomic relations everywhere. The balance between all antagonistic polarities should be based on 'justice', which Proudhon sees as the mutual recognition of opposed persons and communities.

Contemporary personalist philosophy was developed in the late 1920s and the early 1930s by philosophers such as Maurice Blondel, Isaac Stern and Max Scheler (who was the subject of Pope John Paul II's doctoral thesis). The Protestant theologian Karl Barth, the Catholic writers Gabriel Marcel and Jacques Maritain and the Orthodox Russian Nicolas Berdiaeff directly participated in the Personalist Movement by contributing to the journals *L'Ordre nouveau* (no connections with the extreme right movement of this name, which took its title in the 1970s) and *Esprit*. Major writers in these journals included Arnaud Dandieu, Alexandre Marc, Emmanuel Mounier, Robert Aaron, Daniel Rops and Denis de Rougemont. After the end of World War II they were joined by Henry Brugmans, the first Rector of the College of Europe in Bruges, who had become a personalist federalist in the Dutch Resistance movement. Brugmans summarized personalist federalist position as follows: 'Everyone thought that the individualism inspired by the Jacobins led logically towards an atomization of society, which in its turn would bring out the absolute state as the counterpart of this disintegration – "the cement of the totalitarian states is made of the dust of individuals" (Denis de Rougemont)' (1965: 62). For Brugmans, each person is responsible and free, committed and autonomous, a being in himself and yet related to his fellow men by his responsibility.

Hence, personalism rejects both individualism and collectivism. It is opposed to the neo-liberal or conservative pure market economy ideology based upon the assumption that the summing-up of all egotistic and anti-social attitudes will lead to general welfare and freedom. At the same time federalist personalism is opposed to the collectivist priority given to an overwhelming state where manipulated individuals have no freedom at all. Personalist thinkers discovered that federalist principles were the condition necessary for personal fulfilment. A person's autonomy and liberty as well as their capacity to participate in decisions of various communities, institutions or organizations at different levels will only be achieved if grass-roots communities, which allow for real personal relations, are also autonomous.

The principle of autonomy promoted by personalist federalism means the destruction of the oppressive centralism which often characterizes mass organizations. Autonomy may be reached either by devolution or decentralization of decision-making power to the grass roots, or by the establishment of new communities of human dimensions, such as neighbourhood organizations in urban areas, the reinvigoration of trade-union cells and the regrouping of workers in autonomous work-teams in factories or administrations. Of course, autonomy can only work if it is based on adequate legal statutes and sufficient financial resources. But the protection of traditional and the creation of new autonomous communities should not lead to the juxtaposition of absolute sovereignty or liberty. There is also the need for autonomy of neighbouring groups, just as the individual liberty of each person is limited by that of others. Hence the application of the principle of autonomy inevitably generates conflicts if it is not counterbalanced by cooperation, checks and balances and the adequate distribution of power through the principle of subsidiarity. Conflicts should be resolved by generally accepted covenants, constitutional rules, freely engaged contracts and law.

Finally, the real principle of participation is seen by the school of personalist federalism as the most important transcendental act of the person in society. But it is only in small grass-roots communities that the person can understand the decision-making procedures and participate in full awareness. In addition, democratically elected representatives of these small living communities should be delegated to participate in the solving of problems which they share with others, either through horizontal cooperation with representatives of other communities at the same level or through their presence at the immediately superior level.

Personalist Federalism as a Model for Contemporary Society

Opponents to personalist federalism often accused this movement of being no more than an ideology. They would be right if this doctrine were either a simple justification of an existing system or an abstract projection of an ideal 'perfect world' into the future. In both cases, an ideology is usually characterized by an important gap and contrast between an internal logic and a very different reality which usually does not confirm the system or theory. Ideologies are consequently tempted to deny or to minimize this contrast: 'too bad for reality'. In fact, aspects of reality are either denied or, in the worst cases, discriminated and persecuted or even condemned to disappear.

Personalist federalism does not use this kind of methodology. It is neither trying to justify an existing system nor proposing a kind of abstract paradise on earth. Personalist federalism tries to give an answer to some of the major problems of our contemporary world, in which traditional values, structures and institutions are constantly questioned, whereas relations between individual human beings, on one side, and the natural environment as well as advanced technologies and finally relations with other human beings, on the other, have become more and more depersonalized.

In Western countries most people have no or little personal relations with nature. Most of us, in particular those who live in industrialized urban areas, have lost direct experience of, and therefore knowledge of, nature. Under these circumstances, it seems almost normal that a large majority does not care too much about the destruction of nature. Although nobody likes polluted air or water, not enough people are ready to stop polluting activities. Even as relations between man and nature have become unbalanced, a general nostalgia about the environment may be observed.

The same phenomenon of depersonalization characterizes relations between man and technology. On the one hand, technology progresses with an ever-growing speed and is constantly promoting globalization and making communication, travel and practically all of our daily life much easier. On the other hand, we control it less and less, since over-specialization has led to a very large loss of transparency. Depersonalization becomes most obvious when we look at human and social relations. Small communities such as families, small shops and enterprises, villages and small towns have been declining ever since the industrial revolution. Most people today live anonymously in big cities, working for non-transparent mass organizations, with tens of thousands of employees, in the shadow of numerous public and private sector bureaucracies. Consequently, our society shows an increasing trend towards individualism. More and more young people refuse to take on the long-term commitments of marriage; unions and political parties complain about decreasing membership; the egotistical pursuit of individual goals and success has become the rule.

The lack of transparency observed in the area of advanced technology also becomes obvious in our globalized society, in spite of all the new and technically perfect media of communication. Beyond our personal relations and acquaintances, mankind continues to appear to us as a juxtaposition of monolithic labels. We speak of the French or the Americans, of Catholics or Protestants, women, farmers, workers, etc. as if they all represent the same unique attitude, opinion and behaviour. Indeed, all these terms describe one particular dimension of a human community, neglecting all the others. By using one of these labels, we immediately violate the rich complexity of our real society.

As a reaction to growing depersonalization, the Personalist Movement proposes the global and general application of the above-mentioned federalist principles: autonomy, cooperation, contractualism and mutualism, subsidiarity, checks and balances, individual and collective participation. Of course, personalist federalism could rightly be accused of being an utopian ideology if there were not real cases of effective achievements of federalism in different and important areas, as shown in the following examples.

1   The European Union has reached a remarkable degree of federation. Economic and monetary integration has established a customs union, a common or single market with free circulation of persons, goods, capital and services, as well as a single currency and a number of common policies. In the area of economic and monetary integration, the EU's institutions and decision-making procedures are somewhat similar to a federal government, parliament and supreme constitutional court. The Commission looks like the Swiss government, where, traditionally, all important political parties, ethnic and religious communities are represented. Like a federal government, the Commission takes the initiative for EU legislation. Members of the Commission are nominated by both the Council representing the member states and the European Parliament representing the people of the Union.[2] This federalist bicameralism reminds us of the German Bundestag and Bundesrat or the American House of Representatives and the Senate.[3] It also applies to the procedure of adopting the Community's budget. The Commission proposes a draft budget which is then amended and adopted by the Council and Parliament.[4] In 1987, the European Single Act and, in 1993, the Treaty of Maastricht gave Parliament powers of cooperation and co-decision in the legislative field. Although this is limited to amending or rejecting the Commission's proposals and the Council's 'common positions', which are established by qualified majority, this was seen as the first step to greater legislative power. The Amsterdam Treaty extended the co-decision procedure to most areas of economic integration, thereby replacing the former cooperation mechanism which gave the right of final decision to the Council.

2   The Court of Justice is the supreme jurisdictional authority on all questions related to EU treaties, the Single Act and the Maastricht Treaty. There is no appeal against decisions taken by the Court and its interpretation of European Community law.

3   The federalist model has also been partially achieved by regionalism and devolution within some of the EU's member states, such as Germany, which had gone through the most extreme experience of centralism under Hitler after World War II, and Spain, which also

experienced authoritarian centralism under Franco. Democratization also initiated the establishment of autonomous communities. Belgium went from centralism via regionalism to federalism. Italy and even France established elected regional councils and governments. More recently, the UK accepted the creation of parliamentary assemblies in Scotland and Wales.

4   In Central and Eastern Europe, Marxist-Leninist ideology was quickly replaced by a general rise of nationalism. Federalism has been compromised by the so-called federalist constitution and failures of the USSR, Yugoslavia and Czechoslovakia. But federalism is popular in Hungary, the major reason probably being the existence of Hungarian minorities in neighbouring states such as Romania, Serbia and Slovakia. Hence the concept of a Europe without borders as well as regional autonomy for ethnic minorities receives a large approval amongst Hungarian intellectuals.

Of course, the personalist federalists' macro-economic proposals of the 1930s need to be modernized today. It would be extremely difficult to promote the simple replacement of the social security system by the 'minimum social income for all'. Nevertheless, this concept could be gradually introduced. And although neither devolution within corporations and companies, nor workers' participation, automatically establishes federalist structures and an example of personalist society, a number of important steps towards this model have been achieved by structural reforms of business. After all, while globalization seems to favour a new kind of centralization by the concentration of financial power, it also creates opportunities for more autonomy and initiative for local and regional decision-makers.

In conclusion, I would suggest that all those subscribing to progressive communitarian ideas or to personalist federalism should cooperate with each other and with other like-minded thinkers and activists – whatever label they may prefer for their beliefs – in the development of a strong progressive front in the politics of the global age. We should never underestimate the sociological rule of power. Political, economic, social or cultural leaders are generally reluctant to accept a new power-sharing concept if they find themselves in a commanding position. Even politicians who previously embraced federalist or progressive ideals prefer, once they win power, taking moderate steps that will not endanger their own controlling and commanding position. We have to persuade them and the wider public that political power is best vested in and sustained through not just the promise, but the delivery, of long-term progressive reforms.

Notes

1 Proudhon proposed a European 'confederation', but his description showed that he meant a federation.
2 The Amsterdam Treaty gives the Commission's President, who is chosen by the European Council, the right to propose his colleagues to the Council and the European Parliament.
3 Until this century, American senators were not directly elected but delegated from the individual states.
4 The Council has the right of final decision on expenditures resulting from the original EU treaties (agricultural price policy, costs arising from international trade agreements), whilst Parliament has the right of final decision on expenditures introduced more recently (education, social programmes, regional development fund, cohesion fund, environmental and cultural projects), and at the end of the procedure Parliament adopts or rejects the global budget.

References

Brugmans, H. (1965) *L'Idée européenne* (Bruges: De Temple).
Etzioni, A. (1995) *The Spirit of Community: Rights, Responsibilities and the Communitarian Agenda* (London: Fontana Press; 1st edn 1993).
Marc, A. (1970) *De la Méthodologie à la dialectique* (Paris: Presses d'Europe).
Tocqueville, Alexis de (1968) *Democracy in America*, trans. George Lawrence; ed. J. P. Mayer and M. Lerner (London: Fontana).

4

Solidarity in Theory and Practice

Wlodzimierz Wesolowski and Aneta Gawkowska

In theory and practice, solidarity – one of the most powerful ideals in progressive thinking – has been a notable driving force in Polish intellectual and political history. Following the collapse of Soviet-backed totalitarian communist regimes in Eastern Europe, engagement with the communitarian ideas of thinkers such as Charles Taylor, Alasdair MacIntyre, Michael J. Sandel, Michael Walzer, Amitai Etzioni and Henry Tam has brought out a number of common strands within our respective traditions. Through an appreciation of what solidarity has meant in our struggle to free ourselves from authoritarian state socialism and laissez-faire capitalism, and how it relates to the wider debate on the future of progressive politics, we can begin to map out the core concerns for reform movements, not just in Poland, but possibly in other countries as well.

The holistic perspective present in Charles Taylor's writings often refers to the Romantic (though mostly German) tradition (Taylor, 1995). Similar currents can be identified in Polish intellectual heritage. Moreover, contemporary attempts to deal with the world's diversity and multiculturalism can be deeply enlightened by coming to grips with their roots in the broader Romantic tradition, including the Polish one. Charles Taylor proves to be an astute student of nineteenth-century history, in helping to teach his Canadian compatriots how to make a positive use of their diversity by means of mutual exchange and complementarity (Taylor, 1998). Another deeply communitarian element present in Polish Romanticism is the idea of carrying out debates between various communities and establishing stable links based on (partly) shared values. Today, the need for such dialogues is strongly emphasized in the writings of Amitai Etzioni (1996: 128, 191, 224–5) and in 'The Responsive Communitarian Platform' (in Etzioni, 1998: xxv–xxxvii). The motives of broadness, openness and inclusive character of communities, as well as the universal nature of some basic values constituting the core of community order, lie at the heart of Henry Tam's argumentation in his analysis of communitarianism (1998).

The Forerunners of Solidarity

Let us start by considering the writings of Jan Strzelecki, an exceptional and very significant figure among Polish intellectuals. In his collection of essays published in 1974, he gives considerable thought to the impact of the Second World War on the self-awareness and transformation of socialist ideas. The specific experience of the war in Poland, in particular the atrocities and the extreme suffering, together resulted in the creation of a certain community of fate, a community of the endangered who felt a strong need to defend basic human values. For all those who went through the war, but for socialists in particular, it was the point when they realized that there were strong bonds of community beyond the world of workers. Strzelecki writes about the importance of the nation, a common language, the symbols of culture and their unifying role in the process of discovering and experiencing an essential brotherhood (1974: 11–16, 51, 68). The issue of the nation has also been crucial for older Polish socialists, as is noted in the literature on the subject (for example, Jan J. Lipski describes the links between early Polish socialist thought and the concept of nation in his essay in Wesolowski, 1990). Strzelecki must have been aware of this fact, so his stress on the experience of war gave the theoretical musings a special flavour: 'During the wartime years the socialist fight became the fight for the values of European culture' (1974: 112, trans. AG). The voice of the oppressed nation gained a universal character because it defended universal values. The bonds of the nation were the bonds of common duties and responsibility for the fate of an endangered humanity (ibid. 53). The positive meanings of the concept of nation have been realized by many contemporary Western intellectuals, for example David Miller, who notes that 'nations are the only possible form in which overall community can be realised in modern societies' (1992: 93). The importance of particular traditions for the continuation of our practices and our definitions of justice is described widely by many philosophers mentioned earlier (see MacIntyre, 1984; Walzer, 1983).

Another substantial source of human bonding whose positive impact came to be discovered during the war was Christianity. It strongly defended the dignity of human beings and advocated the ethics of brotherhood in God against the power of militarized collectivities, by which Strzelecki meant fascism and communism (1974: 46–7). The great potential of Christianity and its affirmation of the human being are more recently emphasized by Charles Taylor (1992).

During the war, paradoxically, the common causes of the oppressed became identified with the voices speaking in the name of individual freedom. The person and the community were perceived as mutually supportive. Consequently, individual freedom, collective national liberty and social justice became intertwined ideals. They all served as the fundamental tenets of Strzelecki's socialist humanism, where the brotherhood would successfully overcome the conflict between social and individual life in a society that would be characterized by openness and solidarity (1974: 29, 65, 77, 90).

Strzelecki's socialist humanism seems to have essentially communitarian characteristics, not only because it managed to put the care for the individual's development at the centre of community's concern but also because his socialism was to be rooted in society, not based on the institutions of the state. According to Strzelecki, the statist economy could not guarantee the proper realization of social justice. The people themselves had to undergo a transformation into being more socially active and open, i.e. ready to work for others and open to the acceptance of such new values as well-being, equality, creative freedom and solidarity (ibid. 91–2, 221). In claiming the need for both statist and societal involvement, Strzelecki invoked the authority of Stanislaw Ossowski, a prominent Polish sociologist, who postulated the necessity of both the rational planning of the economy and the polycentrism of the remaining areas of social life (ibid. 231).

Strzelecki's experiential conclusions about the nature of freedom was a powerful warning against the naive hopes of classical liberals. He wrote that the ideal of freedom in itself is not the ultimate goal of the human being, but an important tool that can be used in either a good or a bad way, depending on our choice of the value it is going to serve. The case of Nazi Germany was the clear example of a badly used freedom. Equally dangerous consequences happen whenever the means of economy and technology are put in the position of being goals in themselves, while we forget about the proper goals of human and community development (ibid. 30, 77, 221). The critique of both capitalism and fascism awakened in Strzelecki a real fascination with Emmanuel Mounier and his promotion of personalism. The personalist perspective seemed to him attractive because it was so close to his envisioned integration of both individual and community flourishing. Strzelecki was alone among the socialist thinkers of 1945–89 to express open sympathy with 'progressive' Catholic thinkers. (For the connections between progressive thought and the personalist tradition, see Kinsky, ch. 3 this volume.)

Mounier's thought also influenced Polish Catholic intellectuals gathered around the monthly *Wiez* (Bond). The periodical was established in 1958 by a group of Polish lay Catholics (Tadeusz Mazowiecki, Wojciech Wieczorek, Stefan Frankiewicz, Cezary Gawrys and others) who aimed to revitalize Polish Catholicism, taking advantage of the wind of political change in Poland after 1956. The group was fascinated first by Mounier and then by Vaticanum II. They wanted to plant the ideas of Vaticanum II into Polish Catholicism, which was rather traditional.

In a discussion among the past and present editors of *Wiez*, Tadeusz Mazowiecki emphasizes that the philosophy of personalism was a guiding idea (Mazowiecki et al., 1998: 139). The fundamental tenets of this position embrace the central value of the human person as an end, not a means, and the crucial value of solidarity that is realized in a human community. Following Mounier, the group professed their allegiance to the form of personalism that was based on Christian anthropology and which perceived this basis as the most solid guarantor of the preservation and realization of human dignity (Mazowiecki, 1990: 47; Wieczorek, 2000: 29). Christianity has not only stood for the community but also defended the freedom of individual human beings. Particularly in the context of 'real socialism', Christian social teaching that warned against the total state ownership of property was well received and understood by Polish Catholics. For them it was clear that the defence of private property was a defence of human freedom, while state ownership resulted only in state domination (Mazowiecki, 1990: 47–8). To avoid the latter and, yet, allow the individuals to realize their community calling, the most promising form of ownership for the future times seemed to be that of socialized property. And that is why the encyclicals devoted to social issues by John Paul II (1986, 1991) fell on such ready ears among the *Wiez* authors, who in the figure of Cezary Gawrys described the Pope's teaching as 'their spiritual land' (Mazowiecki et al., 1998: 160). The truly communitarian concern for personal and community flourishing made them repudiate both liberal individualism and communist collectivism.

It is interesting how both the older and younger generations of authors have understood personalism as a kind of openness to another human being, who is always worthy of respect and from whom we can always learn. This way of conceptualizing the issue appears in the discussion about the lineage of *Wiez*, where both Tadeusz Mazowiecki and Zbigniew Nosowski (a younger-generation representative) accentuate the fact that the periodical has always intended to stay above some political, social, religious and other divisions in order to promote a dialogue between various options and slowly create civil society (Mazowiecki et al., 1998: 148, 152, 161). Among the sources of inspiration for Polish Catholic thinkers, Mazowiecki mentions Jacques Maritain and his possibility of joining Christian and non-Christian efforts in common actions around the social issues of humanity. Similar currents were found inspiring in the developing social teaching of the church in the second half of the twentieth century (Mazowiecki, 1990: 50). The motive of dialogue plays a crucial part in many modern philosophies. Jürgen Habermas is well known for devoting a lot of attention to discourse ethics, according to which different world-views are brought into the debate, idealized and enlarged in order to reach a perspective common to all discourse participants (Habermas, 1984/1987, 1990, 1993). Dialogue is also a vital element of Taylor's writings, as he shows that the essential nature of human beings consists in our dialogical character (Taylor, 1991: 305, 312–14).

Another communitarian element in the *Wiez* group was the new perception of politics as the mechanism of serving the common good, not merely an area for fights between particular interests. The common good was to be the motivation for publishing the political texts in *Wiez* in the opinion of Cezary Gawrys (Mazowiecki et al., 1998: 161). Thus, the intellectuals who were gathered around *Wiez* for more than two decades participated in preparing the ground for the appearance of the Solidarity Movement.

The Solidarity Movement

The eruption of strikes and the spontaneous creation of the Solidarity trade-union movement, which almost instantly developed into a national movement embracing all strata of society, has received philosophical and sociological interpretations by several Polish intellectuals. The most comprehensive depiction of the movement was given, however, by Reverend Jozef Tischner, a Catholic academician, and a politician, Jacek Kuron, who was the prominent member of democratic opposition, many times arrested and sentenced to prison under the communist regime. Tischner was a theologian and a philosopher, who became the outspoken chaplain of the Solidarity Movement. He formulated the core value system of the so-called 'Solidarity ethos', the nature of which consisted in a combination of Catholic theology with such liberal and even social democratic tenets that can be acceptable to every Polish person. In his elaboration of current religious and social problems, the reference to God as the ultimate inspirer of everything ended on the most general level. He incorporated, first of all, many liberal ideals into his presentation of problems of the collapse of communist society and the need to create a new social order. Jacek Kuron was a civic opposition activist, who was, to start with, of social democratic persuasion, but who later incorporated the liberal ideas of civil society into his thinking. The new strands of Tischner's Catholic philosophy together with Kuron's civil society doctrine made them the thinkers closest to the communitarian ideas of contemporary Western philosophers.

Tischner deliberately strove to merge the Catholic concept of the 'person' with the liberal concept of the free individual. Moreover, he genuinely linked some leftist ideas of the role of work (including the Marxist view) with problems of individual freedom and creativity. He was also very sensitive to the question of the practical aspects of the democratic order. At the top of his interests was the concept of the freedom of the Polish nation, which he conceived in a liberal rather than a conservative or populist way. (His main ideas were presented in *Etyka solidarnosci* (The Ethics of Solidarity), published by several underground presses, amongst which was Pryzmat in 1989.)

Although individual liberty should be achieved within a community (the civil and the national), the ultimate goal of human communities is to serve individuals, not vice versa. Tischner tells us about various mundane conditions that make individual freedom possible. One of them is the need to act for the good of the community, but the act should come first, followed by the concept of 'we'. This is the reversal of the traditional or the nationalistic concept of 'we', which is the prime condition of action. We find the same approach when we look at the concept of work and its significance for both civil society and the nation. In purely civic terms, Tischner writes about the national communality of work as the distribution of tasks to different people and strata. In a sense, it is the whole complex of national work that creates civil society, with its division of labour and duties. These duties consist of working to serve the needs of 'others'. In this way, in the work process, society is maintained in the most tangible dimension. But the process of work is also the process of communication between individuals maintaining their symbolic ties. This remark refers mostly to industrial work, which has both a horizontal aspect (cooperation) and a vertical aspect (management). What is emphasized by Tischner is work for others and the utility of products for others. If work is spoilt either by the poor quality of products or by unfair rates of pay, which fall below a minimum basic level, we witness the phenomenon of moral exploitation. In the communist system of work many products are spoilt at the very beginning because they produce unnecessary pain and have morally debilitating effects. All such considerations indicate the interest in mundane problems, which had been taken up a century earlier by many thinkers, including Marxists. Tischner is at odds with Marxism on one key point: the most important dimension of exploitation cannot be considered solely in terms of an economic theory of surplus value; it has much broader manifestations.

The struggle for national independence is conceived by Tischner as a communal problem. However, the liberty of the nation is conceived in a very modern and liberal way. God gave people a piece of land, but that is where the direct role of God ends. The people with their own land must then carry out the task of building their nation. In the case of Poland, Catholicism played an important role in its creation and in the survival of its people in the face of many traumatic experiences throughout history. One of Tischner's specific concepts emphasizes the role of cultivated land inherited by subsequent generations, which, finally, constitutes the fatherland. The cultivation and fertilization of land inherited from one's forefathers depicts in the best way the individual/personal contribution to the formation of the national community. In an allegoric form, Tischner says that the farmer who cultivates the land is maintaining his ties with other members of the national community. He serves them and he enters the community; by keeping the land in his hands he serves the national cause (Tischner, 1989: 55–9).

In Tischner's view, the individual is a prime factor, the real actor in the arena of the battle for national independence. The systematic work of individuals is primary to any feeling of pride or superiority of a given nation. Here we have, evidently, an anti-nationalistic and solely patriotic dimension of the theory of nation. Another similar feature is found in Tischner's consideration of democratic order. It is created by free individuals, who are able to conceive themselves as actors and sovereign subjects of history. In some respects he defends the liberation theology of Latin American Catholics. Here is a telling quotation: 'How can one save the someone who is not aware of himself . . . deprived of his own will, full of fear of survival? . . . Such an individual lives below the level of "person". Such a person cannot become the child of God because she has not matured to the level of personality' (Tischner, 1991: 201). Tischner claims that similar ideas emerged within the Polish Solidarity Movement at the popular level. The striking feature of this statement is the assumption that even God's action at saving the individual requires the previous development of the individual. Moreover, the conditions for the maturity of the individual are created by society itself.

Tischner's conception of democracy unites the individual and the communal dimensions. The task of political democracy is to provide effective human rights to citizens: this is the liberal component. On the other hand, the development of democracy, its maintenance and effectiveness may be secured solely by fully developed personalities.

Tischner's philosophy has Christian roots. His Catholicism has a definite ecumenical appeal. Paradoxically, his 'preachings' are well received by agnostics and even atheists. This is so because his absorption of dilemmas of modern times and his attempts to elucidate them have an 'elective affinity' to the contemporary popular way of thinking. People are interested in a form of social life that would provide them with theoretical and moral guidelines. And ordinary people, at least in Poland, do not think that a mere replica of a timely version of liberalism, which says nothing about the conditons of the contemporary period, will satisfy their aspirations. Tischner's message, which is individualistic in a personalistic incarnation, fits their needs. Simultaneously, this teaching somehow eliminates the conflict between the individual and the community. Moreover, it postulates the view that individual efforts serve to strengthen the community and the community allows the individual to flourish.

Jacek Kuron is a civic philosopher who was among the group of opposition politicians with some inclinations to conceptualize the emergence of the Solidarity Movement and to increase its impact on the new reality that solidarity itself had created. Like Tischner, his general aim was to increase cooperation within society and diminish the conflictual aspects of people's daily lives. His concepts appeared in an elaborated form later than Tischner's, but they have the same roots in liberal, social democratic and, finally, communitarian inspirations. Kuron became involved in practical politics after the victory of the Solidarity Movement. He was the Minister of Labour in the Mazowiecki cabinet, the first Solidarity government. He presented his considerations on the state and the nation in two major essays: 'A Republic for Everyone: Thoughts on the Program of Action' (1994a) and 'Modernization and Dignity' (1994b). He was disillusioned with crude liberalism and its visionless, insensitive way of implementing market reforms. He has emphasized that the former communist regime deprived the economy of efficiency and as a result ruined it, while at the same time depriving the people of their freedom and possibility of independent civic action. However, introducing a new type of economy requires the participation of the people, so Kuron became the most prominent proponent of reconstructing the Solidarity Movement into focused civic associations that would support government actions towards reforming the various spheres of life inherited from the communist past.

Kuron saw the political disruption of the early Solidarity Movement into fragmented party groupings as inevitable under formal democratic rules. However, he considered the fragmentation of the political scene as detrimental to the long-term process of reforming the country. Reforms can only be achieved with the support of the people, but, at least to start with, the people were disillusioned, confused and frustrated by all the change. If it is impractical to strive for the re-establishment of a united Solidarity Movement, grouping people according to special interests is the only alternative solution. Kuron has accused the government of technocratic distortion. He accepts privatization, but argues that employees should play a greater role in the process of developing it without social and political conflicts. He opposes dismantling the welfare state in its many forms. The democratic state has a duty to construct and execute various social programmes of educational reforms, of the pension system and of reconstructing the health service. These programmes have to be designed in cooperation with civic associations conceived as active movements.

Kuron proposed to establish a system with the three main actors of reforms: the government, social movements and expert groups. Each has a different role to play in the transformation process, and each needs to be stimulated by the other two. To start with, it is the government's role (a Solidarity-led government) to make the first move, because it has more resources with which to act: a budget, an institutional network and a means of communication. This very realistic view on resources and organizational frameworks was the step forward (or away) from earlier beliefs of many Solidarity militants that the spontaneous activity of ordinary people would be the catalyst of every change.

Kuron also criticizes the alienation of the political elite from the opinions and sentiments of the common people. In his opinion, the ruling elite moved too far in the liberal direction, treating individual interests as the sole motivation for action and, moreover, rather egoistic pursuit; economic man is the real actor on the historical scene. But Kuron contradicts this opinion. Man is, historically, a social creature, not insensitive to 'the common good' and mostly destined to act in groups, both small and large. He sees civil society as organized on various levels and for different purposes. Politicians should act in concert with activists of civil society, which is the tool used to increase the participation of every citizen and to bridge the gaps between various philosophical orientations by practical endeavours.

It seems to us that looking at the concept of civil society, together with its practical implementation, in the context of the Polish transition indicated the need to find an intellectually guided route to the future. Kuron has been aware that any simplistic copy of Western capitalism will not provide proper instruments for the rapid development of post-communist societies. It is an unsolved question whether the reason for this is that there must be a natural diversity of capitalist orders under various conditions. We do not know what makes Poland's quest for a satisfactory post-communist society so difficult to realize. It could be the negative heritage of communism itself, or it could be the Polish people's own idealistic striving for a social order that will incorporate some of the demanding ideals brought over from Western societies, such as the concept of an active civil society. With his belief in the real innovativeness of human beings organized in goal-oriented groups, and his accentuation of the active and creative character of human beings, Kuron is possibly the closest to the position of many progressive communitarians.

Both Tischner's and Kuron's ideas were reactions to the harmful experiences of communism and its dangerous illusions. In their opinion, the analyses of totalitarian experiences pave the way for a fundamental rethinking of the universal problem of social order. Tischner has attempted to broaden the meaning of 'work' both on land and in industry. Work creates, one might say, cooperative associational relations and communal, symbolic ties. In this respect, Tischner may be regarded as a genuine contributor to the development of a progressive communitarian social philosophy. Kuron's originality is related to the way he conceives the market economy and democracy amidst cross-cutting currents of aspirations of people who find themselves under conditions of apparent personal and political freedom, on the one hand, and being left to their own devices with neither an adequate income nor public support, on the other. Hence, both the capacity for self-organization and the significant role of the government are present in his deliberations and vision.

Conclusion

The central challenge for progressive communitarian thought is to define the kind of cooperation, coherence and social ties which should be provided for each individual. Evidently, the strength of communitarian analyses lies in identifying the many wrongs of contemporary modern or supra-modern societies (including the very weak nascent market economies and fragile democracies of Central Eastern Europe). What kind of solidarity ties, including emotional warmth and economic security, may be designed and implemented? Some intellectuals consider the question itself an inappropriate one. However, they are overlooking a historical-social fact that bare spontaneity of development occurs more and more rarely. It is necessary to monitor economic, social and cultural phenomena, so as to guide them and prevent them from destroying the lives of vulnerable individuals. The real problem consists in delineating the scope of interference in view of the vast number of people being drawn into the 'global flow'. Postulating non-interference under the cover of 'benevolent spontaneity' simply does not measure up to our human capacities or our collective aspirations.

References

Avineri, S. and De-Shalit, A. (eds) (1992) *Communitarianism and Individualism* (New York: Oxford University Press).
Etzioni, A. (ed.) (1998) *The Essential Communitarian Reader* (Boston: Rowman and Littlefield).
Etzioni, A. (1996) *The New Golden Rule: Community and Morality in a Democratic Society* (New York: Basic Books).
Habermas, J. (1984/1987) *The Theory of Communicative Action* (2 vols), trans. T. McCarthy (Boston: Beacon Press).
Habermas, J. (1990) 'Justice and Solidarity: On the Discussion Concerning "Stage 6"', in Michael Kelly (ed.), *Hermeneutics and Critical Theory in Ethics and Politics* (Cambridge, MA: MIT Press).

Habermas, J. (1993) *Justification and Application. Remarks on Discourse Ethics*, trans. Ciaran P. Cronin (Cambridge, MA: MIT Press).

John Paul II (1986) *Laborem exercens* (Lublin: Wydawnictwo Katolickiego Uniwersytetu Lubelskiego).

John Paul II (1991) *Sollicitudo rei socialis* (Warsaw: PAX).

Kuron, J. (1994a) 'Rzecspospolita dla kazdego. Mysli o programie dzialania' [A Republic for Everyone: Thoughts on the Programme of Action], *Zcie gospodarcze*, 21, 22 May: 1–16.

Kuroñ, J. (1994b) 'Modernizacja i godnosc' [Modernization and Dignity], *Gazeta Wyborcza*, 5 October.

MacIntyre, A. (1984) *After Virtue: A Study in Moral Theory*, 2nd edn (Notre Dame, IN: University of Notre Dame Press).

Mazowiecki, T. (1990) 'Spotkania Chrzeœcijanstwa z ideami socjalistycznymi i kontrowersje miedzy nimi' [Encounters of Christianity with the Socialist Ideas and the Controversies between Them], in Wlodzimierz Wesolowski (ed.), *Losy idei socjalistycznych i wyzwania wspólczesnoœci* [The Fate of Socialist Ideas and the Challenges of the Modern Times] (Warsaw: Polish Association of the Club of Rome).

Mazowiecki, T. et al. (1998) '*Wieziowe* pokolenia, *wieziowe* oblicza' [The Generations of *Wiez*, the Faces of *Wiez*], *Wiez*, February.

Miller, D. (1992) 'Community and Citizenship', in Shlomo Avineri and Avner De-Shalit (eds), *Communitarianism and Individualism* (New York: Oxford University Press).

Strzelecki, J. (1974) *Kontynuacje (2)* [Continuations (2)] (Warsaw: Panstwowy Instytut Wydawniczy).

Tam, H. (1998) *Communitarianism. A New Agenda for Politics and Citizenship* (London: Macmillan).

Taylor, C. (1991) 'The Dialogical Self', in David R. Hiley, et al. (eds), *The Interpretative Turn. Philosophy, Science, Culture* (Ithaca and London: Cornell University Press).

Taylor, C. (1992) *Sources of the Self: The Making of the Modern Identity* (Cambridge: Cambridge University Press).

Taylor, C. (1995) *Philosophical Arguments* (Cambridge, MA: Harvard University Press).

Taylor, C. (1998) 'The Dynamics of Democratic Exclusion', *Journal of Democracy*, 8(4), October: 143–56.

Tischner, J. (1989) *Etyka solidarnoœci* [The Ethics of Solidarity] (Krakow: Znak).

Walzer, M. (1983) *Spheres of Justice: A Defense of Pluralism and Equality* (New York: Basic Books).

Wieczorek, W. (2000) 'Emmanuel Mounier po latach' [Emmanuel Mounier after Years], *Wiez*, June.

Wlodzimierz, W. (1990) *Losy idei socjalistycznych i wyzwania wspolczesnosci* [The Fate of Socialist Ideas and the Challenges of the Modern Times] (Warsaw: Polish Association of the Club of Rome).

Further Reading

Bellah, R. N., Madsen, R., Sullivan, W. M., Swidler, A. and Tipton, S. M. (1985) *Habits of the Heart: Individualism and Commitment in American Life* (New York: Harper and Row).

Bellah, R. N., Madsen, R., Sullivan, W. M., Swidler, A. and Tipton, S. M. (1991) *The Good Society* (New York: Knopf).

Etzioni, A. (1991) *A Responsive Society: Collected Essays on Guiding Deliberate Social Change* (San Francisco: Jossey-Bass Publishers).

Etzioni, A. (1993) *The Spirit of Community: Rights, Responsibilities, and the Communitarian Agenda* (New York: Crown Publishers).

MacIntyre, A. (1970) *Herbert Marcuse, an Exposition and a Polemic* (New York: Viking Press).

MacIntyre, A. (1983) *Marxism and Christianity* (Exeter: A. Wheaton and Co.).

MacIntyre, A. (1995) 'Is Patriotism A Virtue?', in Ronald Beiner (ed.), *Theorizing Citizenship* (New York: State University of New York Press).

Mulhall, S. and Swift, A. (1992) *Liberals and Communitarians* (Oxford: Blackwell).

Sandel, M. J. (1982) *Liberalism and the Limits of Justice* (New York: Cambridge University Press).

Sandel, M. J. (1988) 'Democrats and Community', *The New Republic*, 22 February: 20–3.

Sandel, M. J. (1996) *Democracy's Discontent: America in Search of a Public Philosophy* (Cambridge, MA: The Belknap Press of Harvard University Press).

Taylor, C. (1991) *The Ethics of Authenticity* (Cambridge, MA: Harvard University Press).

Taylor, C. (1993a) 'Modernity and the Rise of the Public Sphere', in Grethe B. Paterson (ed.), *The Tanner Lectures on Human Values*, XIV (Salt Lake City: University of Utah Press).

Taylor, C. (1993b) *Reconciling the Solitudes: Essays on Canadian Federalism and Nationalism* (Montreal: McGill-Queen's University Press).

Tischner, J. (1991) *Polski mlyn* [The Polish Mill] (Krakow: Nasza przeszlooeæ).

Walicki, A. (1982) *Philosophy and Romantic Nationalism: The Case of Poland* (Oxford: Clarendon Press).

Walzer, M. (1970) *Obligations: Essays on Disobedience, War, and Citizenship* (Cambridge, MA: Harvard University Press).

Walzer, M. (1981) 'Philosophy and Democracy', *Political Theory*, 9(3), August: 379–99.

Walzer, M. (ed.) (1982) *The Politics of Ethnicity* (Cambridge, MA: Harvard University Press).

Walzer, M. (1987) *Interpretation and Social Criticism* (Cambridge, MA: Harvard University Press).

Walzer, M. (1990) 'The Communitarian Critique of Liberalism', *Political Theory*, 18(1), February: 6–23.

Walzer, M. (1994) *Thick and Thin: Moral Argument at Home and Abroad* (Notre Dame, IN: University of Notre Dame Press).

Walzer, M. (1998) 'Pluralism and Social Democracy', *Dissent*, Winter: 47–53.

5

A Quest for Community

Philip Selznick

In the United States and Europe a number of politicians and thinkers have tried to formulate a 'Third Way' to transcend the political ideologies of Left and Right, and renew the tradition of progressive politics. Such an attempt is in part a revisionist response to the perceived failures of American welfare liberalism and European social democracy. Both have relied too much on government programmes and bureaucracy, allowed the development of welfare dependency, showed too little concern for crime, family life and the vitality of civil society and were insufficiently appreciative of free enterprise as the key to prosperity. At the same time, Third Way advocates have argued that unfettered enterprise and unregulated markets too often undermine the public interest. They weaken the capacity of the community to provide needed resources for health, education and environmental protection. Left to themselves they exacerbate social inequalities and reinforce patterns of discrimination. Therefore, unbridled capitalism will not do either. The quest is for a middle way, a 'Third Way', which will retain the virtues and correct the deficits of both systems. This quest, it is said, is made especially urgent by the great changes taking place in modern society, especially the spread of information-based technology and the globalization of culture and economic life.

These messages draw important lessons from the experience of the twentieth century. Nevertheless, to date, proponents of Third Way thinking have not come up with an intellectually coherent public philosophy to reorientate, let alone revive, progressive reforms in the global age. In response, some politicians have looked to the idea of community for guidance. In the United States, for example, the Democratic Leadership Council – a political organization closely associated with Third Way ideas – has chosen 'Opportunity, Responsibility, Community' as a self-defining slogan. Some Third Way writers, however, being uncertain about the meaning of community, are sceptical and even hostile (Giddens, 2000: 63). In this chapter, I try to meet this challenge by offering what is, I believe, a valid interpretation of the experience of community, and of its promise in shaping progressive politics for the future.

The Principle of Community

When we appeal to 'community' as a guiding ideal, we have in mind the moral bonds of membership and leadership. These are the obligations people owe one another and the whole of which they are parts. Bonds of community arise from interdependence and from an awareness of shared identity. They are peculiar in this, that they protect as well as demand. In a genuine community people are not mere means or resources, to be deployed, manipulated or sacrificed without concern for their interests as individuals. Here, we can discern the animating principle of community, which we may call the union of solidarity and respect.

This principle has great practical significance. It comes into play not only as a result of moral understanding, but wherever the quality of human relations is important, wherever more than minimal levels of morale and performance are desired. Thus it is that in business or military organizations – which try to mobilize human energies in disciplined ways for predetermined ends – many efforts are made to approximate (or fake) the principle of community.[1] That is so because employees and soldiers tend to accept discipline, do their jobs better and cooperate more effectively when they are treated with respect, when their connections are personal as well as instrumental, when they feel protected and nurtured as well as controlled and when they sense that they are included as valued members of an enterprise, which both requires and gives loyalty.

So community is about respect and nurture as well as solidarity. Thus understood, solidarity takes on a special character and is subject to moral judgement. When solidarity is divorced from personal well-being, it is likely to be a caricature of community, not a fair representation of its meaning and promise. To give up personal dignity and integrity in exchange for pay, or for the satisfaction of serving a leader or cause, is a betrayal of community, not a fulfilment of it.

There is a close kinship between the moral bonds of community and those of friendship and family. These attachments share a commitment to the union of solidarity and respect. In each we see a balance struck between the needs of individual persons and what they owe to one another because of their relationship. In an ideal friendship, marriage or family, members show one another mutual respect, and they readily grant the freedoms respect requires. If demands are too great, if members or partners are neglected, humiliated or abused, relationships suffer and may dissolve. In these familiar contexts, we have no trouble understanding that excessive control and inappropriate dependency are pathological states which must be treated or avoided. They do not lead us to reject the ideal or to think of it as unattainable.

In one important respect, however, the model of community differs from family and friendship. Those connections, together with the identities and obligations they create, are characteristically special, local and particular. In contrast, the idea of community draws us outward as well as inward, towards inclusion as well as exclusion. Community builds on the limited and intimate associations of kinship, acquaintance and locality, but it also looks towards farther horizons and broader loyalties. Although many communities are parochial and exclusive, the ideal of community accepts diversity and pledges inclusion.

Diversity and inclusion are familiar themes in ordinary conceptions of community. In many contexts we understand community as an ensemble of relatively loosely coordinated activities and groups. Thus, the 'Catholic community' includes all communicants, lay and clerical, as well as a variety of schools, orders, publishers and sports teams. Loyalty and cohesion are certainly important, but so is an implied promise of caring and concern for everyone's interests. Much the same may be said of expressions such as 'the university community', 'the law school community', 'the medical community', 'the intelligence community'. Inclusion is the leitmotif: in colleges, staff and students as well as professors; in government, a cluster of cooperating agencies. For the sake of 'community', boundaries are broken down. The focus shifts to a common enterprise and a common life.

Indeed, communities are strengthened when belonging takes many forms and when people are animated by diverse and compelling motives – when they can pursue their own interests within the framework of community. Among religious or ethnic communities, where shared identities are stressed, solidarity is enhanced when opportunities are provided for childcare, education, recreation, charity, and self-improvement. Similarly, social or political movements often look for solidarity in a rich internal life.

The Experience of Community

My argument thus far suggests that community is best understood as a framework within which ordinary lives can go forward. In such a setting there must be leeway for autonomy and allowance for differences among families, localities and occupations. The experience of community is distorted or undone – may become a parody of itself – when unity is too tight or discipline is too rigid. Nevertheless, the community and its institutions must be strong enough and resilient enough to provide the benefits of a common life. Most important for strength and resilience are a shared history, shared beliefs, accepted authority and rules defining social obligations. Every effort to create, build or improve a community must supply these needs. The trick is to do so while recognizing the limits of social control.

A shared history (or 'community of memory', see Bellah et al., 1985: 152–5) may be the high drama of sacred origins, acute suffering or glorious victories. It may also be more homely and modest: family pictures in a treasured album. Splendid or modest, sacred or mundane, a shared history will fade without reminders: anniversaries, re-enactments, orations, legends. In these ways, memories are touched up and identities are formed.

A community's history is the source of shared beliefs, thought ways and rules for right conduct. This is, for the most part, a world taken for granted, accepted unconsciously in the course of growing up and as a result of unquestioned practice. However, rules and beliefs are not equally compelling. Some are fully internalized and strictly observed; others are frequently evaded, ignored, misunderstood or self-interestedly misconstrued. Some obligations are accepted uncritically; others are closely scrutinized and often challenged. Some rules are quite specific about what they require; many are ambiguous and open to interpretation. This 'normative order' should not be thought of as a solid cake of custom. Even in relatively stable and 'simple' societies, we find lively controversy and subtle argument.

In a thriving community, moreover, something more is wanted than a 'sense' of community. Communities are sustained by the realities of everyday life, including interdependence, reciprocity and self-interest. If people do not need each other, if little is to be gained from participation and commitment, communities are not likely to emerge or endure. This rational element is often overlooked, perhaps more often by theorists than practitioners. It is no surprise to anyone who has had hands-on experience in community organization. Self-interest is not necessarily an enemy of community. On the contrary, it is an engine of community, a reliable basis for cooperation and commitment. This is no disparagement of friendship, love or loyalty. Love and reciprocity need each other; they wither when apart.

Not All or None

A simple but essential conclusion must be drawn from the sociology of community. Groups can be more or less full-blown communities, and they can be communities in different ways. Some arise mainly from kinship and locality, others from shared ideals or a common enterprise. If we want a definition we can say: A group is a community in so far as it embraces a wide range of interests and activities, in so far as it takes account of whole persons, not just specialized contributions or roles; and in so far as bonds of commitment and culture are shared.

These 'in so far as' conditions shift attention from the question, 'is this a community?' to 'how far and in what ways does this group experience the bonds, benefits, and deficits of community?'. We can then focus on the difficult process of building or strengthening communities. Most importantly, we can more readily recognize that the values we associate with community can be sought, with different strategies and varying success, wherever sustained human interaction takes place – family life, work, education, politics, healthcare, urban design. In each sphere we can find ways of encouraging responsible conduct; we can find a proper recipe for a healthy union of solidarity and respect.

Kinds and Contexts

The elements of community I discussed (and some I have not discussed)[2] are not always equally important, and they occur in different combinations. In some communities a shared history is crucial; others make the most of a religious or political identity. All communities have rules, but, as I have pointed out, rules are not equally sacred, nor do they spell out what people must do in great detail. These differences remind us that communities vary in kind, as well as in the extent to which bonds of community exist. Monastic communities are closely controlled and turn life inward. Professional or occupational communities – police, military, legal, medical – are unified by craft values or by distinctive style of life. Extended family communities, based on common ancestry, are sustained by inheritance, family traditions, patronage and other special claims and obligations. In short, all communities have recognizable but often distinctive ways of bonding.

It is sometimes thought that the most tightly knit community is also the most genuine or ideal community. That is a mistake because a very tightly knit community is likely to be distorted in one way or another, overly exclusive and withdrawn, or demanding too much commitment and conformity. Such communities – for example, some religious or therapeutic groups – need special justification, and they are recognized as special by the larger community within which they exist as isolated and perhaps protected enclaves. A more normal or natural community is less disciplined, less insistent on conformity, not governed by a closely specified ideal, such as a monastic way of life. In a normal community, we must take account of how people actually live, and want to live, not only how we would like them to live.[3]

The pull of normality is recognized in the following account of 'hippie' enclaves in the 1960s:

> Typically, communes were made up fairly uniformly of young people who identified with the subculture of drugs, rock, and voluntary poverty. . . . By contrast the community embraced a greater diversity of people, not just the hip and the young. Where communes left finances, work and decision to the fickle will of group consciousness, communities leaned more heavily on definite structures: work systems, treasurers, and corporations. . . . The physical as well as the emotional distance was greater in a community than in a commune. Traditionally, a community was made up of separate houses rather than a large common dwelling. (Houriet, 1971: 205f)

The commune seeks communion, not community, psychic unity, not the tempered discord of ordinary life.

A democratic community has special features, notably free speech and association, and uncoerced voting. But politics is not all of life. The political system strives for harmony with, not opposition to, the non-political incentives, relationships, purposes and demands of civil society.

In his writings on the history of science, Thomas Kuhn (1970) emphasized how much good science depends on shared standards and ways of thinking (see also Selznick, 1992). These include basic requirements of scientific method, such as accuracy, objectivity and more specific criteria of respectable and creative work in geology, physics or chemistry. Each discipline is governed by rules of argument and evidence, including mathematical arguments, and by other norms of good science, including what knowledge should be taken as settled, at least for the enquiry at hand. Transmitted in the course of scientific education, these norms are reinforced when new professors and research scientists are appointed, and in peer review of applications for research grants.

As in other communities, the norms of science create personal and group identities. They say what it means to be a self-respecting physicist or entomologist. But what Kuhn calls the 'disciplinary matrix' – the special premises and rules of a science – is only incidentally about identity. It is mainly about the benefits of community for creativity, productivity and excellence. The ethos of science encourages initiative, challenge and dissent, but the challenge must be credible, the dissent responsible.

In thinking about kinds of community, we have to know what each kind requires, what each has to offer and what sacrifices each demands. Despite the differences, however, the essential features of community are present. From them we can draw lessons about the benefits and costs of community in the context at hand. For example, in the scientific communities, the benefits of sharing a common perspective. We can learn something about how to create or repair a particular kind of community. We would not want to create a counterfeit community or a parody of community. If we want a special kind of community, such as a democratic community, a religious community, or a community of scientists or scholars, we should have reason to believe it is a *community* we are creating.

Virtues and Deficits

There is nothing unusual about the coexistence and interdependence of good and evil. We can safely say, with little exaggeration, that every virtue has a humbling vice. Hence, we often need to defend 'genuine' love, freedom, friendship, religion, democracy, law, education or science from the corruptions that arise from their own weaknesses and temptations. Love may create emotional dependency; religion is corrupted by superstition, science by mindless 'scientism', democracy by populism, journalism by bottom-line pressures for news as entertainment. That we are aware of these deficits does not lead us to spurn love or reject science. Instead, we redouble our efforts to discover what is genuine and make it prevail.

Like family, friendship, knowledge and statesmanship, community is a prima facie good. The favourable presumption is justified by what we have learned from experience. But in a given case, the presumption is rebuttable by showing that the evil outweighs the good. We do this when, for example, communities are distracted and distorted by ideological extremism or by corrupt or criminal activity.

The fundamental virtue of community is an ethos of open-ended obligation. Marriages are supposed to endure, through good times and bad, 'for richer for poorer, in sickness and in health'. Parents have open-ended obligations to their children, and children to their parents. In these relationships people do make choices – whether and whom to marry, whether to have children and how many – but choice fades in importance once the commitment is made. Parents must care for the children they have, not for those they would have liked to have; and children have the same problem in caring for their elderly parents.

The principle of open-ended obligation extends well beyond marriage and parenting. It has force wherever caring and commitment matter. The effect is to enlarge the obligations fixed by contract or by a closely specified role. We see this in many settings – among employers and employees, teachers and students, doctors and patients, business firms and communities. Wherever open-ended obligation prevails, people are treated as multifaceted persons and as members of a community. In this way the experience of belonging is thickened. It may begin in limited ways, but it gravitates towards wholeness, interdependence, loyalty and commitment.

There is of course a downside to this virtue. When obligations are diffuse and unclear, too much may be asked of us, as many family dramas reveal, and as do the demands of organizational, political and professional life (Whyte, 1956; Coser, 1974). We do not respond to this problem by rejecting the principle of open-ended obligation, or the settings within which it is wholesome and appropriate. Instead we narrow obligations when that makes more sense. Caring and commitment are surely needed, but we do not need them all the time, nor do we have to find them everywhere. The rule is: look for nurture in a proper place.

The weakening of community in modern times is partly due to the ascendancy of limited obligation in social life. Liberal culture has celebrated 'freedom of contract', thereby advancing economic prosperity as well as ideals of choice, dignity, consent and rationality. But the modern contract is a contract of *limited* obligation; ideally, its terms are specific and the cost of a breach is known. Its spirit is wholly opposed to the ethos of open-ended obligation.

The idea of contract works best when relationships are temporary or can be readily changed. The model is less appropriate, and less effective, when continuing relationships are contemplated or required. In continuing relationships, whether in business or in family life, people want to stay connected and retain the benefits of cooperation, despite changing circumstances. Therefore, they try to resolve problems by negotiation, without necessarily insisting on the specific terms of a contract. In other words, as we approach community the principle of limited obligation loses force, is pushed into the background, invoked only when a breakdown is expected or desired.

Open-ended obligation fosters trust, depends on trust and encourages communication. Trust and good faith prevail when people can rely on one another to honour their commitments: as parents, friends, or business associates; when they can appeal to shared purposes instead of demanding literal compliance; when all can appreciate taken-for-granted understandings that underlie a promise or policy. The transition is from arm's-length bargaining to a spirit of cooperation.

Trust is the great mortar of group life. It is a kind of social capital, a resource people can draw on when they need help or when they form new families, enterprises or institutions. Like love and friendship, trust is only a prima facie good, since it can be misplaced or self-destructive. Similarly, social capital creates vested interests, inertia and resistance to change. These are drawbacks, but hardly anyone would deny on that account the benefits of trust and other forms of social capital.

A less well-understood virtue of community is the contribution it makes to responsible judgement. To participate in community is to be aware of and responsive to a complex set of interests and values. Therefore, the goals we seek and the ideals we embrace are tempered by concern for how they affect other goals and other ideals. Artists, businesspeople, scholars or politicians cannot be wholly or single-mindedly committed to their specialized concerns. The more sensitive they are to the communities they belong to, the less free they are to act in irresponsible and ultimately self-defeating ways. A corollary is the enhancement of personal rationality. We do not think of participation in communities as irrational or self-destructive. On the contrary, without community rationality is often precarious and may be lost. If an electorate consists of detached individuals, without anchors of interest and association, it is vulnerable to manipulation by political demagogues. Young people tend to gain in rationality as they settle down, accept obligations and choose goals that are genuinely satisfying and attainable. It is in and through the stable friendships we make, the education we get, the groups and institutions we embrace that we make self-preserving life-plans and rational choices.

This is not to deny that the experience of belonging can also limit rationality. It may also restrict horizons, stifle initiative and foster uncritical attitudes towards tradition and authority. Here again, the virtue has a humbling vice; here again, the virtue is genuine, despite the vice.

An Irrepressible Tension

It is obvious that community is not a comfortable idea, blessed with simplicity. On the contrary, it is one of those great concepts from which we learn the perplexities and burdens of social life. Most important is the conflict between exclusion and inclusion. There are good reasons to make communities open or permeable in some ways, even if they are closed in other ways. There are benefits to be gained from local attachments. But those attachments are routinely transcended when people recognize the advantages of broader identities and ideals. In the language of sociology and moral philosophy, the tension is between 'universalist' and 'particularist' ways of choosing, judging and relating. This conflict is pervasive and irrepressible, but it is not irreconcilable. Finding ways of accommodating the abiding values of particularism and the just claims of universalism is a major part of the communitarian project.

The Promise of Community

The common good – the good of community – cannot rest on a narrowly political or economic ideology. Broader interests are at stake. Among these are the challenges of modernity, especially the problems created by new technologies and new forms of family life, work, education and politics. The great task is to retain and strengthen the benefits of modern life – prosperity, health, longevity, political freedom – while repairing damage done to the social fabric.

Two closely related principles are centrepieces of communitarian thinking, and they ought to underpin any serious attempt to renew progressive politics. These are personal and social responsibility and social justice. Responsibility has been a dominant theme, indeed a trademark or watchword, of the contemporary communitarian movement. Amitai Etzioni edits a journal called *The Responsive Community: Rights and Responsibilities*. And, as I have noted, 'responsibility' is highlighted in the programme of the Democratic Leadership Council. The aim is to enhance responsibility at all levels and in all sectors of the community: among individuals, groups and the community as a whole. Guided by ideals of principle, honour and self-respect, responsible conduct is in part self-regarding; it is also and essentially other-regarding. Responsible parents, teachers, physicians or public officials protect their own integrity, and they do so by attending to the interests of children, students, patients and citizens, especially when what they do or fail to do affects those interests in serious ways. They cannot be indifferent to the conditions that make social cooperation possible, necessary and effective. Therefore, they honour the obligations they have inherited or assumed.

We cannot divorce individual or personal responsibility from social or collective responsibility. We expect adults to be self-restrained and self-reliant, to take care of themselves, avoiding distractions, temptations and addictions, and to help others when necessary, especially those who can be hurt by misdeeds and failings. This concern for personal responsibility cautions respect for conventional morality – in so far as the conventions uphold baseline standards of respect, restraint and helpfulness. On the other hand, character is a product of social experience. To become morally aware and morally competent, individuals need the nurture and support usually supplied by families, friends, schools and churches. When this support is absent or inadequate, for whatever reason, including the fragmenting pressures of modern life, new policies, practices and institutions must be put in place. New ways must be designed for providing childcare, preventive medicine, early education, vocational training and other social services. These programmes call for collective will, intelligence and sacrifice, which in turn requires personal responsibility. Being willing to pay taxes is a start.

In a communitarian public philosophy, an ethic of responsibility governs the activities and frames the self-conceptions of all institutions, including business, healthcare, education, science and government, which have become such prominent features of the social landscape. Each enterprise should be seen (and see itself) as a civic-minded member of a community from which it draws vital resources. Of course, autonomy is needed, so that every institution can do what each does best. However, institutional autonomy, like personal autonomy, is conditional, not absolute. No enterprise can justify injuring employees or consumers, or degrading the natural environment by invoking a supposed right to do as it pleases, or whatever seems necessary to reduce costs and maximize gains.

Social responsibility is fully realized when social justice prevails. If a community cares for all its members, it will strive for a just ordering of rights and duties, needs and contributions, privileges and opportunities. The balance struck is history's best judgement as to how the promise of community may be realized. Although often criticized and even scorned, social justice remains a powerful and resilient expression of the human spirit. It is a fluid, historically contingent, yet inescapable standard for judging regimes, policies and social systems. We speak of *social* justice when we have in mind the structural conditions which largely determine the life chances of individuals: how much security, health, comfort and esteem they will have, relative to others and the available resources; how far they can rise in the social scale; how vulnerable they will be to bad choices and bad luck. These issues make inequality the chief concern of social justice.

The great problem is how to achieve moral equality within a community that must accept many forms of inequality as necessary and proper. Moral equality is the principle that every person is equally worthy of respect and concern. This is a foundation of community, whose defining principle, I have argued, is a union of solidarity and respect. It is also the keystone in the arch of social justice. Thus the promise of community is also a promise of social justice.

An ideal of moral equality makes two demands. First is the imperative of inclusion: bridging differences, discouraging alienation and seeking reconciliation. Especially important is the divisiveness created by extremist ideologies and parochial passions. An ideal of inclusion underlies the American constitutional mandate that 'all persons born or naturalized in the United States are citizens of the United States, and of the State in which they reside'. This provision of the Fourteenth Amendment, made possible by the Union victory in the Civil War, was a long step towards full legal equality for all Americans, regardless of their special backgrounds or origins.

The second demand of moral equality is that it should serve as an ever-present judgement on existing patterns of social inequality. For many purposes, including effective government, economic prosperity and cultural creativity, we need leaders, managers, artists, professionals and investors. To get them, we offer special incentives, in the form of special privileges and rewards. These concessions are proper because they benefit the community, but they do not advance, indeed they often threaten, the principle of moral equality. In response, we insist on equality of opportunity, effective as well as formal. This is, indeed, the main contribution of liberal society to social justice. Beyond equality of opportunity, however, lies a broader horizon of caring and concern. In the competitive race, many are left behind and left out, with disastrous consequences for their capacity to live decent, healthy, self-respecting lives. They too are moral equals, and must be recognized as such in a fully realized community.

Notes

1 It has often been noted that business firms and other organizations try to create a sense of community without providing for the reality of community. But this should remind us of the adage that 'hypocrisy is the homage which vice renders to virtue'.
2 For example, legitimate authority, strong institutions, leadership.
3 On the sociology of a tightly knit community, see Zablocki (1971).

References

Bellah, R., Madsen, R., Sullivan, W. M., Swidler, A. and Tipton, S. M. (1985) *Habits of the Heart* (Berkeley: University of California Press).
Coser, A. (1974) *Greedy Institutions* (New York: The Free Press).
Giddens, A. (2000) *The Third Way and its Critics* (Cambridge: Polity).
Houriet, R. (1971) *Getting Back Together* (New York: Coward-McCann).
Kuhn, T. (1970) *The Structure of Scientific Revolutions*, 2nd edn (Chicago: University of Chicago Press).
Selznick, P. (1992) *The Moral Commonwealth: Social Theory and the Promise of Community* (London: University of California Press).
Whyte, W. (1956) *The Organizational Man* (New York: Simon and Schuster).
Zablocki, B. (1971) *The Joyful Community* (Baltimore: Penguin Books).

PART II

FAMILIES, CITIZENS AND THE STATE

6

Citizenship Begins at Home: The New Social Contract and Working Families

Linda C. McClain

Introduction

Attempts in America and Britain to renew progressive politics have focused from the outset on the need to rethink citizens' entitlement to welfare support from their government. The Clinton Administration, for example, promised to 'end welfare as we know it', and sought to develop welfare policies to 'put people back to work' and 'empower' them through a time-limited period of 'education, training, and childcare' to 'break the cycle of dependency' (Clinton and Gore, 1992: 164–5). This 'Third Way' approach deserves credit for its recognition of a place for public responsibility to foster the political economy of citizenship, that is, the institutional arrangements that are vital to persons' personal and democratic self-government. A consistent theme in Third Way political rhetoric has been that of a new social contract premised on mutual responsibility, or demanding personal responsibility and governmental provision of opportunity (ibid.; Marshall et al., 1996: 7–8). In short, '[p]utting our people first means honoring and rewarding those who work hard and play by the rules' (Clinton and Gore, 1992: 14).

However, in championing 'welfare to work' as its core element and extolling market labour as the source of the dignity of a 'real' job, the Third Way approach suffers from its inability squarely to confront the role of care – and care work – in the political economy of citizenship (or, the institutional arrangements that foster self-government). This leaves care, which should be affirmed as a core public value and as a vital component of social reproduction (i.e., the reproduction of society from one generation to the next) in a precarious state. The welfare policy debate cries out for more explicit attention to the vital role of care needed by children in order to meet their developmental and material needs and to prepare them to take their place as responsible, self-governing citizens. Too often, the problem of care surfaces as an incidental issue or as an obstacle to successful market participation, as welfare reformers stress that parents cannot be successful market participants if they are unable to find safe, affordable, quality childcare for their children.

Yet Third Way proponents must, inescapably, return to the issue of care, because they envision strong families as undergirding or underwriting a successful democracy. Families feature as perhaps the most important among the institutions of civil society and are to be a source of values and a generator of human capital (Marshall et al., 1996). However, this recognition of the crucial role of families in fostering democratic self-government leads to a seeming paradox: the same political leaders who championed moving mothers from welfare to work – and away from their children – to bestow upon them the dignity of a real job and put them back in touch with core American values of work and responsibility now urge governmental support for 'working families', because the job of raising our children is 'one of the most important jobs of all' (Gore, 2000b). Perhaps even more surprising is the gendered dimension of some of these appeals. If phase one of welfare reform was encouraging personal responsibility by moving mothers from welfare to work, these political leaders now speak of phase two, or the next step, as intensifying efforts to strengthen families through promoting 'responsible fatherhood', or the idea (which enjoys widespread bipartisan support) that fathers should provide not only financial support for their children but also take a more active role in caring for them, since 'the most important job anyone will ever have is the job of parent' (Gore, 2000a).[1]

This emerging rhetoric of supporting working families has the potential to open the door for a more robust and sustained focus upon the role of care in fostering human and social capital and to resist the simple equation of personal responsibility with market participation, without attending to the other responsibilities adults must honour and the other roles they must fulfil. And the responsible fatherhood movement may encourage incremental movement away from the traditional male breadwinner/female caregiver model upon which our care economy has been based. Indeed, it would be a welcome, if ironic, development if exhorting workplaces to become more *father*-friendly catalysed the needed institutional restructuring to help parents be market workers and responsible parents (of the sort long advocated by feminists (Williams, 2000)). But to open the door wide enough to allow for better ways to envision the new social contract of mutual responsibility and the types of institutional forms that might support it, we need a more adequate analysis of the public value of care and of the legacy of the gendered structure of caregiving (and its intersection with race and class) in our industrial society.

From Welfare to Work

The neglect of care work

The welfare reforms in the USA of the mid-1990s, championed by the New Democrats and other proponents of Third Way philosophy, such as the Progressive Policy Institute, advanced a new social contract of 'mutual responsibility', or affording opportunity to welfare recipients and asking them to take responsibility and adhere to core values of work, family and responsibility (Clinton and Gore, 1992: 164–8). Government would 'demand that people work hard and play by the rules' and 'honor and reward those who do' (ibid. 164). This required a rejection of a philosophy of 'entitlement', or of 'something for nothing', and the embrace of an 'ethic of reciprocity' (Yankelovich, 1999). It meant that 'those who can work, must work' (Clinton, 2000a). Thus, moving 'from welfare to work' became a key sign of achieving personal responsibility. In effect, this was an implicit repudiation of the social contract thought to underlie previous government proposals to provide assistance so that mothers could stay out of the paid labour force and rear their children, which was judged to be a valuable social contribution (Gordon, 1994; Skocpol, 1992). For, if the 'ethical core of the Third Way' is 'civic reciprocity', which requires that, 'whenever possible, policies should be devised so that citizens who contribute to the community are rewarded, and those who benefit from the community give something back', then, as applied to welfare, public benefits should be linked to the 'bedrock value of work' so that 'everyone . . . put[s] something back in the common pot' (Marshall 1999). So formulated, the notion of contributing to the community seems to neglect the idea that caregiving – that is, attending to children's needs for care – makes a valuable social contribution worthy of recognition and support. The task of social reproduction, of nurturing the next generation and attending to their moral education and character formation, simply seems absent from this idea of 'work'.

Even before the Republicans recaptured the White House in 2000, they had succeeded in pushing Bill Clinton's welfare reform plans into more conservative and punitive guises in the Republican 'Contract with America' and the 'Personal Responsibility Act', which was enacted, in modified form, as the Personal Responsibility and Work Opportunity Reconciliation Act of 1996 (PRWORA). This rhetoric spoke less of providing opportunity than of ending pathological dependency of non-working adults on government subsidies, fighting 'illegitimacy' (or, the birth of children outside wedlock) and restoring marriage and work (Gillespie and Schellhas, 1994; McClain, 1996). It also called for returning power to the states through block grants and experimentation and reducing the federal role (even though, in reality, PRWORA imposed considerable requirements upon states). New Democrats shared these Republican concerns about family forms, work and limits to federal power, but the rhetoric attending PRWORA put less emphasis on investing resources to empower people and foster opportunity and more on ending pathological behaviour and reducing expenditures borne unjustly by hardworking taxpayers (ibid.). Clinton signed PRWORA, while pledging to correct its failings. Incidentally, this willingness to sign the Act brings to mind a frequent criticism of the Third Way approach to renewing progressive politics, namely, that it constantly attempts to position itself in the centre and to mirror public opinion, while the centre itself shifts more and more to the right (Chait, 1998).

Several years into the implementation of PRWORA, as millions of former welfare recipients move into paying jobs, there appears to be an emergent model of 'supporting work' by low-wage workers to 'make work pay' (Clinton, 2000b). The new social contract of responsibility and opportunity requires that government facilitate persons' exercise of responsibility. What is encouraging about this emerging rhetoric is that it appears to reject the model of 'playing by the rules' underlying PRWORA: that welfare recipients failed to play by the rules because they – unlike working families – expected 'outside' help in providing for their children. Instead, the new social contract underlying the post-welfare era seems to be not that responsible parents should have *no* expectation of outside assistance, but that parents who manifest their personal responsibility by working for wages may reasonably expect governmental support in their efforts to provide for their families. Thus, it is one's willingness to 'play by the rules' and work (hard) for wages that makes it appropriate for government to 'honour and reward' that worker.

This way of approaching a model of mutual responsibility holds promise, but, as suggested above, it leaves care in a precarious place, for supporting the care work of parents remains incidental to supporting their market work. Yet Third Way rhetoric itself seems to harbour the potential to break free of this model when it speaks of 'honouring' families and supporting strong families in their vital role in social reproduction. To develop this potential more fully, the model of mutual responsibility and of the political economy of citizenship requires a more explicit focus upon the public value of care and upon care work as socially valuable work, work that the market insufficiently 'honours' or 'rewards'.

The partial recognition of the care crisis

A central problem in welfare reform has consistently been that moving mothers from 'welfare to work' requires finding safe, affordable and appropriate substitute childcare for their children. Similarly, a consistent theme in feminist work on welfare has been that calls to move women from welfare to work renders invisible the value of women's caretaking labour (Kittay, 1999b; Roberts, 1999). There is a care crisis that spans class lines, because the old male breadwinner/ female caregiver model no longer reflects the practice of most American families, but no new regime that embraces both commitment to care and a commitment to women's equality has emerged to take its place (Harrington, 1999). Not only do current economic arrangements, and the demands of employers, constrain parents' ability to spend time with their children, but parents also face a crisis in finding good-quality substitute care for their children. Some studies conclude that 'the vast majority of children receive care that is of poor to moderate quality; few receive care that is good enough to stimulate their development' (Kisker and Ross, 1997). Poor and low-income people suffer disproportionately from a shortage of safe, affordable and accessible childcare (Annie E. Casey Foundation, 1998; White 1999). Many low-income jobs fail to offer workers the financial resources necessary for them to make safe and developmentally appropriate arrangements for the care of their children. Also, the terms and conditions of many low-income jobs make the task of finding such childcare especially difficult, if not impossible (Annie E. Casey Foundation, 1998).

The childcare problems faced most acutely by low-income workers are a serious obstacle to many former welfare recipients' successful participation in the workforce (GAO, 1997; Henly, 1999; Kisker and Ross, 1997). Although PRWORA made provisions for funding child-care, serious unmet needs remain and will increase as more former welfare recipients with dependent children engage in market labour (GAO, 1997, 1998; Cohn, 2000). As well as jeopardizing parents' ability to work, this childcare crisis also imposes large costs on employers in terms of lost productivity, as well as hurting children and society as a whole (Annie E. Casey Foundation, 1998; Kisker and Ross, 1997). When market work takes caregivers away from the unpaid work that is the ' "glue" that keeps low-income families from falling apart', and no adequate substitute care facilities are made available, this also imposes very human costs on families (Dodson, 1999). Thus, although empirical studies concerning the impact on mothers working at paid employment suggest that such employment may be beneficial for children (Moore and Driscoll, 1997; Zaslow and Emig, 1997), some studies caution that the terms and conditions of the low-income jobs that many former welfare recipients are likely to find may actually be detrimental to the quality of children's home life, their safety, and to the quality of the parent–child relationship (Annie E. Casey Foundation, 1998; Parcel and Menaghan, 1997). Without a more explicit focus upon the public value of care and of care as a valuable form of work, it is difficult to bring these types of human costs, incurred from a shortage of good-quality substitute childcare as well as by insufficient parental time for caring for children, to the foreground of public discussion.

To be sure, many of those concerned with the renewal of progressive politics recognize that accessible, affordable, quality childcare is vital to the success of 'welfare to work', and that states have not yet done enough to ensure that success (Waller, 1997). There is a real risk of the problem of childcare being inadequately addressed if it continues to feature merely as incidental to 'supporting work'. Undeniably, it would be a positive step forward if government were to strengthen efforts to support working families through such measures as education and training and by expanding the Earned Income Tax Credit, so that the new social contract would reward (market) work by ensuring that working families were not in poverty. But it is also vital to affirm not only the public value of care work, but also the importance of such work as part of what 'working families' – as well as other caregivers – do.

Recognizing Care as a Public Value and Care Work as Work

A better approach would be to think about childcare not only as a precondition for parents' successful participation in the workforce, but also as a component of their responsible self-government. An expanded conception of responsible self-government should affirm other forms of personal responsibility. In other words, government should foster parents' personal responsibility by supporting their caregiving work. This should encompass not only helping parents obtain safe, good-quality substitute care, but also helping them to meet their own responsibilities to provide care for their children. Focusing on care as a dimension of family 'work' would invite more explicit recognition of the public values at stake in ensuring the nurture of children. Not only should society care that the immediate physical and emotional needs of children are met, but the reproduction of society from one generation to the next depends upon the moral development and education of children, so that they develop the capacities for responsible self-government. The family, of course, is not the only institution responsible for social reproduction, but it has a special role to play with respect to the development of children (Rawls, 1997) – as well as for the adults within the family.[2] It is necessary to develop a more robust principle of public responsibility to support the work of families.

Support for such a principle exists in the work of a growing number of feminist, liberal and progressive thinkers, who have urged greater attention to care work as essential to human health and development (Fineman, 2000a; Fineman, 2000b; Harrington, 1999; Kittay 1999a). For example, in an article in *Nation*, Deborah Stone (2000: 13) calls for a national 'care movement', premised on the idea that 'caring for each other is the most basic form of civic participation', and she argued for a 'right to care', i.e., to give and receive care. Human development literature looking at the issue of care in a more global perspective finds that 'the role of care in the formation of human capabilities and in human development is fundamental' not only for children, but also for adults, and that 'the expansion of markets tends to penalize altruism and care'. It also finds that 'both individuals and institutions have been free-riding on the caring labour that mainly women provide' (United Nations, 1999). Feminist scholars such as Martha Fineman similarly argue that this caring labour, which addresses 'inevitable' human dependency, such as that of children, affords a subsidy to society and that it is appropriate for society to recognize a public responsibility towards support carework (Fineman, 2000a). Feminists have long argued that the prevailing political and legal order pays insufficient attention to values such as care and interdependency, as well as to the disproportionate responsibility of women for care (as paid and unpaid caregivers) (Kittay, 1999a; West, 1997). They persuasively argue for a redistribution of responsibility within families and among families, corporations and government, so that families no longer bear the sole burden of social reproduction (Fineman, 2000a, 2000b).

Another source of support for the recognition of the important caregiving work that families do to foster human development and for the fact that institutional arrangements would be a better way to support parents' ability to provide that care – as well as to find high-quality substitute caregivers to help in that task – may be found in communitarian thought, in much of the literature calling for a renewal of the institutions of civil society, such as families, and in some Third Way writings. This common concern seems a promising start for a national conversation about care and care work and about a public responsibility to support such work (Fineman, 2000a; Harrington, 1999). It also promises to challenge definitions of personal responsibility that exhaust themselves by focusing upon market work to the exclusion of family work. For example, the Responsive Communitarian Platform affirms the responsibilities of parents for the moral education of children and proclaims that workplaces should provide the maximum flexibility so parents can preserve an important part of their time for such family work (Etzioni, 1993: 256–7). Illustrative of a Third Way approach, the New Progressive Declaration argues that society 'pursue new public and private strategies intended to support parents' efforts to fulfill their responsibilities' to their children (Marshall et al., 1996). Recent calls to renew civil society similarly affirm the vital role of families as 'seedbeds of virtue' and exhort corporations to facilitate, rather than hinder, parents' exercise of responsibility (Council on Civil Society, 1998; National Commission on Civic Renewal, 1998; McClain and Fleming, 2000).

One way to frame the question that may help keep the focus on fostering care work and recognizing it as work is: 'How could public policy encourage and enable parents of both genders, at all income levels, to play a major role in caring for their own children, without either reinforcing the gendered distribution of care work or the marginalization of caretakers from waged work and public life?' (White, 1999; 138). One helpful approach may be a 'universal caregiver' model, which uses the norm of most women's current life-patterns, combining breadwinning and caregiving, and redesigns institutions so as to eliminate the difficulty and strain in meeting these dual responsibilities (Fraser, 1997). Although concerns for sex equality and family diversity counsel some caution about the 'responsible fatherhood' movement embraced by some Third Way proponents,[3] the movement's calls for 'father-friendly' (as well as parent-friendly) workplaces and new definitions of fatherhood may be a catalyst for some of that institution redesign (Gore, 1996, 2000a). Whilst I will not elaborate further on how, in practice, we should 'honour' and 'reward' the work of families, in the next chapter David Anderson sets out a progressive family policy – the Family Unity Act.

I will conclude with two observations on the future direction for locating the role of care in progressive political thinking. First, it is important to affirm a strong principle of public (and corporate) support for the work families do in social reproduction, but Third Way suspicion of 'big government' and its enthusiasm for markets may conflict with a robust call for such public support and lead to expecting too much of families (Marshall et al., 1996).[4] This retreat from ambitious governmental programmes and the embrace of the market seems less 'progressive' than an approach that recognizes that market forces are not necessarily compatible with civic health and focuses upon care as a vantage point from which to critique the ways in which current economic arrangements impinge upon families, devalue care and impose human costs justified in the name of 'efficiency' and productivity (Fineman, 2000b, McClain and Fleming, 2000; McCluskey, 2000). Here, it may be that alliances across the political spectrum are possible.

Secondly, there is also a risk that if Third Way proponents too closely identify supporting families with 'shoring up' a particular form of the family – i.e., the two-parent, marital (heterosexual) family (Marshall et al., 1996), in an era of diverse families, they miss an opportunity for a more inclusive and apt family policy. Elsewhere, I have argued for an approach that focuses less on form than on how to support the functions families serve (McClain, 1998; McClain and Fleming, 2000). Here, I simply second the family policy advocated by David Anderson which supports both more traditional families and less traditional families (see next chapter). Further, because most American families rely on some substitute caregiving, a more inclusive approach to family work should train its lens upon some issues of equity raised by such caregiving. Those include, for example, the low wages generally afforded caregivers, the disproportionate role of women (especially women of colour) in such work and the human costs of the 'global nanny chain', or 'invisible ecology of care, linking rich and poor countries', when first-world mothers depend on nannies who have emigrated from other countries, who in turn depend upon other caregivers to care for children left behind (Hochschild, 2000).

Any policy which couples the demand for personal responsibility with recognition of governmental responsibility to provide opportunity deserves credit for validating an appropriate role for government in fostering human capacities for responsible self-government. As applied to welfare policy, however, the simple emphasis upon 'welfare to work' and on no more 'something for nothing' leaves out care work as work. As former welfare recipients now feature in policy discussions as 'working families' who deserve support, the rhetoric of 'supporting working families' runs the same risk if it focuses only on market work, to the exclusion of the important work families do in caring for children and fostering their human capacities, thus ensuring social reproduction. This leaves care and care work in a precarious place. A better way is for Third Way thinkers to embrace more fully their commitment to families and build upon the idea, already in their rhetoric, that caring for children is an 'important job', deserving of societal support. This would give care work a more secure place in policy discussions and also invite closer attention to the idea of care as a public value.

Notes

1   The 'responsible fatherhood' movement first gained national prominence several years ago with the publication of such books as David Blankenhorn's *Fatherless America* (1995). The basic premise of the movement is that the absence of fathers from families – through divorce, female-headed single-parent families and also 'emotionally absent' fathers who are physically present in the home – is America's foremost social crisis and a source of many other problems. In 1995, Clinton directed all federal agencies to review their programmes and policies with the goal of strengthening the role of fathers in families (Clinton, 1995).

2   In this chapter, I focus upon one dimension of the care work done by families and how that work fosters the capacities for self-government: caring for children. But I also believe that families potentially serve as important sites for the development and exercise of the moral capacities of adult members of families and allow for the realization of important moral goods.

3   I have elaborated on some of these concerns, which relate to the

underlying gender ideology about men's natures and the need for taming through marriage, elsewhere (McClain, 1996). Also I think claims about the 'unique' and 'irreplaceable' role of fathers in families are more in the category of apologetics or advocacy than well-founded empirical ones, and may also open the door to more patriarchal notions of male authority within families. However, I welcome the emphasis upon empowering low-income men, on teaching men non-violent conflict resolution and on defining fathers' roles more explicitly in terms of caregiving.

4   For example, the New Progressive Declaration states: 'It is because Americans can turn less and less to big government that we should look to family as the primary source of the security, socialization, and investment necessary to prepare the next generation and sustain the present one' (Marshall et al., 1996). Some critics of the Third Way approach to welfare fear that the demand for personal responsibility will apply only to the poor, and not to the corporate sector in the way necessary to address the economic conditions contributing to poverty (Edelman, 1999).

References

The Annie E. Casey Foundation (1998) *Kids Count Data Book* (Baltimore: The Annie E. Casey Foundation).

Blankenhorn, D. (1995) *Fatherless America: Confronting Our Most Urgent Social Problem* (New York: Basic Books).

Bush, G. W. (2000) 'Governor Bush Addresses National Summit on Fatherhood', Presidential Campaign Press Materials, 2 June (www/lexis.com).

Chait, J. (1998) 'The Self-Contradictions of the Third Way', *The New Republic*, 16 November.

Clinton, B. and Gore, A. (1992) *Putting People First* (New York: Times Books).

Clinton, President (1995) Memorandum for the Heads of Executive Departments and Agencies on Supporting the Role of Fathers in Families (http://aspe.os.dhhs.gov/fathers/pclinton.txt).

Clinton, President (2000a) 'Clinton's Address to Party: Extolling 8 Years of Change in America', *New York Times*, 15 August: A17.

Clinton, President (2000b) Statement by the President (Office of the Press Secretary).

Cohn, J. (2000) 'Child's Play: Why Universal High-Quality Day Care Should Be Elementary', *American Prospect*, 19 June–3 July: 46–9.

Council on Civil Society (1998) *A Call to Civil Society: Why Democracy Needs Moral Truths* (New York: Institute for American Values).

Dodson, L. (1999) *Don't Call Us Out of Name: The Untold Lives of Women and Girls in Poor America* (Boston: Beacon Press).

Edelman, P. (1999) 'Welfare and the "Third Way"', *Dissent*, 46: 1.

Etzioni, A. (1993) *The Spirit of Community: Rights, Responsibilities, and the Communitarian Agenda* (New York: Crown Publishers).

Fineman, M. A. (2000a) 'Cracking the Foundational Myths: Independence, Autonomy, and Self-Sufficiency', *American University Journal of Gender, Social Policy and Law*, 8: 13–54.

Fineman, M. A. (2000b) 'The Family in Civil Society', *Chicago-Kent Law Review*, 75: 531–54.

Fraser, N. (1997) 'After the Family Wage: A Postindustrial Thought Experiment', in Fraser, *Justice Interruptus* (New York: Routledge).

GAO (Government Accounting Office) (1997) *Welfare Reform: Implications of Increased Work Participation for Child Care* (Washington, DC: GAO).

GAO (Government Accounting Office) (1998) *Welfare Reform: States' Efforts to Expand Child Care Programs* (Washington, DC: GAO).

Gillespie, N. and Schellhas, R. (eds) (1994) *Contract With America* (New York: Times Books).

Gordon, L. (1994) *Pitied But Not Entitled* (New York: Free Press).

Gore, A. (1996) 'Vice President Calls for "Father-Friendly" Workplaces', *US Newswire*, 3 May.

Gore, A. (2000a). 'Al Gore Proposes Next Step in Welfare Reform: Help for Responsible Parents, Crackdown on Deadbeats' (http://www. algore2000.com/briefingroom/releases/pr_102099_welfare_reform.html).

Gore, A. (2000b). 'Gore to Delegates and Nation: "My Focus Will Be on Working Families"', *New York Times*, 18 August: A21.

Harrington, M. (1999) *Care and Equality: Inventing a New Family Politics* (New York: Alfred A. Knopf).

Henly, J. R. (1999) 'Barriers to Finding and Maintaining Jobs: The Perspectives of Workers and Employers in the Low-Wage Labor Market', in L. White and J. Handler (eds), *Hard Labor: Women and Work in the Post-Welfare Era* (Armonk, NY: M. E. Sharpe).

Hochschild, A. R. (2000) 'The Global Nanny Chain', *American Prospect*, 2 January: 32.

Kisker, E. E. and Ross, C. M. (1997) 'Arranging Child Care', *The Future of Children: Welfare to Work*, 7: 99–109.

Kittay, E. F. (1999a) *Love's Labor: Essays on Women, Dependency, and Equality* (New York: Routledge).

Kittay, E. F. (1999b) 'Welfare, Dependency, and a Public Ethic of Care', in G. Mink (ed.), *Whose Welfare?* (Ithaca and London: Cornell University Press).

Marshall, W. (1999) 'The Rule of Reciprocity', *Blueprint: Ideas for a New Century* (http://www.dlc.org/blueprint/spring/default.html).

Marshall, W., From, A., Galston, W. A. and Ross, D. (1996) 'The New Progressive Declaration: A Political Philosophy for the Information Age'. Progressive Foundation.

McClain, L. C. (1996) ' "Irresponsible" Reproduction', *Hastings Law Journal*, 47: 339–453.

McClain, L. C. (1998) 'Toleration, Autonomy, and Governmental Pro-motion of Good Lives', *Ohio State Law Journal*, 59: 19–132.

McClain, L. C. and Fleming, J. E. (2000) 'Some Questions for Civil Society-Revivalists', *Chicago-Kent Law Review*, 75(2): 301–54.

McCluskey, M. (2000) 'Subsidized Lives and the Ideology of Efficiency', *American University Journal of Gender, Social Policy and Law*, 8: 115–52.

Moore, K. A. and Driscoll, A. K. (1997) 'Low-Wage Maternal Employment and Outcomes for Children: A Study', *The Future of Children: Welfare to Work*, 7: 122–7.

National Center for Children in Poverty (1999) *Map and Track: State Initiatives to Encourage Responsible Fatherhood* (http://cpmcnet.columbia.edu/dept/nccp/MT99text.html).

National Commission on Civic Renewal (1998) *A Nation of Spectators: How Civic Disengagement Weakens America and What We Can Do About It* (University of Maryland: National Commission on Civic Renewal).

Parcel, T. L. and Menaghan, E. G. (1997) 'Effects of Low-Wage Employ-ment on Family Well-Being',*The Future of Children: Welfare to Work*, 7: 116–21.

Rawls, J. (1997) 'The Idea of Public Reason Revisited', *University of Chicago Law Review*, 64: 765–807.

Roberts, D. (1999) 'Welfare's Ban on Poor Motherhood', in G. Mink (ed.), *Whose Welfare?* (Ithaca and London: Cornell University Press).

Skocpol, T. (1992) *Protecting Soldiers and Mothers* (Cambridge, MA: Belknap Press of Harvard University Press).

Stone, D. (2000) 'Why We Need a Care Movement', *The Nation*, 13 March.

United Nations (1999) 'The Invisible Heart: Care and the Global Economy', in *Human Development Report* (United Nations Development Programme).

Waller, M. (1997). 'Welfare-To-Work and Child Care: A Survey of Ten Big States' (http://dlcppi.org/texts/social/ccare.htm).

West, R. (1997) *Caring for Justice* (New York: New York University Press).

White, L. (1999) 'Quality Child Care for Low-Income Families: Despair, Impasse, Improvisation', in J. F. Handler and L. White (eds), *Hard Labor: Women and Work in the Post-Welfare Era* (Armonk, NY: M. E. Sharpe).

Williams, J. (2000) *Unbending Gender: Why Family and Work Conflict and What to Do About It* (New York: Oxford University Press).

Yankelovich, D. (1999) 'Sidebar: What's Fair?', *Blueprint: Ideas for a New Century* (http://www.dlc.org/blueprint/spring/default.html).

Zaslow, M. and Emig, C. (1997) 'When Low-Income Mothers Go to Work: Implications for Children', *The Future of Children: Welfare to Work*, 7: 110–15.

7

Towards a Progressive Family Policy: The Family Unity Act

David M. Anderson

This essay supports a progressive politics of the family. In the first section, I briefly explain the main tenets of what has been termed 'Third Way' thinking in relation to the renewal of progressive politics in America. In the second I turn to an account of the implications this has for the family. The third section begins an argument for a national family policy that I place at the centre of a transformed progressive politics, one that I regard as a development of existing American Third Way thought. The remaining sections continue the argument for the national family policy.

American Third Way Ideas

Third Way Democrats, or New Democrats as they often refer to themselves, have replaced the top-down philosophy of governance associated with Franklin Roosevelt and the New Deal and Lyndon Johnson and the Great Society with a leaner, more decentralized, more community-centred philosophy of governance. New Democrats regard themselves as Information Age Democrats. And although they seek to maintain commitments to the leading values of the earlier Democratic eras, they argue that an Industrial Age mentality that suited them no longer works in our society or our world today. A major statement of the philosophy of the New Democrats states:

Our country is being transformed from top to bottom. The industrial order of the twentieth century, with its great concentrations of economic and political power, is giving way to a new society shaped by the centrifugal forces of the Information Age: microchip technologies, global markets, and new communication networks. This historic shift has released tremendous energy and creativity while, at the same time, rocking the economic and social foundations on which our leading public and private institutions rest. (Marshall et al., 1996: 17)

Because the economic structure of our society has changed, New Democrats say that we must change our approach to governing: 'We advocate a new model of progressive governance that does not merely hand down programmatic "solutions" from Washington but instead creates an enabling environment where citizens and communities can fashion their own responses to local problems' (ibid. 20).

Senator Joseph Lieberman, who was the Democratic nominee for Vice-President, and who chaired the Democratic Leadership Council which, along with its think tank the Progressive Policy Institute, is the main source of American Third Way thinking, says that New Democrats must seek to find the 'vital center' (an Arthur Schlesinger, Jr. concept) rather than a moderate, compromise position. The New Democrat philosophy 'does not simply navigate a middle course between left and right. . . . [It] . . . lifts us up to a new level. . . . It defines a rational way of governing that adapts America's best traditions to the post-industrial, Information Age world in which we, and especially our children, live' (ibid. 221). The language of moving beyond left and right has been important to numerous movements and important books in recent years, most notably the Communitarian Movement led by Amitai Etzioni and the Third Way writings of Anthony Giddens (Etzioni, 1993, 1996, 2000; Giddens, 1998, 2000). Other important writers in this broad tradition include E. J. Dionne, Jr. (1991, 1996), Henry Tam (1998), Sylvia Ann Hewlett and Cornel West (1998), Stanley Greenberg and Theda Skocpol (1997) and Michael Sandel (1996). While some are more progressive than others, they all share a commitment to synthesizing some important aspects of liberal and conservative thought.

It is central to most Third Way arguments that the rich social sector of 'civil society' – which on most definitions includes the family, the schools, religious institutions, voluntary associations and community organizations – be integrated both into our understanding of society overall and into our proposed solutions to our problems. Third Way thinkers thus talk about government, market *and* civil society and seek to avoid polarizing choices rooted in a government–market framework.[1] Moreover, Third Way thinking, especially Etzioni's work, embraces the overarching theme that individual rights come with social responsibilities.

The American Third Way Approach to the Family

One area where Third Way thinking is most visible is family policy (see Marshall et al., 1996: 28–9). The New Democratic Declaration includes important treatments of the family. It tells us that in 'industrial America', it was assumed that large government programmes could rescue families in need. But the 'government's safety net' crippled many poor citizens, especially welfare recipients. The 'loss of well-paying manufacturing jobs', the New Democrats argue, has been destructive to both the middle class and the working class. Amongst the poor, we have witnessed 'a violent trade in illicit drugs' and a dearth of 'marriageable males'. In the middle class, many families have been forced to 'send a second earner to work' and close to 50 per cent of marriages result in divorce.

In the information age economy, where workers must 'master new, knowledge-based work' without the support of 'big institutions', families must be strong and secure. Thus, the New Democrats call for policies and practices that will strengthen what they regard as the best model of the functioning family, the 'intact two-parent family'. New Democrats say that we can no longer afford to be 'neutral' about family structure.

Their vision of a strong family system revolves around the concept of responsibility, but it is by no means a vision of personal responsibility in isolation from institutional support. To the contrary, New Democrats believe that 'we need new public initiatives that reduce taxes on working parents, assist community efforts to discourage teen pregnancy, and ensure that in cases of divorce, children's interests are put first'. William Galston, who has served as the voice for the Progressive Policy Institute on family policy, has supported numerous family policies that require government funding but which aim to empower individuals.[2]

The New Democrats Have Not Gone Far Enough

The New Democrats have transformed a party focused on protecting individual rights that require that institutions fulfil political and economic responsibilities into a party focused on motivating individuals to be responsible who nonetheless can rely on public institutions to protect their rights. But they have not confronted the most basic issue about families, namely the birth of children and the care and attention that is required in order for children to develop into responsible adults.

In order to support strong families, it is necessary to support a three-part policy, which I call 'The Family Unity Act' (FUA). The three parts to the Act are as follows:

- paid parental leave;
- tax credits for stay-at-home parents;
- substantial support for childcare across socio-economic classes.

This three-part policy goes well beyond America's existing policies. The Family and Medical Leave Act (FMLA) of 1993 provides unpaid leave for 12 weeks, and only about one half of workers qualify.[3] Still, less than half of them actually take the leave, most because they cannot afford to give up their salaries. Tax-credits are not provided for stay-at-home parents, and most of our childcare programmes, apart from the modest dependent-child deduction and childcare expense deductions, are only open to the most impoverished parents and their children (see Bergmann, 1996: 95–110). As a nation, we are far behind most of the other democracies in the world, especially Europe, where paid parental leave and major childcare programmes are a commonplace (Kamerman and Kahn, 1995: esp. 21–67, 132–50, 167–81). It is the vast middle class as well as the working poor (the lower class) who are left to fend for themselves. Theda Skocpol refers to 'the missing middle' in our social policy (Greenberg and Skocpol, 1997: 115) and Sylvia Ann Hewlett and Cornel West (1998) call on the 62 million beleaguered mums and dads to start a parents' movement.

I call the three-part Act the Family 'Unity' Act because it would help unify families across family structure, race and class at the same time that it would act as a unifying theme for American politics. Others have defended many policies – housing, health and education, to name three – which are also critical to supporting American families. While I support many of these arguments, I concentrate on a set of policies that concern parent–child relationships in the first five years of a child's life. These relationship issues are extremely controversial because they require government intervention into the task of 'parenting'. This highly controversial area speaks to the heart of many of our greatest struggles over the family and that is why I place it at the centre of a new vision of American public philosophy.

Arguing for the Family Unity Act

Young families are truly the source of the next generation of Americans, and therefore it is of the first importance to support them. The primary way that young families need support is with the tasks revolving around the care for children themselves. The childcare needs start as soon as the baby is born and they remain extremely intense until the child enters first grade. This is not to say that childcare needs cease at this point. But the needs that families have during the first year of a child's life and then in the preschool years, including kindergarten which often is half a day, are substantial.

When a child is born, economic, emotional and ethical support should be provided for the family regardless of the way the family chooses to manage its work and parenting responsibilities. Doctors, psychologists and social workers are more or less unanimous in thinking that during the first year of life a baby needs to bond with one or possibly two human beings, preferably the baby's parent or parents. In those families where the woman works, the family must be given a year of paid leave which the woman can either take herself or which she can share with her husband. In those families where the woman does not work or where she works part time, then economic, emotional and ethical support are also needed. In this instance, the family should receive tax credits during the first year of the child's life. The message that is sent to this woman and her family must be the same as the message that is sent to the full-time working mother and her family: it is the collective responsibility of this society, rich and poor, white, black and Hispanic, young and old, to ensure that young families are provided with conditions to give children responsible care.[4]

Needless to say, economic, emotional and ethical support must be provided for single parents as well, 90 per cent of whom are women, and most of whom work. The argument that Third Way Democrats often give in support of intact two-parent families is, in certain ways, misplaced. The fact is that three out of ten families in America today are single-parent families, and those families need support. It is problematic to have a platform that rallies around the concept of intact two-parent homes when a third of families do not fit into this description. This is not to say that ways should not be found to promote the stability of new two-parent families; indeed, the FUA does that. It says that no viable philosophy of the family for our time can have a single message that applies to all families. On a more controversial front, since the FUA calls for respecting diversity, it must also support gay and lesbian families. It is conceivable that this important feature could get squeezed out of a major bill, but that would be unfortunate.

The same line of argument that applies to newborns applies to children from the age of 1 to 5. Families who choose to leave their children with a babysitter or relative or in family or professional day care must be given economic, emotional and ethical support for their choice. Only a small percentage of American families can afford safe, secure, stimulating day care for their children, which can cost $8,000 or more a year. Therefore, we must ensure that funds and facilities (including higher wages for childcare workers and adequate background checks on childcare workers) are available to enable parents to choose an approach which most suits them. While the more economically well-off families will always have options not open to other families, the FUA would close this gap considerably. At the same time, young families who choose to have one adult as the stay-at-home parent during the first five years of the child's life – or indeed parents may split this role – must also be supported. The tax credits that are given to parents who stay at home during the first year of life must also be given to parents during the second, third, fourth and fifth years of the child's life.[5]

Democrats who criticize and stigmatize stay-at-home mothers must change their attitude about work, women and family. They must recognize that the gains won in principle for American women over the last generation do not identify a model of existence that is right for all women or all families. Thus, Democrats must concede that women who, with their mates, choose to stay at home with their children must be treated with respect. That respect is due as much to the women as to the children who need their care and attention. Republicans who talk about the importance of raising children to have good character but who will not support government measures that would provide economic support for young families must finally admit that if they want virtue in the family it is going to cost money. In order to improve the chances that a new child receives love, attention and guidance, measures must be found to fund the families who cannot afford to have the mother and/or the father stay at home with that child.

Where the Republicans go wrong is that they argue for responsibility without recognizing the injustice, suffering and oppression that exists; where most Democrats go wrong is that they talk about injustice, suffering and oppression without talking about personal responsibility and virtue. A realistic approach will unite these two languages and find economic support for all young families.

It is also important to consider benefits more directly related to the public good. One critical benefit concerns the costs that are associated with delinquency and crime. If we can create a childcare system where children are likely to receive responsible childcare, then we reduce the likelihood that children will act in irresponsible ways towards other children and towards private and public property. This issue is primarily about male development, since the vast majority of delinquent and criminal acts are committed by males. If we can raise boys to be more self-controlled and responsible, as well as more empathetic and caring, then we will save a lot of money. If boys behaved like girls, the yearly cost of crime in the United States would be reduced from $112 billion to $20 billion (Anderson and Austin, unpublished paper).

A second argument in favour of the FUA is that it would lift morale throughout the American workplace, the benefits of which should not be underestimated, especially during a time when the concept of the traditional job has dissolved and the forces of globalization have increased anxieties as much as they have increased opportunities for educated and well-trained workers. If American working parents were provided with economic support from their companies as well as from the government, this would reduce economic and emotional stress for them. Corporations would benefit over the long run as well, since workers would be more productive if they had less stressful lives. Working parents would be more loyal, staff turnover would decrease and recruitment would be easier.

The work–family balancing problem is extreme in the United States today (see, e.g., Hochschild, 1989; Friedan, 1997; Berry, 1993). Working parents, especially working mothers, feel overwhelmed with their work and family responsibilities. Only employees at the very best American companies benefit from 'family-friendly policies'. If all employees could benefit from government-mandated family-friendly policies (in addition to corporate initiated flexi-time and part-time policies), employers would have no choice but to see their employees as fully human-workers rather than as knowledge-workers. Supporting young families would provide them with some stability during a time when job security has vanished.

Financing the Family Unity Act

I write here and elsewhere in defence of a federal family policy. While I continue to think that this is necessary, it may be that the best strategy towards passing major legislation at the federal level is to promote a similar policy at the state level. The states are, of course, regarded as laboratories of change, and thus a major federal effort may have to rise up from the state level. In this section I want to emphasize a few general points about the cost of the FUA, but I will focus on federal legislation.

First, the FUA would be expensive. Most of the major social programmes of the American welfare state have been expensive – social security, Medicare, Medicaid, the GI bill. The same can be said of major infrastructure expenditures, such as the Interstate Highway Act of 1956, and of major defence expenditures during the world wars, and the Korean and Vietnam wars. Endeavours of minor importance are not likely to require major financial commitments. The FUA, were it funded at a level that it truly deserves, could cost between $75 billion and $100 billion dollars a year. But even if the three-part package – leave, tax credits and childcare – was made into law at $25 billion, this would still be regarded as a major pro-gramme. This would represent about 1.5 per cent of our current budget of $1.7 trillion, but in American terms $25 billion out of $1,700 billion for young families is still regarded as a huge expense.

Secondly, the cost of the FUA would not be borne by one institution or group of people. It would be borne by three sources and not one: the federal government, companies and, apart from the poorest families, citizens themselves. The more well-off a family is the more funds they would have to find – for example, through tightening their belts – to finance their own approach to balancing work and family responsibilities.

Thirdly, the law should be written in such a way that companies are required to split the cost of each of the three parts of the package with the government, but the cost-sharing must be worked out so that larger companies pay more than smaller. Likewise, as Heidi Hartmann and Barbara Bergmann (1995) argue, a viable childcare programme should be developed on a sliding scale for families, so that the least advantaged families (the lowest 20 per cent) receive free childcare, while remaining families receive assistance on a sliding scale.[6] Paid parental leave should be handled in a similar way. Middle- and upper-middle-class women would receive up to 50 per cent wage replacement, while lower-middle-class and lower-class women would receive between 75 per cent and 100 per cent wage replacement.

Fourthly, in the last few years America has been anticipating a budget surplus, with some estimates as high as $4.6 trillion in the first decade of the new century, or over $460 billion a year. A robust progressive politics can find a way to unite fiscal conservatism (especially to reduce the long-term debt) and some new spending programmes. It is also worth noting in this context that Herbert Simon, the former Chairman of President Nixon's Council of Economic Advisors, argued famously in 1992 that there is always $50 billion to be found in the federal budget for a good federal programme. The problem, he said, was to develop the programme. Were Simon alive today, he would no doubt change the figure to $75 billion.

Fifthly, it is very important that we do not conceal the moral arguments in favour of supporting leave, tax credits and childcare support under the heading of tax cuts, however targeted and however large. First of all, the funds might not be directed towards children's well-being. They might go towards the parents' personal interests and needs, including entertainment and vacations, even drug habits and gambling. But, more importantly, it would be a case of weak leadership if the importance of supporting childcare was not backed by specific programmes about the care of children and the development and respect of parents. Recognition of a problem cannot be achieved if people are given complete liberty to identify the areas that they choose to recognize as of vital importance. We do not grant citizens these rights when it comes to many aspects of the public good, ranging from defence to the transportation infrastructure to social security.

Sixthly, contrary to the media coverage about the retrenchment of family policy spending in West European democratic countries, spending has, as a rule, been increasing. Janet C. Gornick and Marcia K. Meyers argue convincingly that 'against the backdrop of limited overall retrenchment, we find multifaceted evidence for widespread protection and expansion of family benefits, including family allowances, maternity and paternity leave, and child care' (forthcoming). They also document the 'distorted media coverage' and discuss the scholarly literature associated with media distortion and public opinion. While policy formation in Washington and the states has not been tightly connected to what is happening in Europe, or the rest of the world for that matter, the end of the Cold War and the rise of globalization have made the world smaller for us. Advocates of the FUA should not have to confront the objection that the European welfare states have given up their commitments to young families if this objection has no rational basis.

The Wider Perspective: Psychological and Historical Arguments

A viable politics of the family today requires that we relieve women of some of their responsibilities at the same time that we call on men to shoulder more responsibilities. The language of restoring social order by balancing social responsibilities with individual rights obscures the fact that women are in most cases carrying a disproportionate share of responsibility in their families today. The New Democrats, like many others, are guilty of obscuring this reality as they seek to strengthen all families. New Democrats, like Old Democrats, find injustice in our political and economic institutions, especially regarding women and minorities. But, again like Old Democrats and some of the most progressive thinkers about the family, they still shy away from discussing injustice that arises *within* families.[7]

These issues centre around power relations, and the New Democrat public philosophy needs to talk more about them.[8] Working mothers, as a rule, are more overburdened by their work and family responsibilities than working fathers. And women overall, as a rule, are more likely than men to be victims of domestic violence, emotional manipulation, adultery and rape. These problems arise in part because males, as a rule, are raised to have a predominantly masculine gender identity which is based on the denial of feminine capacities for relatedness. Denial of the feminine leads males to devalue females in various ways. If more parents shared parenting responsibilities, sons would be more likely to develop more balanced gender identities (see Anderson, 1994, 1999, 2001).

The New Democrat oversimplification of the task of balancing individual rights with social responsibilities is rooted in their explanation of social problems largely as the result of economic and technological changes. New Democrats are wrong to assume that the onset of the Information Economy essentially underlies the transformation in the American family. While it is true that many middle-class families needed a second wage-earner to maintain their standard of living, an era of consciousness-raising propelled women into the workplace for emotional and ethical reasons as well as economic. No reasonable account of the changing dynamics of the American family will overlook what Weber (1958) would call 'ideational' reasons in additional to 'materialistic' reasons (see also Etzioni, 1988).

The very suggestion that we live in an age analogous to the Progressive Era is strained. It is true that we are experiencing a major transformation in technology and the economy, just as Americans did at the turn of the twentieth century. Where they moved from an agricultural to an industrial economy, we have been moving gradually from an industrial to an information economy. But in this past generation we have also experienced major social revolutions in gender and race relations – the women's movement and the civil rights movement – whereas the generation preceding the Progressive Era was almost as racist and sexist as that of the Progressive Era itself. The slaves, of course, were freed, but racism was still extremely intense.

The real challenge for a viable politics of the family during this time of great economic and social change is to find a way to acknowledge two things: first, that women who want to combine work and family in the early years of a child's life have been treated unfairly; and, secondly, that women who would prefer not to work full time during the early years of a child's life have *also* been treated unfairly. The public philosophy which articulates this message, and the political leaders who carry it, will no doubt be accused of inconsistency by some of their critics. But real politics and much political and social philosophy (Plato, Machiavelli, Emerson, Hobbes, Locke, Mill, Dewey) is not about delivering the same message to every constituency. Even more, our times of ambiguity and ambivalence require that everyone acknowledge that there is no simple solution to our hardest dilemmas about family structure and parenting roles. The main reason the Family Unity Act is an ideal unifying theme is that it aims to unify people around a theme that smacks of major tensions. If we admit that these tensions cannot be entirely eliminated, then we can channel them in constructive ways.

New Democrats have also failed to treat what Arlie Hochschild (2000) and Rhacel Parrenas (2001) call the 'globalization of care'. The globalization of care is the development of 'nanny chains' (which admittedly are most relevant to upper-middle-class and upper-class families), where women from developing nations, like the Philippines, are forced to emigrate to the United States. These women end up displacing the love they have for their own children onto the children for whom they become nannies. This is a bad situation for them and for the parents of the American children. The upshot is that America's family policy, like its environmental policy, cannot be made in isolation from foreign policy (see Christopher, 1996; 81–5; Shuman and Harvey, 1993). Because New Democrats only see the 'globalization of markets', their view of globalization and international relations needs to be expanded.

Language and Leadership: Arguments for the Family Unity Act

The next stage of Third Way philosophy needs leaders who will speak with courage about the very complicated emotions that millions of Americans experience but may not fully understand. It is not a time where dichotomies speak to the interest of most people – capitalists versus communists, whites versus blacks, corporations versus employees, men versus women. The inspiration that must be summoned today requires a more subtle kind of leadership than what was needed during times of manifest crisis – times of economic depression, civil or international war.

For all the value of economic support for childcare, whether it comes in the form of parental leave, tax credits or day care, the drive and confidence that people need to deal with the daily struggles of life require external emotional and ethical support as well. Where laws are needed, they are always necessary but not sufficient; enforcement and encouragement are also necessary. The ultimate value of the Act would probably lie more in the actions that people – parents, children, employers – would take based on and inspired by the statute, but not required by it. These actions will require a change in attitude – although it is likely that they will affect attitudes and vice versa.

Great leaders are needed today who will not be afraid to encourage fathers to face their own insecurities even as they strive to rise to new levels of responsible conduct with their children and their partners. Great leaders will look the media in the face and say that men need to heal their own wounded sense of self even as we compel them to pay their child support and participate more in childcare and housework. Great leaders will stand up in front of millions of people and say that the cynicism and distrust that people feel towards politics and business are, in part, an expression of the cynicism and distrust they feel within their own families. Great leaders will craft policies and language to overcome cynicism and distrust throughout our society.

Having heard the words spoken to them, citizens will be inspired to speak their own words in their own dialogues. Moreover, the opportunities for local as well as national dialogues on the Internet cannot be ignored. Nor can the value of online issue advocacy campaigns that could bring important ideas to our politicians, who could then join the leaders of these campaigns in affirming these ideas and bringing them into law.

In the years ahead, people will fight for the FUA and related Acts at both the national and state levels because the human heart will not take no for an answer. The moral crisis in the American family must be addressed at its roots. Our politics must continue to grow, and our people must continue to grow. Communitarian and Third Way thinkers, in reshaping and restraining traditional liberalism, have actually opened the way for a richer liberalism, one that promotes the values of dignity and community. The Family Unity Act could be the unifying theme for a new generation of Americans, a generation that rose above Left and Right and found a way to overcome seemingly intractable disputes about the family by providing economic, emotional and ethical support for everyone.

Notes

I am grateful to many people for their help in thinking through the issues discussed in this. I wish especially to thank Paul Churchill, Amitai Etzioni, Bill Griffith, Daniel A. Bell, Vicki Lovell, Christopher Van Hollen, Jr., Mark K. Shriver, Kumar Barve, Louise Gallun, Martha Burk, Stiv Fleishman, David DeGrazia, Robert Eisen, Ellen Chubin, Gary Laden, Ben Jones, Ingrid Creppell, Mark Nadel, Seymour Martin Lipset, Betty Friedan, Heidi Hartmann, Jacqueline Fralley, Joyce S. Anderson, B. Robert Anderson, Jonathan Slade, Stephen Darwall, Elizabeth Anderson, Allan Gibbard, Don Herzog, David Hills, James Austin, Maria Gregoriou, Michael Edwards, Ed Grefe, Michael Cornfield, Hugh Wilder, Martin Perlmutter, Jane Braaten, Harvey Mullane, Angela Curran, Melinda Hogan, Stephen Downes, Henry Tam and Ron Willis. Special thanks to Andrew Altman and Adrienne Oleck.

1   For an instructive discussion, most of which I support, of various approaches to civil society, see McClain and Fleming, 2000; also see Linda McClain, ch. 6 this volume.

2   See, e.g., Galston, 1996. Galston supports reducing the tax disadvantages of marriage, a mentor system for vulnerable children, 'second chance' homes for single mothers and a new system of foster care. I discuss

Galston's approach in the context of communitarian economics in Anderson, 1998.

3 FMLA is an extremely important piece of legislation even though it is not about paid leave. The Act, to simplify, provides 12 weeks of job-protected, unpaid leave to persons to care for newborns, adopted children or seriously ill relatives, so long as they have worked a minimum of 1,250 hours for 12 months in an organization with at least 50 people that is within 75 miles of their home. Under the Congressional leadership of Representative Patricia Schroeder, FMLA, after nine years of work, was signed into law by President Clinton in 1993. For part of the story of the Act's life, see Schroeder, 1989. All subsequent efforts for family leave, including the Campaign for Family Leave Benefits launched at the state level in June 1999 by the National Partnership for Women and Families (http://www.nationalpartnership.org/work&family/fmleave/expansion/2PGFACTSHEET_0699.HTM), build on the leadership of Schroeder and other leaders in Congress and the non-profit sector. These leaders include Connecticut Senator Christopher Dodd, Marian Wright Edelman, President of the Children's Defense Fund, and Edward Zigler and James Comer, originators of the 'COZI' school which provides childcare and educational programmes through schools that stay open 7 to 7. On 10 June 2000, the US Department of Labor issued a regulation that created the opportunity for states to use surplus unemployment funds for paid parental leave. Fifteen bills were proposed in 2000; none made it into law, although Massachusetts got as far as the Governor's office and met a veto.

4 Note that since Etzioni (1993) defends a year of paid parental leave (to be shared by corporations and the federal government), he is more progressive, at least on the issue of parental leave, than New Democrats. I support Etzioni's approach to the family, with recommendations for revisions (Anderson, 1998/9)

5 A similar approach is adopted by Hewlett and West (1998: 248–50). I would add here that policies for elder care should be linked in mobilization efforts to policies for childcare. AARP and the Children's Defense Fund both supported FMLA; they could both support FUA as well.

6 Bergmann (1996) later develops the argument, focusing, like the essay in The Nation, on childcare as well as healthcare. She also focuses on child poverty and not universal support for families across socio-economic classes. Hartmann is founder as well as Director and President of The Institute for Women's Policy Research in Washington, DC, one of the leading sources of economic research concerning women.

7 In the feminist tradition, the theme of treating 'injustice within families' is often associated with the work of Susan Moller Okin (especially 1989). Also see Anderson (1999), where I treat this issue explicitly, and Anderson (2001). I still hold to significant components of an earlier article (1994).

8 The person who has done the most in the communitarian tradition to make oppressive power relations a central feature of a communitarian

public philosophy is Henry Tam. While he has not addressed issues of gender oppression in any detail, the main line of argument of his book (1998) shows how communitarians can criticize unfair power relations throughout the body politic without slipping into a traditional leftist critique of mainstream liberalism. As a progressive communitarian, then, I am a Tamian about power relations and community-building.

References

Anderson, D. M. (1994) 'False Stability and Defensive Justification in Rawlsian Liberalism: A Feminist Critique', in Robert Paul Churchill (ed.), *The Ethics of Liberal Democracy* (Oxford: Berg Publishers), pp. 47–70.

Anderson, D. M. (1998) 'Communitarian Approaches to the Economy', in Herbert Giersch (ed.), *The Merits and Limits of Markets* (Berlin, Heidelberg, New York: Springer-Verlag), pp. 29–52.

Anderson, D. M. (1998/9) 'Communitarian Families: A New Center, Not a Compromise', *The Responsive Community*, 9, Winter.

Anderson, D. M. (1999) 'A Viable Strategy for Women's Progress', *Women's Progress: Perspectives on the Past: Blueprint for the Future* (Conference Proceedings), Institute for Women's Policy Research.

Anderson, D. M. (2000) 'Family Unity Act Needs – and Deserves – Sponsor', *The Hill*, 8 February.

Anderson, D. M. (2001) 'Part of the Project of Building a Progressive Coalition: Uniting Working Mothers and Welfare Mothers Behind a National Family Policy', in John Abbarno (ed.), *Inherent and Instrumental Values: Excursion in Value Inquiry* (Lanham, MD: University Press of America).

Anderson, D. M. and Austin, J. (Co-Director of the Institute on Crime, Justice and Corrections, George Washington University) (unpublished paper), 'What if Boys Behaved Like Girls? Redefining the Solution to the Crime Prime'.

Bergmann, B. (1996) *Saving Our Children From Poverty: What the United States Can Learn From France* (New York: Russell Sage Foundation).

Berry, M. F. (1993) *The Politics of Parenthood* (New York: Penguin Books).

Christopher, W. (1996) 'American Diplomacy and Global Environmental Challenges of the 21st Century', *Environmental Change and Security Project Report*, The Woodrow Wilson Center, Issue 2, Spring: 81–5.

Dionne, jun., O. E. J. (1991) *Why Americans Hate Politics* (New York: Simon and Schuster).

Dionne, jun., O. E. J. (1996) *They Only Look Dead: Why Progressives Will Dominate the Next Political Era* (New York: Simon and Schuster).

Etzioni, A. (1988) *The Moral Dimension: Toward a New Economics* (New York: Free Press).

Etzioni, A. (1993) *The Spirit of Community* (New York: Simon and Schuster).

Etzioni, A. (1996) *The New Golden Rule* (New York: Basic Books).

Etzioni, A. (2000) *The Third Way to a Good Society* (London: Demos).

Friedan, B. (1997) *Beyond Gender: The New Politics of Work and Family*, ed. B. O'Farrell (Washington, DC: Woodrow Wilson Center Press, distributed by The Johns Hopkins University Press).

Galston, W. (1996) 'A Progressive Family Policy for the Twenty-First Century', in Marshall, W. (ed.), *Building the Bridge: 10 Big Ideas to Transform America* (Lanham, MD, New York, Boulder, CO, Oxford: Rowman and Littlefield), pp. 149–62.

Giddens, A. (1998) *The Third Way* (Cambridge: Polity).

Giddens, A. (2000) *The Third Way and its Critics* (Cambridge: Polity).

Gornick, J. C. and Meyers, M. K. (forthcoming) 'Lesson-Drawing in Family Policy: Media Reports and Empirical Evidence about European Developments', *Journal of Comparative Policy Analysis: Research and Practice*.

Greenberg, S. B. and Skocpol, T. (eds) (1997) *The New Majority* (New Haven, CT, and London: Yale University Press).

Hartmann, H. and Bergmann, B. (1995) 'A Program to Help Working Parents', *The Nation*, 1 May.

Hewlett, S. A. and West, C. (1998)*The War Against Parents* (Boston: Houghton Mifflin Company).

Hochschild, A. R. (1989) *The Second Shift* (New York: Avon Books, 1989).

Hochschild, A. R. (2000) 'The Nanny Chain', *The American Prospect*, 11(4), 3 January.

Kamerman, S. B. and Kahn, A. J. (1995) *Starting Right* (New York and Oxford: Oxford University Press).

Marshall, W., From, A., Galston, W. A. and Ross, D. (1996) 'The New Progressive Declaration: A Political Philosophy of the Information Age', in Marshall (ed.), *Building the Bridge: 10 Big Ideas to Transform America*, Foreword by Vice-President Al Gore (Lanham, MD, New York, Boulder, CO, Oxford: Rowman and Littlefield).

McClain, L. C. and Fleming, J. E. (2000) 'Some Questions for Civil Society-Revivalists', *Chicago-Kent Law Review*, 75(2): 301–54.

Moller Okin, S. (1989) *Justice, Gender, and the Family* (New York: Basic Books).

Parrenas, R. (unpublished) 'The Global Servants: (Im)Migrant Filipina Domestic Workers in Rome and Los Angeles', Dissertation, Department of Ethnic Studies, University of California, Berkeley.

Parrenas, R. (2001) *Servants of Globalization: Women, Migration, and Domestic Work* (Stanford, CA: Stanford University Press).

Sandel, M. (1996) *Democracy's Discontent: America in Search of a New Public Philosophy* (Cambridge, MA: Harvard University Press).

Schroeder, P. (1989) *Champion of the Great American Family*, with Andrea Camp and Robyn Lipner (New York: Random House).

Shuman, M. H. and Harvey, H. (1993) *Security Without War: A Post-Cold*

War Foreign Policy, Foreword by Senator Paul Simon (Boulder, CO, San Francisco, Oxford: Westview Press).

Simon, H. (1992) 'The 50 Billion Dollar Option', *Wall Street Journal*, June.

Tam, H. (1998) *Communitarianism: A New Agenda for Politics and Citizenship* (New York: New York University Press).

Weber, M. (1958) *The Protestant Ethic and the Spirit of Capitalism*, trans. Talcott Parsons (New York: Charles Scribner's Sons).

8

Family and the Politics of Community Life

José Pérez Adán

The Coming-of-Age of a Progressive Communitarian Way of Thinking

The communitarian paradigm describes community as a collective subject that possesses a certain sovereignty of its own, and proposes that the community be granted conceptual independence from the two dominant, monopolizing forces of sovereignty, as it is understood by modernity, the individual and the state. Communitarianism does not define community in a univocal manner – rather, it refers to communities – nor does it describe community in geographical terms – social borders cannot be drawn or seen on any map. The community is any human setting where virtue is seen to have a social dimension and where, moreover, there is a shared sense of morality. Some communities may be defined by geographical location (residential groups, for example) but other forms of community, which are not based on spatial boundaries, also exist: those based on ethnic background and heritage, shared religious affiliation, similar work forms and practices, or on technology, as with the more recent emergence of 'virtual' communities.

The impulse of modern communitarian thinking originates in problems relating to the environment and to the family. These two human situations (the natural world and the home) manifest in the clearest possible way the fact that diachronic change is an intrinsically social phenomenon. The individualism of our culture has to a great extent made it more difficult to think about our society as a collective subject, existing in and through time, before and beyond the life and times of individuals and their actions. Without a sense of social history, there can be no responsibility due to the next generation, nor can environmental conservation and protection be said to be necessarily better than its opposite. Without an understanding of social history, the liberal thinker, in order to justify his support for the existing social and environmental balance, is obliged to act in contradiction to his own principles. He must place a very high price on such a balance, but without considering the beneficiaries of his choices and actions (including potential beneficiaries, that is, future generations) and how much it may be worth to them – that is, the liberal ends up making decisions about what is in the best interest of others.

From a progressive communitarian point of view, not all societies are good in the same way or to the same degree. Values are frequently a matter of dispute – for example, in some societies the environment is a good to be conserved and protected, while for others it is merely 'potential' to be exploited. For this reason, the highest social goods can be said to exist to the degree that we can discern human settings or environments with a higher degree of social well-being. This is a qualitative conception of social life and living. The community is not simply a 'space' in which human relationships take place; it is also and above all a sharing of values. These values are reinforced, preserved and spread within and by each community because they are considered to be the best possible values, values which act for the betterment of all in society.

It is important to qualify what has been outlined so far by saying that a commitment to shared values is not necessarily to be regarded as a defence of the state that has taken on the role of defining what values are to be shared. On the contrary, the greater emphasis on the notion of society takes attention and focus away from the powers of the state, and exposes the state when it blinds us to the good, and the potential for good, of society. In affirming the importance of making the invisible (society, community, family) visible, the social need to revitalize collective subjects against the monopolizing power of the state is also being highlighted. We need to look for the signs of collective values in social realities, as defined by the values they embody, and not in uniforms, flags, anthems and sports – a superficial sense of community often presented by the state.

The discovery of the characteristics of the social good through an understanding of social needs and priorities rooted in values is synonymous, for progressive communitarians, with the commitment to recognizing the complete equality of all persons. For example, the recognition of the superiority of the right to life over the right to own private property is the basic guarantee of a just juridical order in a society of equals. In the same way, the protection of the natural world is judged to be superior to the individual's right to choose a particular sporting activity. Likewise, in such a society, the values held and practised by the Red Cross take precedence over those of a casino-hall card game. The communitarian defence of the family is based precisely on this line of argument, an evaluation of values: each value is assigned its place on a scale of values ordered by social priority. In an article entitled 'Which Values Matter Most?' (1995), Amitai Etzioni was unequivocal in this regard, arguing that 'without a basic agreement on what constitutes and defines the family, there can be no discussion of stable social policies, or of basic social improvement'.

A majority of the electorate in most developed countries are now demanding that there be less state and government control and interference in the social and personal lives of citizens. At the same time, nevertheless, this demand is accompanied by a call for a substantial improvement in the public services provided by the state. The wish-list of the people, then, runs something like this: lower taxation and an increase in the range and quality of social services, shorter working hours and higher salaries, fewer restrictions on consumption and greater regulation of the market, less military spending and greater national security, cheaper petrol and cleaner air. Political action is reduced to voting down every government that fails to get the electorate to clarify or moderate its demands. What is really at issue in this distortion of political activity is whether or not the welfare state has succeeded in convincing people that the government alone can provide them with adequate social security. The surest way of meeting legitimate public demands, which are much less contradictory than they may seem, is to offer public services in a more organized way, not by increasing the bureaucracy of the state but rather by inviting the participation of the community. In order to achieve this involvement, however, the key roles played by various communities in society must be recognized. In the first place, by recognizing the sovereignty of the family in areas like education and public representation, the family can be 'put to work' in a way that is socially visible and beneficial.

The Treatment of the Family in the Spanish
Parliamentary Elections 2000

In 1998, the average Spanish household spent 4,500 euros per person; living and food costs accounted for the greater part of the family budget. The Spanish family spent 14 per cent more in that year than in 1992. Ageing of the population accounts for the fact that spending on private healthcare went up by 19.5 per cent and spending on education fell by 16.6 per cent with respect to the 1992 figures. These statistics show very clearly the importance of the family as a consumer-unit in Spain.

More important than this, however, is the fact, demonstrated by recent studies, that the family in Spain shows signs of a genuine aspiration to develop along the lines of the communitarian framework. The family continues to have the highest importance for people, according to surveys of public opinion. The *Informe Jovenes Espanoles 99* (Survey of Young People in Spain 1999) also shows clear communitarian inclinations among the members of this sector of the population, a sector that, according to the principles of comparative sociology, is most inclined to the affirmation of individuality. Family life has the highest priority for 70 per cent of young people in Spain, and ranks ahead of friends and acquaintances, and of future work-life (in that order). Unemployment, nevertheless, continues to be considered by young people as the most pressing social problem.

If we want to find out about the society of the future we have to examine the available statistics about the family. The low birth rate, along with other indicators about family life, will determine the future of Spanish society; at the moment, the fertility rate of 1.07 is the lowest in the world. The scale of the UN projection for population-ageing predicts that 43 per cent of the population of Spain will be over 60 years of age in 2050, a figure not reached by any other country (nor is any other country expected to do so). This information should stimulate a lively consideration of, and strong response to, the fact that public policy relating to family matters continues to regard the family itself as socially invisible. This invisibility reveals the gap that divides the world of political life from social reality. Politicians in Spain seem to be blind. Even with the above facts as a matter of public record, Spain is the EU country that assigns the least amount of money from its annual budget for the assistance of families with children (calculating the amount of money to be assigned according to the number of children in the family). While the European average for such spending is 7.5 per cent of the public budget, Spain spends only 1.8 per cent.

In October 1999, the government approved a law designed to reconcile work and family life. According to this law, maternity leave can be shared by the spouses: the first six weeks after the birth are exclusively granted to the mother, while the remaining amount of time, up to sixteen weeks, can be shared, as they decide, between father and mother. This law is still in marked contrast, however, with existing legislation in the majority of European countries, particularly that of the Baltic States, where family policies are much more generous.

According to findings made public in 1999 by the National Institute of Statistics (cf. Indicadores Sociales de España, 1999), the number of childless couples has risen by 9.5 per cent with respect to the 1990 figure, and that of couples with two children has fallen by 12.2 per cent over the same period. Likewise, between 1990 and 1997 the figures for marital separation rose by 50 per cent, the number of divorces by 47 per cent and the average marriage age has risen to 30 for men and 28 for women. Shifts in the structure of the family constitute the most significant social changes taking place in Spanish society at this time. In this context, the introduction of a progressive communitarian analysis to the debate about society becomes pertinent and interesting not only from an intellectual or academic point of view; it also has an unquestionable socio-political importance.

In some countries, periods of right-wing rule have at times shown an unexpectedly harsher stance taken against the family and a lower appreciation of family life – the British Conservative government led by Margaret Thatcher is a case in point. Meanwhile, in other countries, parties that act according to standards derived from a stale left-wing inheritance play this anti-family role, the paradigmatic example being that of the Spanish Left. Thus, paradoxically, in the policy area that most clearly defines political differences in Spain – namely, family policy – Margaret Thatcher and Joaquin Almunia, the Spanish socialist candidate in the latest election, have been in complete and remarkable agreement. The Spanish Left, unlike the left-wing movements in other countries, has simply chosen not to differentiate itself from its political opposition by referring to economic performance and policy, or through its understanding of public administration or by the focus it thinks ought to be placed on educational, health or social welfare policies. It entered the dressing-room of the theatre of modern politics and reappeared on the political stage in the last election, ready to propose conceptual alternatives to the most basic and common understanding of the family. For those who still believe in participating in the democratic process in order to bring about a society based on justice and solidarity, in the social regeneration brought about by the appreciation and rewarding of work well done, and in the possibility of bringing socio-economic development to the furthest corners of the world, this is a travesty of the generous effort made and all the good work done in and through the left-wing tradition. A survey of the 2000 election manifestos will shed light on some of these issues.

Differences between various programmes for political action can be depicted and summarized in many ways. The selection presented below, though it takes some of the material out of its immediate context, is relevant to the point being made and will illuminate the line of argument traced so far. Only textual phrases, taken directly from the different and, at times, lengthy manifestos are included.

(i) Key proposals from the agreed programme of the PSOE (Socialist Party) and IU (United Left: communists and affiliates) put forward just before the elections:
   • increasing the status of the autonomous regions from a federal perspective;
   • a reduction of the working week to 35 hours;
   • a revision of the regulatory system for businesses engaged in seasonal work;
   • abolition of the Public Health Foundations (Fundaciones Públicas Sanitarias);
   • replacement of energy production by nuclear means;
   • design of the future Public Business Sector (Sector Público Empresarial);
   • reassessment of fiscal responsibility and of the types of taxation;
   • equalization of personal and family deductions for all taxpayers;
   • Deduction of the minimum personal and family exemption from the imposed quota;
   • achieve more balanced public representation in terms of gender;
   • a new abortion law that will remove current limitations.
(ii) Proposals specific to the IU:
   • dedicate 0.7 per cent of the National Budget to cooperative work in developing countries, and to the remittance of the

Public External Debt (Dueda Externa Pública) owed to the Spanish state by Third World countries;

- dissolution of the Spanish Foreign Legion and Spain to leave NATO and the EU defence force;
- grant same-sex couples the rights to marry and to adopt children;
- recognition of the right to free and open-access abortion in the first sixteen weeks of pregnancy;
- decriminalization of squatting (the occupation of vacant houses).

(iii) Proposals specific to PSOE:
- Free educational text books;
- maximum number of students in the class during the years of compulsory education: 22 (a maximum of 10 in language classes);
- the provision of non-discriminatory sex education on an optional basis;
- educational institutions (schools, colleges, universities) to remain open 11 months a year, 7 days per week and 12 hours per day;
- reform of the Electoral Law to ensure balanced representation on election lists – in a ratio of not more than 60 per cent nor less than 40 per cent, men to women;
- approval of an abortion law that ensures a complete programme of medical treatment for any woman who chooses the procedure;
- removal of the legal, social and economic obstacles that limit or prevent the individual's freedom to choose his/her personal lifestyle;
- proactive policies to encourage an increase in the birth rate.

(iv) Proposals of the PP (Centrist Party):
- A National Programme of Kindergartens and Schools for young children; places guaranteed for all under-3-year-olds;
- release from social security costs during a period of two years after the birth of a child, and reduction in other financial charges;
- permit voluntary extension of the working life;
- provide free schooling for all between the ages of 3 and 6;
- promotion of the use of school libraries outside school class hours;
- creation of the Spanish Institute of Tele-education (Instituto Español de Teleeducación) and of a Public Administration and a Health Internet portal, with open access to all;

- liberalization of the postal services sector and transformation of the existing Public Postal System;
- National Plan for home-help services and a new law to meet the needs of large families;
- combat discrimination on the basis of sexual orientation;
- introduce legislation as the basis for the establishment of a National Commission on Bioethics (Comisión Nacional de Bioética).

Leaving aside the expected differences in emphasis here and there, and the different political personalities and histories, the most identifiable difference between Right and Left in Spain today, the one that will have the greatest effect on the ordinary social life of its citizens, is in the particular family-type and family social life which the respective parties are prepared to support in legislation and with public finance. With hindsight, it is clear that PSOE's position on these issues contributed greatly to its second consecutive defeat in parliamentary elections (and, on this occasion, to an absolute majority). In PSOE we have an example of a political party being held to ransom by its past, and by a language and understanding of the family that is at odds, at least on paper, with its progressive aims. On the other hand, in PP we have a self-proclaimed centrist party escaping, on paper too, from its right-wing legacy. In both cases the family and not the economy is the vehicle that shows the colours. It is not surprising that both parties are showing a deep interest in communitarian ideas.

Progressive Communitarian Conception of the Family

Robert Bellah has denounced the politicization of visible social realities and the deliberate neglect and exclusion of the invisible carried out, in the name of individual freedom, by conservatism in the structure of the state, and liberalism in workings of the market. Bellah says:

> society as it is envisioned by these two world views, which are only apparently contradictory, is composed of the same parts: autonomous individuals, states and markets. It is not the world of normal living, not even for the proponent of free trade and enterprise, nor for the

ideologue of the welfare state: it is an idealised world, a state without families. (Bellah, 1995; see also Bellah and Sullivan, ch. 1 this volume)

The family embodies in social life and practice the connections that the political community seeks to make between the active and passive populations, between the past, passing and future generations. The consequences of economic risks taken by the present generation, or of a reduction in quality of life, can be understood, in this context, not only as the failure of a certain economic policy or policies but also as a moral failure. In so far as the public deficit or debt contributes to an unfortunate economic legacy to the coming generation, its reduction to a minimum is not only one possible political option among others, but a moral duty. Those who understand rational (and political) choices in the way they are defined by neo-classical economists will and do find this a difficult position to accept.

That the family is only one among the many communities of which the individual may form a part is self-evident. The family, nevertheless, retains its primary importance. Studies in social science show clearly that a deterioration in family life leads to a corresponding rise in crime. However, there is also evidence to suggest that a good family background, backed by a quality education system, does not necessarily mean that the members of the family are prepared for and situated in a socially healthy environment. This evidence indicates that other communities, from informal residential groupings to civil society as a whole, require a basic social recognition by which each can see and organize itself as a collective subject. The strengths and weaknesses of each socially visible community can then be evaluated both from within, by the people of whom it is composed, and from without, by those who do not belong to that particular community. We should continue to harbour a healthy scepticism of any well-meaning sensibility that advocates only a rebirth in the personal responsibility of each individual; this concern is partial, and its intention selective. The argument for individual responsibility is rarely furnished with the social context that would also mark out the wider need to meet collective responsibilities, and the individual's role in the development of social life.

The family unit, seen in terms of the good or well-being it brings to social life, requires autonomy and power if it is to perform the functions that are expected of it. Progressive communitarians advocate that it is important to grant the family this power, and, therefore, that the sovereignty of the family as a social agent be recognized in a formal way. It is generally known that the notion of sovereignty, as it is articulated and exercised in contemporary societies, is a closed shop. Two dominant agents closely guard the doors of this idea on the modern social stage: the individual and the state exercise, between them, each in its own way, an absolute and monopolizing sovereign power. The current distribution of power, the existing definition of personal and social freedoms, legal and penal codes as they stand today, all reflect clearly that, in practical terms, there is no place for a third form of sovereignty in our highly structured modern societies. The various declarations of human rights, as well as the constitutions of many independent nations, claim a monopoly on sovereignty for the individual and the state. In this context, the status of the family, as a cultural and social reality, can only be advanced with great effort, and at a cost to the family itself; development, when it does come, is principally (if not only), in the sphere of what is called 'private life'.

The division of labour within the family is an area of key importance to this discussion. Neo-classical economics tended to deal with the family as a single unit in terms of market activity: the decision of the head of the family was the decision of all. However, when Becker began to study how decisions were made within the family, economists of the neo-classical school saw that it became necessary to reconfigure the household as a domestic market in which two autonomous individuals, husband and wife, have a mercantile relationship that involves the exchange of goods or commodities (cf. Becker, 1974). They go on to argue that time is the commodity in shortest supply within the family, and that the division of domestic chores, as a result, acts as a mechanism by which time can be maximized for each of the individuals who together make up the family unit. A 'normal' structure of the family follows: the husband's role in domestic work is taken over by his spouse, so that he (in his external profession) and she (in the household) derive the highest time-profit possible and thus ensure that the overall productivity of the family is increased.

The image of the family as a community of equals, and as more than merely a collection of individuals, gives the family a new and identifiable status as a collective subject. This new paradigm of the family goes to the heart of the debate about the relative autonomy and compatibility of the public and private spheres of life. Progressive communitarian thought puts forward the model of society as a community of communities. This model could not be further from the notion of society articulated in the neo-classical mercantile approaches that envision society as a place where communities battle against one another, where it is every man for himself. In particular, according to this economic view, the family-as-community is in direct opposition to the professional community. As a result, many people are engaged in a never-ending battle between their professional life and performance, and their private life and self-fulfilment. But the time has come to abandon the idea of an absolute separation of the public from the private. A new understanding of the integrity of the public and private lives of each person will form the basis of personal and social goods of great importance: improvements in social well-being, and in the quality of family and professional life.

It is vital that our professional culture recognizes that the goods and values of family life complement the goods and values of professional life. In considering the workforce, an employer should see persons who work rather than employees who spend some time outside their working hours attending to private concerns. The workplace and, more importantly, the community in and for which work takes place, are enriched when the employee is treated as a person and not simply as a worker. The family life and personal abilities of each working person brings an added value to the company that cannot be produced in the same way as an increase in quantifiable profits can be generated by an employer in the short term by encouraging internal company competition.

Similarly, it is important to see that the values and benefits of professional life constitute goods for family life as well. The culture of the family should take professional values into account and incorporate them into its lifestyle through a fair understanding and an appropriate recognition of professional life. The public and private spheres of life must permeate one another in the unity of life (psychological identity) of the person who participates in both areas of life. The harmony of the communities that together form society is based on the flexible and adaptable identity of the person who recognizes and respects both family and work relationships.

There is, unquestionably, a need to reformulate our understanding of gender roles – especially masculine roles – as part of the process of achieving a new relationship between the public and private. Moreover, some form of public recognition of the community in which professional organizations function and serve is necessary in a world where work is becoming increasingly specialized, and forms of work are very narrowly defined. A key response to this situation will be the re-evaluation, in social terms, of domestic relationships and domestic work: time spent at home, carrying out domestic chores or not, should be given its proper social significance. In practical terms, public recognition for the 'feminine man' would play its part in the attempt being made by all in society to overcome the dichotomy

between public and private. At least one key political goal can be
derived from this argument: new legislation dealing with professional
working practices and conditions should be introduced, based on a
consideration of the whole person, a person who is more than simply
a worker or public professional.

The Family as a Collective Subject of Rights

The proper understanding of society comes through a consideration
of the intermediate bodies (communities) that make it up, the most
important of which is the family. The family is being discussed here
in terms of its importance as a social instrument; in so far as it fulfils
the functions that society expects of it, the family is made legitimate
by society. The new form of family being described in this chapter
and for which we call for a restoration of social sovereignty, the
functional family, is a community based on equal relations between
its members, which has a clear set of responsibilities to the coming
generation.

This reformulation of the family involves it in a power struggle.
Public recognition of the discretionary freedom that the new family
must have in the face of social changes implies that there must be a
reorganization of sovereignty. Without a reconfiguration of power,
the family will not be able to adapt to new situations or to preserve
and guarantee basic standards of social well-being. Neither the
individual nor the state will regard the implementation of this social
necessity attractive: in the re-evaluation of sovereignty, both will be
denied the monopolizing power to which they have become
accustomed.

In order to achieve even the minimum level of empowerment for
social subjects, the redistribution of power must follow two basic
principles of action: (i) a wider extension of democracy according to
place and geographical sectors, and (ii) the introduction of more
intensive forms of democracy so that everybody (citizen and for-
eigner; the collective, as well as individual, subject) is included in the
decision-making process. The family can and should empower itself
as a collective subject through this more intensive exercise of the
democratic means.

Needless to say, collective responsibilities can only be fulfilled
collectively if there is a genuine and just distribution of power among
the social agents who are subject to such responsibilities. The social
agent is responsible to the degree that it has the power to act. To use

the language of contemporary democratic culture: participation in the process of social democracy brings responsibility for its progress. It is on this basis, too, that we can argue that the social recognition of the family as a sovereign subject will bring about a reconciliation of all the social agents that are involved in working for a better society.

The path of social improvement is strewn with obstacles. Individualism, which constantly asserts the range of its power, and which is doing so in a particularly vehement way today, may be the greatest obstacle to be faced. Systematic individualism gives rise to a fundamental error in the notion of privacy that specifically excludes (personal and social) interdependence. Taken to its logical conclusion, this understanding of the autonomy of the individual subject undermines any and every notion of society or social living. In contrast, an understanding of privacy or autonomy that retains the notion of interdependence – between the individual and others, the natural world, his or her heritage and expectations for the future – underscores the social and relational nature of the individual subject. Arguments for the social recognition of intermediate social groups like the family find support in this characterization of the individual. Relations of dependency can be socially legitimated in the same way, and, as a result, it becomes possible to speak of the sovereignty of the family and of the family as a social subject. This social grouping – one that has a basic social status, the right to act on its own initiative, a (socially determined) form of public protection and a charter of freedoms, rights and duties (in particular, those that are currently denied to femininity) – is what we call a communitarian family.

The acceptance of this new definition of the family would, without doubt, make for a great improvement on the legal contracts between autonomous subjects that reflect the contemporary model of the family. The contractual arrangement appears to ensure the equality of the signatories and claims to provide the grounds on which each individual can assert his or her privacy. Nevertheless, in as much as it also refers to non-signatories (future children, for instance), it is not truly representative. In this way, non-signatories are exposed to the types of social problem that individualism causes and exacerbates when those with power decide for those without it. The family constituted by contract is a social grouping whose sovereignty, as a subject, is not fully recognized; it is, therefore, denied fundamental (human) rights, and is left without the power to transform and adapt itself to the demands of the modern world. In response to this, we would suggest that future policies for the family should reflect the following: children should be the first priority when it comes to the drafting of social policy; indirect benefits, in the form of tax deductions, for example, should be replaced by direct financial contributions in proportion to the size of the family; the active discouragement of divorce; transfer of state power to communities directly involved in the education of children; the introduction of a school curriculum to provide a virtues-based character formation that prepares the child for social living; and, finally, the reform of fiscal, administrative and labour laws to allow both parents the maximum amount of time in the home.

References

Becker, G. (1974) 'Is Economics Theory With It? On the Relevance of the New Economics of the Family', *American Economic Association*, 64(2), May: 775–86.

Bellah, R. (1995) 'Community Properly Understood: A Defense of Democratic Communitarianism', *The Responsive Community*, 6(1): 49–54.

Etzioni, A. (1995) 'Which Values Matter Most?', *The Weekly Standard*, 20 November.

Further Reading

Bell, D. A. (1993) *Communitarianism and its Critics* (Oxford: Clarendon Press).

Bellah, R. (1991) *The Good Society* (New York: Vintage).

Bellah, R., Madsen, R., Sullivan, W. M., Swidler, A. and Tipton, S. M. (1985) *Habits of the Heart: Individualism and Commitment in American Life* (Berkeley: University of California Press).

Etzioni, A. (1988) *The Moral Dimension: Towards a New Economics* (New York: The Free Press).

Etzioni, A. (1993) *The Spirit of Community: Rights, Responsibilities and the Communitarian Agenda* (New York: Crown).

Etzioni, A. (1996) *The New Golden Rule: Community and Morality in a Democratic Society* (New York: Basic Books).

Nisbet, R. (1962) *Community and Power* (New York: Oxford University Press).

Nisbet, R. (1977) *The Social Bond* (New York: A. Knopf).

Pérez Adán, J. (1997) *Sociología: concepto y usos* (Pamplona: Eunsa).

Pérez Adán, J. (1999a) *La Salud Social* (Madrid: Trotta).

Pérez Adán, J. (1999b) 'La familia funcional como paradigma comunitario', in A. García Cabrera and A. Lucas Marín (eds), *Formación y Participación; las organizaciones en el siglo XXI* (Las Palmas: SI RC10 of ISA).

Putnam, R. (1995) 'Bowling Alone, Revisited', *The Responsive Community*, 5(95).

Selznick, P. (1992) *The Moral Commonwealth: Social Theory and the Promise of Community* (Berkeley: University of California Press).

Tam, Henry (1998) *Communitarianism* (London: Macmillan).

9

Dignity, Citizenship and Welfare

Joseph Romance

In Michael Ignatieff's thoughtful essay, 'The Needs of Strangers', he asks 'whether societies can ever reconcile freedom and solidarity' (1984: 18). At times it appears that the political debates of the twentieth century constantly returned to this dilemma and resolved it with the disheartening answer, 'no'. We must choose either individual freedom or collective equality. Yet, the old political certitudes that animated past Left–Right disputes appear less compelling today. In the United States and Western Europe, a new generation of left-of-centre politicians have been casting aside traditional understanding of what policies work and offering new solutions to the old political conundrums. While policy innovations are adopted, what is also needed is a more public debate about the principles that underlie this attempt to revive progressive politics. If this is not done, then any 'Third Way' will be summarily dismissed as an act of political expediency (see Chait, 1998).

In many ways, this debate has occurred in the work of such writers as Anthony Giddens, Benjamin Barber and Amitai Etzioni, to name but a few. One of the themes that emerges, which sets this new movement apart from previous conceptions of politics, is a renewed concern about what it means to be a citizen. My contention is that, whereas previous political theorists worried incessantly about the freedom or equality of people, a new progressive politics must elevate the notion of dignity in our discussions about what it means to be a citizen. This does not signal the rejection of freedom and equality as useless concepts; rather, it denotes that an old idea – that of dignity – must be added to our conversations about politics as we enter the twenty-first century. By doing this, not only do we advance the idea of dignity, we may also think afresh about those old ideas of freedom and equality. In contemplating the meaning of dignity and how it is related to the life of the citizen, we can begin to see past the tired trade-offs between freedom and equality that stifled much political debate in the twentieth century. At the same time, a new kind of politics would require that citizens have the wherewithal to lead a dignified political life. In so doing, creating the conditions by which such citizens can live might bother those on the Left and on the Right, because we could expect much of individual citizens and of the state in providing minimal conditions for the attainment of civic dignity. Such actions would lead to greater civic dignity and make it more likely that citizens are strong supporters of their communities.

But what exactly does this phrase civic dignity mean? That is what I want to address in this chapter. To do this I would like to address three broad questions: What is dignity and why does it matter to a progressive politics? What should a dignified form of citizenship involve? Finally, how does welfare reform in the United States work (and fail to work) as a model for maintaining dignity and citizenship. In addressing these questions, we will see that freedom and equality are not realized by simply letting people participate in the free market or giving people government entitlements. We need to think hard about the ways people can successfully take part in their communities and lead the life of the citizen. If citizens can become part of their communities, they can realize a sense of freedom within a community of equal political actors.

Why Dignity Matters

What does dignity mean and why is it important to progressive politics? Dignity is being worthy and honourable. While such words are not usually associated with politics in general, or democratic politics in particular, I think such ideas are central to a new kind of politics, which we need. Such a concept goes to the idea of self-worth and ultimately rests upon a notion of self-respect. To be dignified means that one has the respect of others and that we respect ourselves. Much of the twentieth century was spent working out the ideas of liberalism and the notion of individualism often associated with liberalism. At first glance, dignity and ideas of honour seem far removed from liberalism. After all, a liberal society seems predicated upon the idea that people can do what they want, within reason.

However, I would argue that liberalism is built upon an idea of dignity. Citizens can exercise their freedom because we believe that once given freedom, people will act in a dignified way. Burke, though no liberal, forcefully reminded us, 'The effect of liberty to individuals is that they may do what they please; we ought to see what it will please them to do, before we risk congratulations which may be soon turned to complaints' (1987: 8). We don't believe that dishonourable people deserve to be free. Someone who lacks dignity demeans himself and those around him. Or, to put it another way, when we are visited by indignities, either of our making or by the actions of others, we are less able to exercise our freedom. The entire notion of granting freedom demands that people are worthy of that freedom. We limit the freedom of criminals because they have committed crimes and are, thus, not worthy of exercising their freedom. However, this extreme example is indicative of a more fundamental idea. Freedom can only exist in a healthy society and such a society needs to create conditions of trust among its citizens. If we can no longer trust our fellow citizens then the proper functioning of liberal democracy is jeopardized. When citizens live under conditions that are conducive to their dignity, they are more likely to trust their fellow citizens and this will bolster the practices of democratic society (see Fukuyama, 1995; Putnam, 2000).

To clarify this idea further, I believe that political dignity includes four key concepts. As we have seen, dignity implies a certain elevation or nobility. One of the continuing criticisms of contemporary politics, particularly in its liberal, democratic manifestations, is that it creates a shallow life, unconducive to a thoughtful politics. As Michael Walzer writes:

> I imagine a human being thoroughly divorced, freed of parents, spouse, and children, watching pornographic performances in some dark theater, joining (it may be his only membership) this or that odd cult, which he will probably leave in a month or two for another still odder. Is this a liberated human being? (quoted in Kautz, 1995: 19)

There is a strand of liberalism, which I would identify as liberationist liberalism, that expects little of citizens (see Nozick, 1974; Rawls, 1971: 424–32). However, that is only one prospect for liberal democracy. There is also something potentially ennobling about liberal democracy and the idea that citizens are capable of managing their own affairs. The roots of liberalism hark back to John Locke, and the Lockean citizen is a fairly remarkable and moral person – capable of managing his own affairs, raising a family and even administering justice. Such people are perfectly willing to recognize their responsibility to the broader community and willing to accept something we can identify as the common good. Later, liberals such as J. S. Mill found the life of citizens in a liberal society admirable and it was for just this reason that citizens deserved liberty (1986: esp. ch. 2). Thus, to worry about dignity is not to reject the idea of personal liberty.

This idea of public responsibility is the second principle of political dignity that deserves our attention. Namely, progressive citizens accept that demands will be made upon them as citizens. The idea of dignity, as Jedediah Purdy forcefully and eloquently argues (1999: 194–200), is intimately tied to the idea of a commitment to the common good. Citizens are willing to live up to the demands that the public make. This could mean paying your taxes, voting, doing your jury duty and providing help in a national or local emergency. The situation may vary, and there may be spirited debates about what the common good is, but there is a willingness to agree that such a good exists and can only be maintained by all of us.

This, then, connects to the third principle of civic dignity – that citizens are worthy of politics. This may at first glance appear to be no different from the previously mentioned point. However, there is an important distinction between willingly serving the common good and taking part in decisions about what the common good is and entails. In a democratic and progressive society citizens are devoted to discussions about what needs to be done. Progressive politics assumes that citizens are worthy and interested in engaging in politics. And the idea of dignity, if we accept that people should have it, necessitates the idea that individuals are capable not only of making decisions about how they lead their own life, but that individuals have something to add to collective political decisions. If they are honourable, responsible and committed to an idea of the public good, then they must also be allowed to take part in decisions about that public good. As we have seen, dignity includes in it an idea of elevation or nobility. When politics was the subject of aristocracies or monarchies, the assumption was that only the king or nobles had the requisite dignity to care about public matters. Active citizenship was effectively restricted to the few. It might be the case that many people were legally citizens and entitled to a certain, often a limited, set of rights; however, they lacked the intelligence or virtue necessary for actually making important political decisions that concerned society as a whole.[1] Progressive politics assumes that all who are citizens are capable of ruling. This does not mean that all are equal in matters of intelligence, or looks or talents.

It merely means that all are worthy of politics. Since decisions are being made that concern me, I should have some part in making those decisions. People can have vastly different talents and still be honourable enough for politics.

Finally, we must consider the fourth key concept connected to dignity and politics – that dignity means self-respect. Again, this may be implicit in the previous points, but deserves a separate discussion. As Avishai Margalit argues, in discussing dignity and self-respect, 'A person with dignity, in contrast [to self-respect], demonstrates her self-respect through positive acts which are not responses to provocations' (1996: 51). A progressive politics does not merely allow citizens to be political, it assumes that they want to participate in political life. This does not mean that citizens are forced to participate. Any such coercive action would damage a citizen's sense of dignity. Progressive politics assumes that given the right conditions, people will engage in politics, at least some of the time. There is no sense of Rousseau's 'forced to be free'; rather, progressive politics will try to create the conditions under which political participation can occur.

The Meaning of Citizenship

Part of the problem with the idea of dignity and citizenship is that we have forgotten much of what citizenship means. Historically, as Dennis Hale (2000) reminds us, citizenship had an aristocratic heritage, and the concept has spread out from the upper classes to include more and more people who reside in a given geographic location. Yet, even though the concept underwent a process of 'plebianization', it nonetheless retains some of the ancient ideal first articulated by Aristotle (1981) – namely, that citizens are people who are capable of ruling and being ruled. Furthermore, such citizens are equal and free. The extension of citizenship to so many others may have attenuated the ways in which people engage in ruling and it may make people less equal and free; however, these ideas remain bound up with the very notion of what it means to be a citizen. Thus, citizenship is not merely about having certain rights – rights that mean protection from encroachments by others and the state – and entitlements to certain privileges. Instead, the very idea of citizenship means that people can and must be a part of the political world. Citizenship demands things of people. It is 'open to those whose participation was essential to the creation and the continuing functioning of the association' (Hale, 2000: 156). What is radically different today is that participation has been extended to so many. The older ideal of citizenship aligns uncomfortably with the large nation-state. But, what does that extension of participation to so many do to the concept of citizenship?

One of the problems with our contemporary discussion of politics is that the very idea of citizenship is debased. We expect little of citizens and often the very idea of citizenship is conflated with a different concept – that of the client. Bureaucrats often refer to citizens – to welfare recipients in particular – as clients (see Elshtain, 1995: 3). But what does the use of the word 'client' reveal? Clients, historically, meant someone bound to a patrician – clients have patrons. Later, the idea developed into a consumer. Consumers need others to produce the things they need to consume, and this is usually thought of in material terms. But we should reflect on this for a moment. Either sense of the word client is a bad one for the concept of citizen. If clients need patrons, then they are subservient to someone else and this undermines the ideal of equality that is essential to the concept of citizenship. The more contemporary use of client as consumer is hardly better. Of course, to defenders of capitalism, this is not so bad, and some maintain a notion of ruling through the market. Thus, the client status is supposed to be good and powerful because citizens, qua consumers, can force democratic outcomes through market pressures. However, this is built upon an assumption that the market is good and just, and that market exchanges are all that should define who and what we are in the political world.

At best consumers can exercise choice; however, exercising choice is only one part of the democratic ideal of citizenship. Citizenship implies a shared sense of community where choice is employed after debate and deliberation. These debates concern what we share collectively and do not reflect choices made privately and singularly. Consumer preferences are not deliberative in the political sense of that word. A client of the ruling elite is not a citizen of the polity. This is not what Aristotle – or later Jefferson – meant by 'citizen'. Instead, we have the idea of the state distributing goods to certain classes of people for a variety of noble or bad reasons. If the market prevails, then the allocation occurs under conditions that are antithetical to the political ideal of democracy, which includes a notion of shared discussion and common reflection.[2]

Of course, things are not that bad. We still retain the word 'citizen' and some of its attendant ideals remain with us. However, in looking at 'citizenship' and its connection to the idea of dignity, we see how different things are today. We also see the extent to which an idea of dignity and citizenship represents a Third Way in politics. Some varieties of liberalism are hostile to the very idea of citizenship because liberals are ill-disposed to the idea of demanding too much of citizens in terms of actions.[3] To those on the political Right, a separate set of objections is raised. They champion the idea of citizens as clients because they distrust the government's need for money. Oddly enough, both traditional liberals and traditional conservatives dislike the idea of citizenship, because both groups are attached to the notion of freedom. The Liberal Left does not embrace the idea of dignified citizenship because to be a citizen might impugn the self-expression of individuals. Those on the Conservative Right know that the creation of citizens takes with it the idea of people being equal. And the need for equality, in anything more than the most limited sense of legal equality, may violate our pocketbooks. The state would have to guarantee certain minimal conditions for the attainment of civic dignity. The effort, to put it bluntly, to requisition the monies necessary to create equalizing political conditions is seen as a limit on personal freedom.

This is why civic dignity is so essential to any form of progressive politics. By taking what is most useful from the liberal and conservative traditions and rejecting the extremes of both the Left and Right, we move towards a politics which is based upon recognizing that individual freedom can only be realized within healthy and robust communities. This notion of community expects much of people and demands that we create conditions under which citizens can flourish. Henry Tam's identification of three communitarian principles (1998: 12–18) – cooperative enquiry, mutual responsibility and citizen participation – aligns closely with this revived sense of civic dignity. One of the common criticisms of the communitarian movement is that it too easily embraces a kind of neo-authoritarianism. Amy Gutmann accuses communitarians of wanting Salem without the witches (1985: 319). However, it is quite clear that what motivates people like Benjamin Barber, Michael Walzer, William Galston and Michael Sandel is a strong desire to end coercive politics. They all draw upon the work of Mill and Dewey to articulate a new vision of participatory, community-oriented politics. Whatever we might say about Mill or Dewey, they are clearly members of the liberal tradition and champions of human freedom (see Tam, 1998: 18–30).

Freedom, and a sense of community, can only exist if we begin to expect things of people – that citizens are not clients of state largesse and modestly entitled to rights. They are not merely consumers of products created by a vibrant society. We expect things of citizens because they have responsibilities to the public, to their local communities and to the maintenance of the common good. At the same time, we should confront the inadequacies of right-wing critics who would devastate the welfare state and cut people loose to face the vagaries of the free market. In a democratic polity, where citizenship is extended to all, all must have the ability to participate in politics. If all are to participate in a meaningful way, we need to create the conditions under which they can realize their full potential. This requires a robust state capable of providing education, healthcare and the work that collectively enables people to enter the public square as dignified citizens. At the same time this robust state can easily expect citizens to do things – within reasonable limits behaviours can be encouraged, even required.

Welfare Reform and Citizens' Dignity

Welfare reform was undertaken in the United States in 1995 and, to a significant degree, these reforms represent the kind of policy innovations necessary to create the conditions under which citizens can flourish. In considering this policy, we can note how work and dignity are aligned to create a responsible citizen who is more likely to take part in the broader community and meaningfully participate in political life. However, we need to think carefully about what exactly welfare reform means and the dangers that accompany these reforms.

While the reality is that the welfare state encompasses a whole panoply of programmes, including various healthcare programmes, social security for the elderly and unemployment insurance, to name but a few, the use of the word welfare is typically restricted to a specific set of programmes, technically entitled AFDC (Aid To Families with Dependent Children). To most Americans, including many politicians and policy analysts, this was welfare. During the 1970s, continuing into the 1990s, this programme came under a withering attack. There were numerous criticisms that it broke up families, discouraged work and kept those on it in a state of dependency that limited their ability to be useful members of society. These criticisms received their most famous and controversial expression in the work of Charles Murray (1984). However, many more thoughtful concerns were raised about the weaknesses of the system by other critics (see Mead, 1992; Teles, 1996; Wilson, 1996). While there continue to be sharp disagreements between those on the Right and Left, substantial reforms were undertaken during the middle of the 1990s. These reforms sought to decentralize administrative control, limit the amount of time one could be on the programme, and to make work an important component of welfare policy. There was built-in flexibility which allowed various experimentation at the state level.

Since these reforms were adopted in 1995, there has been a noted decrease in the numbers of people on the welfare rolls. Government reports show an almost 50 per cent decline in the number of families and people on welfare.[4] Of course, the reasons for this apparent success are highly contested and more research must be done. Some critics of the reforms fear that people are simply being removed from the welfare rolls and, thus, merely disappearing from government statistics, while the reality of poverty continues. These critics also suggest that the economic expansion of the 1990s deserves all, or most, of the credit.[5] We cannot debate the evidence here. However, welfare reforms allow us to think more concretely about our principles and to clarify what progressive politics should mean in theory and in practice.

While the evidence is anecdotal, there are solid reasons to be hopeful about these changes in welfare. The insistence on work has created numerous individual stories of success and a common denominator in those successes is the dignity found by working mothers (see DeParle, 1999). People are often forced to work for their welfare support; they then find work and are able to leave welfare and join the permanent workforce. In some cases, the cycle of poverty is broken. What is crucial, though, to a progressive politics is that people not only escape poverty, but that they are able to maintain families, to take part in the economy and become active citizens. The likelihood that an employed person will become a politically active citizen is much greater than that an unemployed person will do the same.[6]

However, despite some examples of success, there is a plethora of problems that continue to raise concerns about the reforms. Many recipients of welfare feel degraded having to work as they do, many cannot truly escape poverty with the rather low wages they receive (let alone become the active citizens one would hope for) and many are simply lost from the system (see DeParle, 1999). In particular, I believe we should be concerned about the restrictions placed on receiving benefits and attending college. A progressive politics should insist upon the importance of education in helping people become productive political actors. Work must be seen as part of a process of encouraging citizenship, and education is a vital part of that process.

What is clear from these success stories is that work requirements are, on the whole, good and that the dignity found in work is extremely meaningful to citizens. Secondly, that much more must be done. As Governor Tommy Thompson of Wisconsin freely admits, welfare reform cannot be done on the 'cheap'. Government must provide money or services that enable citizens to find work opportunities and secure employment, and provide day care for their children and offer decent healthcare. Welfare reform must not be used as an excuse to gut existing programmes. As Governor Thompson insists, real change may cost more than the old programmes. Whether those in government and citizens as voters are willing to pay more will be the true test of our commitment to uniting dignity with citizenship.

Surveys show that many Americans are hostile to the old welfare politics, in favour of reforms *and* sympathetic to spending more money on the poor (see Cammisa, 1998: ch. 1). By making work a requirement and putting limits on how much time people can stay on welfare, reforms tell people that they must take charge of their lives. The principle that citizens must work, but that the state has an obligation to help them, is an excellent one. It means that responsibility is demanded of both citizens and the state. Too often the word 'responsibility' is used to bemoan the lack of it among individual citizens. Welfare reforms insist on citizens becoming more responsible in finding work; however, the state has obligations too. The state has a responsibility to help people find that work and to maintain decent conditions for families while they work.

Welfare reform is only one example of a broader set of progressive political ideas. In making work a central component of welfare reform, citizens are more likely to take part in their communities. They are more likely to become productive citizens – and not merely in the economic sense of that word (see Stodghill, 2000). They are more likely to grow and develop politically. People who work are more likely to vote, join associations and trust their fellow citizens. Of course, there is no guarantee of any of this coming to pass. We are primarily interested in fostering the conditions under which citizens can flourish – if they have the political desire to become active citizens. This illustrates what it means to have dignity – people become more independent from the state, more independent from the direct help of others. Yet, this independence is not used to reject their connections to others; instead they have a greater ability to connect with the broader community as equals and full members of that community.

But to achieve this we must admit that the state has a serious role in helping people get off the welfare rolls, and the principle can be extended to other policy areas. Welfare reform can be a model for how we rethink the relationship between the state and its citizens. The state has an important responsibility in providing the conditions under which people can effectively join their communities as productive members. But, thankfully, such aid does not necessarily lead to dependence; rather, it can be a measure of short-term assistance that leads to long-term freedom and equality. This is the heart of progressive politics. Citizens need to be free and equal. They need to live in a society in which conditions do not conspire against them; rather, conditions are designed to enable them to reach their fullest potential. If government can help create those circumstances, citizens are more likely to lead a dignified civic life. Such a life would recognize our sense of individual independence while at the same time happily accepting the bonds we have with our fellow citizens. In this sense, community becomes a progressive and liberal ideal.

Notes

1 The most powerful critique of democracy is still found in Plato's *Republic*; see 557a–561a.
2 This entire paragraph draws on the work of McWilliams (1977, 1980).
3 I think the version of citizenship I have sketched out would be problematic to whatever version of liberalism is preferred by such diverse thinkers as Robert Nozick or George Kateb.
4 Government statistics can be found at: http://www.acf.dhhs.gov/news/stats.
5 These possible concerns were raised in a personal conversation the author had with Jared Bernstein, economist for the Economic Policy Institute, Washington, DC, 22 February 2000.
6 The difficulty of organizing the poor and the unemployed is explored in Wilson (1995), ch. 4. See also Fox Piven and Cloward (1979), especially chs 1, 2 and 5. Neither writer denies that organizing the unemployed can be done; but it is difficult, as they illustrate.

References

Aristotle (1981) *Politics* (New York: Penguin), bk 1, ch. 7 and bk 3, chs 1, 2, 4.
Burke, E. (1987) *Reflections on The Revolution in France*, ed. J. G. A. Pocock (Indianapolis: Hackett).
Cammisa, A. M. (1998) *From Rhetoric to Reform* (Boulder, CO: Westview).

Chait, J. (1998) 'The Slippery Center', *The New Republic*, 16 November: 19–21.

DeParle, J. (1999) 'Symbol of Welfare Reform, Still Struggling', *New York Times*, 20 April 20: A1, A20–1.

Elshtain, J. B. (1995) *Democracy on Trial* (New York: Basic Books).

Fox Piven, F. and Cloward, R. (1979) *Poor People Movements* (New York: Vintage).

Fukuyama, F. (1995) *Trust* (New York: Free Press).

Gutmann, A. (1985) 'Communitarian Critics of Liberalism', *Philosophy and Public Affairs*, 14(3), Summer: 308–22.

Hale, D. (2000) 'The Natural History of Citizenship', in Hale (ed.), *Friends and Citizens* (Lanham, MD: Rowman and Littlefield).

Ignatieff, M. (1984) *The Needs of Strangers* (New York: Penguin).

Kautz, S. (1995) *Liberalism and Community* (Ithaca: Cornell University Press).

Margalit, A. (1996) *The Decent Society* (Cambridge, MA: Harvard University Press).

McWilliams, W. C. (1977) 'On Equality as the Moral Foundation for Community', in R. Horwitz (ed.), *The Moral Foundations of the American Republic* (Charlottesville: University Press of Virginia), pp. 183–213.

McWilliams, W. C. (1980) 'Democracy and the Citizen: Community, Dignity, and the Crisis of Contemporary Politics in America', in R. Goldwin and W. Schambra (eds), *How Democratic is the Constitution* (Lanham, MD: University Press of America), pp. 79–101.

Mead, L. (1992) *The New Politics of Poverty* (New York: Basic Books).

Mill, J. S. (1986) *On Liberty* (New York: Penguin).

Murray, C. (1984) *Losing Ground* (New York: Basic Books).

Nozick, R. (1974) *Anarchy, State and Utopia* (New York: Basic Books).

Purdy, J. (1999) *For Common Things* (New York: Knopf).

Putnam, R. (2000) *Bowling Alone* (New York: Simon and Schuster).

Rawls, J. (1971) *A Theory of Justice* (Cambridge, MA: Harvard University Press).

Stodghill, R. (2000) 'Off the Dole', *Time*, 12 June: 65.

Tam, H. (1998) *Communitarianism* (New York: New York University Press).

Teles, S. (1996) *Whose Welfare?* (Lawrence, KS: University Press of Kansas).

Wilson, J. Q. (1995) *Political Organizations* (Princeton: Princeton University Press).

Wilson, W. J. (1996) *When Work Disappears* (New York: Vintage).

PART III

POWER AND DEMOCRACY

10

Public Service and Active Citizenship

Kevin Mattson

One of the most challenging legacies of the Clinton presidency is the declaration that 'the era of big government has ended, the era of big citizenship is dawning'. Clinton and his brethren in the Democratic Leadership Council (DLC) – often referred to as 'New Democrats' – attempted to fashion a vision of politics based largely on a commitment to participatory citizenship and an appropriation of the Republican Party's criticism of the welfare state. The objective was to find a progressive alternative – a 'Third Way' – to both traditional welfare state liberalism and a return to laissez-faire. A core component of this vision grew out of a faith in local initiatives, public service and an engaged citizenry. To understand its strengths and weaknesses, we must explore the historical trajectory of progressive thinking and activism in America and ask a fundamental question: can active – or 'big' – citizenship serve as the foundation of a progressive form of politics in the global age? More specifically, can the recent revamping of this tradition by so-called 'Third Way' exponents constitute the basis of a vision of progressive politics in America? This chapter will try to answer this question.

To do so, I suggest we go back in history to the Progressive Era (1890–1917). Many political thinkers have taken this journey recently (see, for instance, Dionne, 1996; Isaac, 1998; Lind, 1996; Milkis and Mileur, 1999; Sandel, 1996; Weisberg, 1996). For good reason too, since this era witnessed the birth of modernity, the ascendancy of welfare state liberalism over nineteenth-century laissez-faire teachings, the growth of governmental power and a great deal of political optimism. Progressive leaders took bold political

action at the time. As President, Theodore Roosevelt decided to build
the executive branch of the federal government in order to combat
the growing power of national corporations. He passed massive
legislation during his presidency, which included the creation of a
Bureau of Corporations, the Hepburn Act (1906) that regulated
railroads, the Meat Inspection Act (1906) that regulated the food
industry along with the Pure Food and Drug Act (1906). He wedded
this activity to a strong vision of national social justice. After his
presidency, and during his failed campaign for a second presidential
bid with the Progressive Party, he called for workmen's compensation
laws, anti-child labour laws, a graduated income tax and massive
spending on public education. In a 1912 speech, he followed the
thinking of the political philosopher Herbert Croly to argue: 'In the
long run, this country will not be a good place for any of us to live
in unless it is a reasonably good place for all of us to live in.' That
required, he believed, 'social and industrial justice, achieved through
the genuine rule of the people'. No better statement could be found
to express the modern liberal belief in a regulatory state assuring
democratic and egalitarian values (for more on state-building at this
time, see Skowronek, 1982).

State-building was accompanied by a great deal of local activism
during the Progressive Era. One of the era's most important and
popular figures was Jane Addams, the founder of Hull House in
Chicago and a leading spokesperson for the settlement house movement in America (see Davis, 1967 and 1973). Addams's settlement
house drew out the local energies of its neighbourhood. Hull House
tried to engage new, immigrant citizens in public problem-solving by
providing them with educational forums on local issues (at some of
which John Dewey spoke) and forging what Addams called a 'civic
consciousness'. Political action became central here, as settlement
house activists tried to improve the conditions of the neighbourhood
(including things like paving streets and improving sewer systems)
and argued for legislation to combat child labour and sweatshops.
Addams distinguished the service she and her fellow settlement house
workers engaged in from charity. She saw her activities as the essence
of democratic citizenship and politics – an expression of obligation
to the public realm to which she and others belonged. For Addams,
these activities were not only necessary for the health of America's
polity but provided enjoyment inherent in active citizenship.

For Addams, service at the local level led directly to political
action at the municipal, state and national levels. As she explained,
'One of the first lessons we learned at Hull House was that private
beneficence is totally inadequate to deal with the vast numbers of the

city's disinherited' (1961: 219). Though she cherished the 'civic cooperation' (p. 222) garnered through local activity, she believed it was not enough. As another democratic thinker of the time who came out of the settlement house movement, Mary Parker Follett, understood so well, government at higher levels had to build itself up through citizen activities at the lower levels (Follett, 1918). And so Addams decided that her local initiatives needed to be connected to a wider national vision. She therefore joined forces with Theodore Roosevelt's run for presidency in 1912. In fact, a famous political poster for the Progressive Party shows Jane Addams shaking hands with Theodore Roosevelt – as if the party was to be a marriage between those who worked at the local and national levels (see Davis, 1973: 190).

The Progressive Era was marked by a faith in conjoint local and national political activity. It saw innovative political thinking that stressed a well-protected public interest along with an overriding belief that a 'sense of satisfaction' flowed 'from active participation in a community' (Kloppenberg, 1986: 348; see also Westbrook, 1991). In terms of activism, the Progressive Era was a time when community organizers opened the doors of public schools in the evenings for citizens to debate national policy and thereby become more politically engaged (see Mattson, 1998a). This was also a period in which political reformers embraced initiatives such as the referendum as a means to engage citizens in formulating policy (see Mattson, 1999a). It might be surprising to some that Theodore Roosevelt – a firm believer in strong executive leadership – endorsed both the initiative and referendum as well as the use of public schools as sites for public deliberation. He did so precisely because he saw these reforms as a way to create the 'rule of the people'. Partnerships between local and national levels of public activism seemed congruent, mutual and complementary to many progressive leaders at this time.

Service and Citizenship During the Progressive Era: The Origins of a Tradition

What was the meaning of public service and citizenship during the Progressive Era? For Addams and others, public service was a means by which citizens could involve themselves directly in public life and begin an entry into political action. This did not necessarily lead to a belief in 'direct democracy' or the sort of self-governance that antifederalists earlier endorsed. Nor did it lead to a belief that voluntary service could, by itself, address social problems. Addams constantly addressed the 'inadequacy of charitable efforts' and the limits of her own non-charitable activities to address poverty (1961: 121). She recognized the need for political leadership and the fact that America was a representative democracy. So too did those who formed social centres in public schools where citizens gathered to discuss the issues of the day. One local civic club in a public school delineated its purposes in its founding constitution in 1907:

> Whereas, the welfare of society demands that those whose duty it is to exercise the franchise be well informed upon the economic, industrial and political questions of today; and whereas by combination of effort the best results may be obtained; and whereas the public school building is the best available place for such a combination of effort; Therefore, we do form a society to hold, in the public school building, meetings whose object shall be the gaining of information upon public questions by listening to public speakers and by public readings and discussions. (Mattson, 1998a: 54–5)

This was no vision of direct rule of the people but rather a belief that even in a representative democracy, citizens needed to be invited to the table of public debate. Here they would help shape their neighbourhood's and nation's agenda. Through service and political debate, citizens could see themselves as political actors, largely by educating themselves and then trying to inform those with the power to make decisions.

This political vision was multi-tiered. On the one hand, it saw active citizenship and local public service as crucial for a healthy democracy. On the other hand, citizenship and service could not serve in the stead of a regulatory government or strong political leadership. The tools of direct democracy should supplement – not replace – representative institutions. After all, the legislation passed by citizens could never abolish representative political institutions. Citizens were to deliberate and then inform their representatives, who still retained a certain amount of autonomy from those demands. Activists and thinkers like Jane Addams and Mary Parker Follett also believed a strong state and regulatory policies did not threaten local participation (what conservative political leaders believed). The two things could work in tandem – sometimes joining up with one another, when for instance, local activists discovered the need for national legislation or political leaders needed to listen to the concerns of local citizens.

This idea of robust citizenship and local public action wedded to an activist and regulatory state continued long past the Progressive Era. Throughout the years, it took on different forms. During the New Deal in America, as Harry Boyte and Nancy Kari (1996) have shown, the federal government created opportunities for 'public work' in order to combat unemployment but also to engage citizens in building common civic spaces. The Civilian Conservation Corps (CCC) created work camps where young men could engage in citizen service by building public parks. In 'some CCC Camps', there were 'citizenship schools alive with intellectual energy and larger democratic vision' (Boyte and Kari, 1996: 109). But more simply, these camps symbolized how Franklin Delano Roosevelt – both a strong leader and a modern liberal – wanted to build a partnership between the local energies of citizens and the power of the federal government.

During the Great Society – the next chapter in modern liberalism after the New Deal – liberals once again tried to build up local initiatives. This was most evident in the Community Action Program (CAP) that President Lyndon Johnson endorsed in 1963. The programme engaged citizens within poor communities to attack poverty, thus ensuring 'maximum feasible participation' (Matusow, 1984: 244). Many of the programme's efforts paralleled the community organizing of Saul Alinsky and Students for a Democratic Society, both of whom were trying to engage poor people in local politics through things like tenant unions. Looking back on this programme, many find it to be a failure (see Lemann, 1991, for instance). It certainly suffered from a number of weaknesses: local programmes often became a haven for irresponsible black nationalists, created a new professional class who treated poor people like clients and generated conflicts between the federal government and local municipal institutions (see Matusow, 1984: ch. 9). Nonetheless, it clearly indicated that liberals, while building up a welfare state, wanted to ensure that citizens played a role in public policy-making.

The Contemporary Remaking of the Progressive Tradition

In the wake of the tumultuous and conflict-ridden 1960s, liberals started to shift away from the political vision embodied in the New Deal and Great Society. During the 1980s 'neo-liberals' (Gary Hart, Paul Tsongas, Al Gore) started having more influence within the Democratic Party. These politicians and thinkers no longer emphasized the 'redistribution of wealth' through welfare programmes but, rather, 'market-oriented solutions in public policy' and an 'affinity for business' (Baer, 2000: 33). A regulatory state started to appear suspect. At the same time, these new liberals believed that government had a role to play in creating national public service opportunities, especially for young people, who seemed increasingly disaffected from public life (Rothenberg, 1984: ch. 18). These politicians set the stage for the DLC, an organization that helped get Clinton elected to the presidency. Made up of politicians, policy advisers and academics (including Al From, Will Marshall and William Galston), this organization has set much of the agenda and philosophical grounding for the Third Way in America.

Throughout the 1980s, the DLC began its long ascent towards influence within the Democratic Party, and by the mid-1980s public service became a central component of its vision. The DLC invited into its orbit Charles Moskos, a sociologist who argued in favour of national public service. By 1988, as Steven Waldman explains, 'The DLC had adopted Moskos's service ideas as its central, defining proposal' (1995: 4). Indeed, public service would become the central policy accomplishment of the Clinton Administration. Going through an amazingly complex set of legislative processes and debacles, national public service became real in September 1993 when Clinton signed the AmeriCorps programme and national service into existence (ibid. 239). Now young people would be provided with the opportunity of doing a year of public service in return for financial aid towards their college education. If Clinton is to be remembered for any major accomplishment, it will certainly be this.

National public service was not just about legislation or bureaucratic programmes. It was about political philosophy too. Perhaps the most important intellectual influence on national service proponents was the communitarian critique of liberalism (see Lasch, 1988; Walzer, 1990). Eschewing individualism or an emphasis on what was often called 'rights talk', DLC spokespeople believed public service cultivated responsible citizenship and the principle of 'equal sacrifice for the common good' (Al From, quoted in Baer, 2000: 112). As Kenneth Baer explains, early arguments for national service were 'premised on a public philosophy in which the relationship between citizens and government was based on reciprocal obligation, not entitlement. . . . Furthermore, New Democrats hoped grandly that this emphasis on mutual responsibility would foster good citizenship and build a sense of community' (ibid.). In the form of national public service, communitarian political philosophy wandered out of the ivory tower into national politics.

Much communitarian thinking before the 1990s had placed an emphasis on morality and character-building. This was true for national public service: 'For Clinton, service was not just about delivering services. It was . . . about building character' (Waldman, 1995: 11; see also Etzioni, 1993). This differed from the idea that political engagement served as the key component of democratic citizenship, and it had an enormous influence on how national public service was framed by political leaders. For instance, legislators 'prohibited AmeriCorps programs from engaging in political advocacy' (Waldman, 1995: p. 243). Soon after starting, the AmeriCorps programme adopted the slogan 'Getting Things Done' – a clear statement of evading politics while emphasizing direct service. Public service and political deliberation were being severed.

A major reason for this might have been the political catastrophes created under the CAP of the 1960s, when federal monies wound up helping fund radical political activism. More important was a desire on the part of many national service proponents to disconnect service from any wider progressive (or liberal) ideology. As Charles Moskos argued, 'There is no better way to insure that national service is a nonstarter than to hint that it is part of a not-so-hidden liberal agenda' (1988: 170). The point is understandable, but, needless to say, it has meant that the ideal of citizenship nurtured by national public service programmes like AmeriCorps has become distinctly apolitical (for more on this point, see Gorham, 1992). No longer was service intended to lead citizens into discussing or creating policies that could address the problems they were facing in local communities. The robust sense of citizenship and the multi-tiered activism of Addams's era seemed to be consigned to the dustbin of history. At times, the New Democrats even suggested that public policy and government in general should be seen only as a negative last resort to problem solving. In their New Progressive Declaration of the mid-1990s, the DLC explained, 'Citizens and local institutions, rather than distant government agencies, should be the public problem-solvers of first recourse' (quoted in Baer, 2000: 235).

From this perspective, citizens were invited into the public realm, but their roles were quickly circumscribed and directed away from political action. The extent of this was most clearly seen in the President's Summit on America's Future held in April 1997. Here, Clinton gathered ex-Presidents Bush and Carter (both of them interested in public service) to come together for a symbolic event in which they would both perform service and discuss its significance. Historians who look back on this event might simply dismiss it as a photo-op for President Clinton, but I would argue that the event held a great deal more metaphorical significance. For it was here that Clinton crafted a political vision based on national service and citizenship. Most importantly, Clinton announced the death of big government and rise of big citizenship – the theoretical touchstone of contemporary Third Way thinking – around the Summit. The Summit served as a civic ritual (to use Rousseau's political terminology) where key political values were defined.

The events at the Summit took place over three days. The central event, though, was held at Marcus Foster Stadium in Philadelphia. Here, citizens assembled in the audience and listened to speeches by Bush, Carter and Clinton (for more on this event, see Mattson, 1998b). Interspersed with these political speeches were cameos by Hollywood and music industry stars. The *New York Times* reported that 'the rally seemed like a rock concert with the President as the main act' (28 April 1997). The blurring of the line between the entertainment industry and political leadership was significant in and of itself (at one point, the master of ceremonies bellowed out, 'We got all the presidents back there waiting to come out here, baby!'). More importantly, in this context, Clinton called upon the citizens in the audience to perform public service by spilling out of the stadium onto the streets of a poor neighbourhood nearby. Journalists and photographers captured the presidents, past and present, assembled with citizens doing such things as painting over graffiti or collecting trash off the streets.

This could be taken as a great populist celebration, in which political leaders intermingled with ordinary citizens, both of them engaged in public work. Unfortunately, the service was of questionable merit. Few if any preliminary discussions were held with local citizens about the event, and one critic called it 'blitzkrieg' service (Rosin, 1997: 14). When journalists talked with local residents, they were told the graffiti being painted over would reappear in a matter of days. The service thus took on an almost surreal, spectacular quality. Citizens were invited into public life, but instead of being invited as political actors – as robust participants in decision-making or even meaningful service – they were invited for their symbolic attributes. Citizens served more as props than as participants sharing responsibility with their political leaders. Of course, some might argue that this makes too much of the event, but the aftermath makes even clearer its significance.

One of the major outcomes of the Summit was the rise of General Colin Powell to fame. He was known for a lifetime of public service, both in community and military circles, and the Summit was a place for him to shine. Here he announced the creation of a new non-profit organization with the forbidding title, America's Promise (it exists to date). Powell suggested that the organization would essentially 'guilt trip' (the term was used in many popular essays written at the time) corporations into donating money and volunteers to charitable service projects. A new political vision emerged here, grounded in a belief that the will of citizens engaged in service – without a regulatory state – could actually produce civic-minded results. All that was needed was the power of guilt. Needless to say, the immediate results were not terribly inspiring. As the *New Republic* reported:

> Under Powell's plan, businesses were supposed to finance the bulk of a $10 million advertising campaign that would have allowed mentoring organizations like Big Brothers/Big Sisters of America to double in size. So far, corporations have supplied practically nothing, according to Catherine Milton, an official running the campaign. (Stricherz, 1998: 13–14)

Even corporations who pledged volunteers fell short (see Alter, 1998).

America's Promise symbolizes a new model of national politics that extends on the energy of citizenship service. It suggests that 'big government' might no longer be necessary to combat certain social ills. Private philanthropy and charity might serve better, and the state's only role would seem to be as a bully pulpit – merely enhancing the civic voices of leaders like Powell. This vision cannot be divorced from the general decline of confidence that citizens have shown in public institutions and government over the last few years. 'Big government' serves as an easy target in a day and age of public cynicism, and service becomes an all-too-easy replacement for state-run public action – the sort that Addams believed should grow out of local initiatives.

Ironically, this brings us to another unintended consequence of the Summit and the political philosophy that has emerged around service and citizenship during the 1990s. When originally proposed, national public service was not simply to address a supposed communitarian deficit; it was to address a specific problem among a new generation increasingly labelled 'Generation X'. Reports during the 1980s found that young people – more than other segments of the American population – expressed increasing amounts of cynicism and disengagement from public life (for more on this, see Loeb, 1994; Mattson, 1999b). Public service, many believed, could tackle this cynicism by providing young people with an opportunity to solve social problems in their communities. But what has seemed to happen over the years is that Generation X spokespeople have taken service as a replacement for political action (for two examples of this tendency, see Mitchell, 1998; Nelson and Cowan, 1994). Politics is seen as inherently corrupt or is associated with baby-boomer protest movements of the 1960s and thus outdated; service, on the other hand, is thought of as noble, 'hands-on', constructive, and free of politics. Building upon the cynicism of many young people, service ironically allows for further disaffection, especially when viewed as an alternative to the rough-and-tumble world of politics. The National Association of the Secretaries of State recently reported on a thorough survey they had made of service participants: 'While youth volunteerism is on the rise, this involvement remains decidedly individualistic and apolitical' (quoted in Mattson, 1999b: 60). It would seem that the original Progressive Era vision that connected local service and citizenship to the wider world of political action has been lost.

A Progressive Rebirth and Alternative?

Certain tendencies in the Third Way thinking of New Democrats – echoed in the pronouncements of New Labour in the UK – suggest that local service and citizenship are separate from the evils of 'big government' and politics as a whole. This betrays a weak form of citizenship disconnected from robust political deliberation and action. Of course, this is not to suggest that every form of service should result in a government programme. Third Way exponents in America are right to redevelop a participatory vision of democracy that has always, I would argue, been associated with the Left and progressives. From the Progressive Era onwards, liberals and progressives have tried to connect citizen activism to the halls of government. Contrary to the Right's recent accusations, progressives have not been whole-hearted celebrants of big government or bureaucracy; they have pointed out the mistakes that have been made in the name of government. Nonetheless, the role of government as an agent of good in people's lives – or at least that possibility – must remain at the heart of Progressive thinking. In relation to local initiatives such as public service programmes, politics should not be ruled out, as it often has been by some recent Third Way proponents and communitarians. We need a view of citizenship and participatory democracy that stresses partnerships between national and local power. We need to return to Jane Addams's conception of service and citizenship as the first – not the last – step into public life and political action.

Of course, a great deal of Addams's political vision grew out of the era in which she wrote, a time in which government's role was beginning to grow. We cannot recreate that world. Yet, as progressives, we should be wary of just how much has been conceded to the Right over the last few years, especially in terms of the foundational language of democracy and citizenship. This seems to be a time in which progressives are regrouping. One of our challenges today is to rethink our conceptions of citizenship, service and localism. How can we formulate a political vision that weds local and national power? How can we envision a form of citizenship that is robust and connected to channels of political power? Recent Third Way thinking and political programmes come up short in answering these questions. To counteract this, progressives must begin to articulate a language of politics that sees the need for deep citizen involvement and engagement, while never severing this from a belief in the need – at times – of 'big government'. I would argue that there is no better way to create this vision than to plumb our history. Creating a political theory informed by historical antecedents is that much stronger than searching for something 'new'.

A progressive alternative will need to embrace the idea that participatory citizenship – which is distinct from moral character – must be nurtured. At the same time, progressives must defend the need for government to protect the public interest. There is a tradition of doing this in America, even with our weak state and predilection for voluntary action. Progressives need not feel boxed into being top-down statists. Instead, we must reconnect local activities and citizenship to the process of building government. This is the ideal that we inherited from the Progressive Era. The challenge remains how to live up to it while facing the changing circumstances of the twenty-first century.

References

Addams, J. (1961[1910]) *Twenty Years at Hull House* (New York: Signet).

Alter, J. (1998) 'Long After the Trumpets', *Newsweek*, 11 May: 41–2.

Baer, K. (2000) *Reinventing Democrats: The Politics of Liberalism from Reagan to Clinton* (Lawrence: University Press of Kansas).

Boyte, H. and Kari, N. (1996) *Building America: The Democratic Promise of Public Work* (Philadelphia: Temple University Press).

Davis, A. (1967) *Spearheads for Reform: The Social Settlements and the Progressive Movement, 1890–1914* (New York: Oxford University Press).

Davis, A. (1973) *American Heroine: The Life and Legend of Jane Addams* (New York: Oxford University Press).

Dionne, Jr., E. J. (1996) *They Only Look Dead: Why Progressives Will Dominate the Next Political Era* (New York: Simon and Schuster).

Etzioni, A. (1993) 'Is Bill Clinton a Communitarian?' *National Civic Review*, 82: 221–5.

Follett, M. P. (1918) *The New State: Group Organization The Solution to Popular Government*. Reissued 1998 with introductory essays by Benjamin Barber, Jane Mansbridge and Kevin Mattson (University Park: Penn State Press).

Gorham, E. (1992) *National Service, Citizenship, and Political Education* (Albany: State University of New York Press).

Isaac, J. (1998) 'The Poverty of Progressivism', in *Democracy in Dark Times* (Ithaca: Cornell University Press).

Kloppenberg, J. (1986) *Uncertain Victory: Social Democracy and Progressivism in European and American Thought, 1870–1920* (New York: Oxford University Press).

Lasch, C. (1988) 'The Communitarian Criticism of Liberalism', in Charles Reynolds and Ralph Norman (eds), *Community in America: The Challenge of Habits of the Heart* (Berkeley: University of California Press).

Lemann, N. (1991) *The Promised Land: The Great Black Migration and How it Changed America* (New York: Vintage).

Lind, M. (1996) *The Next American Nation: The New Nationalism and the Fourth American Revolution* (New York: Free Press).

Loeb, P. (1994) *Generation at the Crossroads: Apathy and Action on the American Campus* (New Brunswick: Rutgers University Press).

Mattson, K. (1998a) *Creating a Democratic Public: The Struggle for Urban Participatory Democracy during the Progressive Era* (University Park: Penn State Press).

Mattson, K. (1998b) 'Doing Good, Looking Marvelous', *The Baffler*, 11: 75–84.

Mattson, K. (1999a) 'Taking Back the Initiative: Renewing Progressive Democracy', *Social Policy*, Summer: 21–7.

Mattson, K. (1999b) 'Talking About My Generation and the Left', *Dissent*, Fall: 58–63.

Matusow, A. (1984) *The Unraveling of America: A History of Liberalism in the 1960s* (New York: Harper and Row).

Milkis, S. and Mileur, J. (eds) (1999) *Progressivism and the New Democracy* (Amherst: University of Massachusetts Press).

Mitchell, M. (1998) *A New Kind of Party Animal: How the Young Are Tearing Up the American Political Landscape* (New York: Simon and Schuster).

Moskos, C. (1988) *A Call to Civic Service: National Service for Country and Community* (New York: Free Press).

Nelson, R. and Cowan, J. (1994) *Revolution X* (New York: Penguin).

Powell, C. (1998) 'Starting with the Young', *Tikkun*, Nov/Dec: 56–7.

Rosin, H. (1997) 'Blah-Blah', *The New Republic*, 19 May: 14–15.
Rothenberg, R. (1984) *The Neoliberals: Creating the New American Politics* (New York: Simon and Schuster).
Sandel, M. (1996) *Democracy's Discontent: America in Search of a Public Philosophy* (Cambridge, MA: Harvard University Press).
Skowronek, S. (1982) *Building a New American State: The Expansion of National Administrative Capacities, 1877–1920* (Cambridge: Cambridge University Press).
Stricherz, M. (1998) 'Any Volunteers?', *New Republic*, 5 and 12 January: 12–13.
Waldman, S. (1995) *The Bill: How the Adventures of Clinton's National Service Bill Reveal What is Corrupt, Comic, Cynical – and Noble – About Washington* (New York: Viking).
Walzer, M. (1990) 'The Communitarian Critique of Liberalism', *Political Theory*, 18: 6–23.
Weisberg, J. (1996) *In Defense of Government* (New York: Scribner).
Westbrook, R. (1991) *John Dewey and American Democracy* (Ithaca: Cornell University Press).

Further Reading

Faux, J. (1993) 'The Myth of the New Democrat', *American Prospect*, Fall: 20–9.
Hale, J. (1995) 'The Making of the New Democrats', *Political Science Quarterly*, 1(10): 207–32.
Judis, J. (2000) *The Paradox of American Democracy* (New York: Pantheon).
Kaus, M. (1995) *The End of Equality* (New York: Basic Books).
Metz, A. (1997) *National Service and AmeriCorps: An Annotated Bibliography* (Westport, CT: Greenwood Press).
Schneider, W. (1998) 'No Modesty, Please, We're the DLC', *National Journal*, 12 December: 2962–3.
Smith, C. (1994) 'The New Corporate Philanthropy', *Harvard Business Review*, May–June: 105–16.

11

Modernizing Government

John Stewart

In America and Britain, many of those associated with the quest for a 'Third Way' to renew progressive politics have put considerable emphasis on the 'modernizing' or 're-inventing' of government. In Britain the Government White Paper, *Modernising Government*, argues that 'we live in an age when most of the old dogmas that haunted governments in the past have been swept away. . . . Now that we are not hidebound by the old ways of government we can find newer and better ones' (CM 4310: 9). Modernization is vital because government has been 'organized too much around the structure of providers rather than the users', 'focused on inputs rather than outcomes', 'is too often risk averse', has paid too little attention to working 'across the board' and has suffered from 'inertia' (ibid. 11).

A similar critique can be found in America in the Gore Report, *Creating a Government that Works Better and Costs Less* (National Performance Review, 1993). That report draws on *Reinventing Government* (Osborne and Gaebler, 1992), a book endorsed by the then Governor of Arkansas, Bill Clinton, in the following terms: 'This book should be read by every elected official in America. Those of us who want to revitalize government in the 1990s are going to have to re-invent it. This book gives us the blueprint.' *Reinventing Government* saw 'the bureaucratic institutions developed during the industrial era' as failing the public. 'Today's environment demands institutions that are extremely flexible and adaptable . . . It demands institutions that *empower* citizens rather than simply *serving* them' (Osborne and Gaebler, 1992: 15).

Modernising Government and *Reinventing Government* recognize that government acts cannot be separated from what government is seeking to achieve. The way of governing is itself part of policies, determining how they are received and perceived by the citizens for whom they were provided. The nature of public management is or should be an expression of the political values pursued and merits study in any analysis of the development of progressive politics. In this chapter I want to argue not only that public management should be geared to the purposes pursued, but more widely that management in the public domain should reflect the distinctive purposes, the distinctive conditions and the distinctive tasks of that domain.

Purposes, Conditions and Tasks of the Public Domain

There is a necessary link between the study of management in the public domain and political theory. The phrase 'management in the public domain' is chosen to indicate a wider concept than the phrase 'public management'. It recognizes the domain of collective action pursued in the search for the public interest and can cover the behaviour of many different organizations. The distinctive purposes can include equity, justice, community and citizenship. The distinctive conditions can include public accountability and the political process. The distinctive tasks can include balancing objectives, demands and interests in public judgement. Any elaboration of purposes, conditions and tasks gives expression to a political theory and can be disputed. What is clear, however, is that the purposes, conditions and tasks are not necessarily those that prevail in the domain of private action.

The purposes, conditions and tasks of the public domain should also reflect the conditions of the polity. The dominant polity in the postwar period was the government of certainty. The problems were seen as clear as were the solutions. Rules were relied upon to guide public action and professionals to apply the right solution. The dominant mode of operation was a combination of bureaucracy and professionalism reflected in the welfare state, particularly in the United Kingdom and the rest of Europe.

Bureaucratic professionalism came under challenge from both the Left and the Right. The necessary rules of bureaucracy were seen as unresponsive. The certainties of the accepted professional solutions came under challenges typified by the reaction to perceived failures in education and to alienating developments in public housing and town centres. The Left stressed the involvement of communities as a counter to bureaucratic professionalism. The dominant idea in the polity of the Right became the market. If the market could be given a place in the public domain it would deliver the right solution – that was the new certainty. The limitations of that approach became apparent as it was realized that for issues such as the environment the market is part of the problem.

In a rapidly changing society there is a change from the government of perceived certainty to realized uncertainty. Problems such as crime, drugs and the environment are matched by the risks of a man-made environment. Services such as health and education are challenged by the new demands and the new conditions of a changing society. The government of uncertainty demands a learning government, but as part of a learning society, for the learning must be with the public and from the public, as the uncertainties faced demand changes in society and by the public. The requirements of a learning society place a premium on interaction in discourse between citizens and government in shared learning. The requirements of a learning government have to be taken into account in considering the purpose, conditions and tasks of the public domain. Societal learning is a purpose, discourse between citizens and government a necessary condition and enabling public learning a resulting task. Management should support the defining process of the public domain as 'public discourse leading to collective choice based on public consent' (Ranson and Stewart, 1994: 88).

The New Public Management

Bureaucratic professionalism had its own pattern of public management or, in the terms of the time, of public administration. The critique developed in the 1970s and 1980s was of an enclosed organization that 'knew' what was required, was dominated by producer interests and unresponsive to those for whom services were provided. Although bureaucratic professionalism was challenged from the Left and the Right, it was the Right's critique which was dominant in what came to be known as the 'new public management'. Kieron Walsh and I have characterized it as involving the following elements (Stewart and Walsh, 1990):

- the creation of markets or quasi-markets;
- an emphasis on the public as customers;

- the growth of contractual or semi-contractual arrangements;
- the separation of purchaser from provider;
- accountability for performance against targets;
- flexibility of pay and conditions;
- separation of the political from the management process.

The 'new public management' sought to emulate the practice of management in the private sector. A rhetoric of an entrepreneurial approach developed. Value was placed on competition and market mechanisms. The public became seen as customers. There was a tendency to simplify management tasks with clear targets and separation of roles. Simplification was achieved by separating policy from implementation, the development of contracts, quasi-contracts or target-governing relationships, and their enforcement by performance management. This replicated an assumed clarity of tasks in the private sector.

The dangers of the private sector model

The 'new public management' approach makes two assumptions, either implicitly or explicitly. It assumes that there is a model of private sector management and that it can and should be applied in the public domain. The danger of an assumed private sector model is that the distinctive features of the public domain are neglected, as illustrated by the emphasis on the public as customer. This emphasis has had a value in focusing attention on those for whom the services are provided. Yet the word 'customer' cannot encompass the variety of relationships between government and the public. For the private sector, the customer is normally the individual purchaser of goods or services. In the public domain there are users of the service but they are not necessarily equivalent to the individual purchaser. For some services there are collective rather than individual customers. For other services there are many different customers whose interests have to be balanced. Who is the customer of a school: the children, their parents, future employers? Many services are provided not on demand as for a customer, but on an assessment of need. In the private sector marketing stimulates demand, while in the public domain the task is often the management of rationing.

The word 'customer' confuses when there is conflict between different members of the public to be resolved. It also fails to capture the relationship in regulatory services. If one is arrested, it is no consolation to be told, not 'we are taking you into custody', but 'we are glad to welcome you as a customer and hope you have a long and happy stay with us'. The relationship with the public as citizens is ignored by the emphasis on the customer. To treat the citizen as customer places limits on citizenship. I am no longer a customer of education, but as a citizen I have views on education and am entitled to have those views listened to. To reduce the citizen to customer is to limit involvement in the process of government. The focus on the public as customer illustrates the danger of basing management in the public domain on an assumed model of private sector management, but the issue is wider, as illustrated by the fragmentation of governance.

The fragmentation of governance

Any system of governance has to have a capacity for differentiation. There will be separate agencies, departments, sections with their own roles. Equally, a system of governance has to have a capacity for integration. A system of governance is fragmented if it has a high degree of differentiation without the requisite capacity for integration.

In the 1980s and the 1990s in Britain there was a tendency to differentiate as part of the 'new public management' regime. Special purpose agencies were created to carry out tasks previously carried out by general purpose agencies such as local authorities. Within organizations, separate units were created to carry out defined tasks either under quasi-contracts or with specified targets. Outside providers were engaged under contracts. The result has been fragmentation of governance because differentiation took place without balancing mechanisms for integration. The process has resulted in a structure of government, in danger of being a series of units each focused on a limited task, without sufficient capacity to work across the units. Yet the public domain is where issues and problems are faced by society and those issues and problems can require action not by one unit, but by many units in ways that cannot always be predetermined.

The growing salience of 'wicked problems' (Rittel and Webber, 1973: 160) has highlighted the problem of fragmentation. Wicked problems are deeply intractable issues which are imperfectly understood and to which solutions are unclear. They include:

- the environment and the aspiration to sustainable development;
- the problems of crime and the aspiration to community safety;

- the problems of social exclusion and the aspiration to meaningful lives.

These are not tamed problems to which response is clear and which can be given to units with a defined task. Such issues are inherent in the public domain where public problems are identified and faced. Fragmentation of governance reduces the capacity to identify and respond to such problems.

A Third Way?

Both *Reinventing Government* and *Modernising Government* assert a Third Way but, with their use of the private sector model, in practice reflect many of the assumptions of 'new public management' thinking. Osborne and Gaebler present their views as a 'third choice', arguing that although the debates have been about 'how much government', they should be about 'what kind of government' (1992: 23). Their rhetoric is, however, very different from advocates of the 'new public management' outlook of the Right: 'We believe deeply in government'; 'We believe that civilised society cannot function effectively without effective government' (ibid. xviii). But their response is to turn bureaucratic institutions into entrepreneurial institutions (ibid. 23). They recommend institutions that

- steer more than they row;
- empower communities rather than simply deliver services;
- encourage competition rather than monopoly;
- are driven by their mission not their rules;
- fund outcomes rather than inputs;
- meet the needs of the customer, not the bureaucracy;
- concentrate on earning not just spending;
- invest in prevention rather than cure;
- decentralize authority;
- solve problems by leveraging the marketplace, rather than simply creating public programmes

The 'third choice' contains elements that played little part in 'new public management' thinking. Empowering communities, funding outcomes and investing in prevention express confidence in government. Yet there is a stress on market forces. Implicitly if not always explicitly, the private sector model remains the basis for public management, as the phrase 'entrepreneurial government' suggests. It has been argued that 'the political theory of reinvention' – since public management expresses political theory – 'founded on a faith in individual self-interest as the engine that drives social good, in fact acts to deny the ideal of citizenship' (De Leon and Denhardt, 2000: 94).

The tension between government and the private sector model is also found in the American National Performance Review. Kettl, while recognizing real achievements from NPR, records tensions which meant that

> for most federal managers, the defining reality of the NPR soon became the work force reduction. Despite the bold phrases in the NPR report about empowerment, customer service, reduction of red tape, creating market dynamics, forming labour–management partnerships, and investing in greater productivity, the immediate threat of fewer employees was what grabbed their attention. (1994: 12)

He saw the fundamental problem as 'balancing the tensions created by contradictory ideas' (ibid.). The problem was in part due to the need for 'establishing and promoting a new definition of the public interest' (ibid. 33). Kettl quotes an interview with Don Hunn, the head of New Zealand's Public Service Commission on the development of the 'new public management' approach there: 'We spent so much time trying to "let the managers manage" that we forgot that government owned these institutions and that there is a set of common, core values' (ibid.).

The British *Modernising Government* programme reflects the same problems. It is structured around five commitments:

1. Policy-making: we will be forward-looking in developing policies to deliver results that matter, and not simply react to short-term pressure.
2. Responsive public services: we will deliver public services to meet the needs of citizens, not the convenience of service providers.
3. Quality public services: we will deliver efficient, high-quality public services and will not tolerate mediocrity.
4. Information-age government: we will use new technology to meet the needs of citizens and business, and not trail behind technological developments.
5. Public service: we will value public service, not denigrate it. (Cm 4310, 1999: 13)

These commitments suggest some of the purposes of the public domain but, implicitly rather than explicitly, 'new public management' practices are accepted. At the same time *Modernising Government* also contains the critique of the weaknesses of 'new public management'. Thus it emphasizes the need to deal with cross-cutting issues (ibid. 17–18), albeit without recognizing that the difficulties have been increased by the fragmentation caused by the impact of 'new public management' practices described earlier.

What is lacking is a consideration of the implications of the distinctive purposes, conditions and tasks of the public domain in present society. There is no emphasis on democratic renewal, on developing citizenship or on public accountability. The special requirements of a learning government are not dealt with adequately. In short, *Modernising Government* lacks a clear theoretical base and, as a consequence, provides an inadequate analysis of existing management practice in the public domain. While problems are identified in past practice, their causes and the extent to which they are due to the 'new public management' approach is not discussed.

The Task for a Progressive Movement

The task for any progressive movement in developing management in the public domain is first to recognize its importance. Management structures and processes are not neutral instruments, but are themselves part of the output. Thomas and Lynda Dalton have made this point:

> [While] some of our ways of appraising private sector performance find expression in public service contexts (for example, productivity, innovations and others), we may characterise an organisation's implementation of public policies as just or unjust, equitable or non-equitable, coercive or non-coercive, or representative on non-representative. (1988: 30)

An adequate approach to management in the public domain requires consideration of its distinctive purposes, conditions and tasks. Taking what has been suggested as those purposes, conditions and tasks, the remainder of this chapter suggests some of the ways in which a progressive approach to management in the public domain can be built.

Building citizenship for public learning

The public domain should enable public learning, and management should support that learning. Public learning is critical to the development of a learning society in the uncertainties of our times. A learning society requires public learning as the necessary condition for its growth and development. 'The public domain provides the setting for public learning in the arena of public discourse' (Ranson and Stewart, 1994: 168). Public learning requires the development of voices, but to be effective it requires discourse rather than a cacophony of voices, each with its own message. Discourse involves interaction in listening and learning. Management in the public domain should develop approaches to strengthen democratic practice to enable discourse. Management must be as much concerned with promoting citizenship as responding to customers.

Failure to appreciate this leads to a restricted concept of public management. A concept of management that has no place for citizens except as customers undermines the public domain, which requires not the passive citizen whose role is reduced to voting, or increasingly not voting, in elections. Instead, an active citizen, who is involved in the processes of government, is sought. It is often supposed that representative democracy is opposed to participatory democracy. The argument here is that representative democracy requires participatory democracy, for without it there cannot be a process of representation. What is required is interaction in discourse both between government and citizens and between citizens themselves, not least in the search for the public interest.

For management the task is to sustain and develop the basic process of the public domain of public discourse leading to collective choice based on public consent. Such a statement may come as a surprise because our ideas about management are informed by private sector models, so that key purposes of the public domain are ignored in management approaches. An approach to management in, for example, building and sustaining citizenship is required that is as rigorous as management approaches in the private sector.

Management would recognize the need for innovation in democratic practice based on interaction, discourse and reflection and would provide a critique of past democratic practice that too often assumed and reinforced the passive citizen. Thus, surveys and often focus groups see the citizen as a source of information which will then be fed into the organization. Many public meetings are domi-

nated by platform and presentation. What should be explored more
are, for example, citizens' juries and other deliberative forums, citizen
panels for the scrutiny of services, or consensus conferences, where
lay people develop their views on technical issues by interviewing
experts. The important lesson that has been learnt from such
approaches is that involvement breeds involvement. The habit of
citizenship is built by experience.

The search for the public interest and the search for balance

The search for the public interest is pursued in the public domain.
It will never be finalized because the public interest can always be
contested. Yet the search has its own importance, as individuals
have to look beyond their particular interests if they are to persuade others. Therefore, the search for the public interest is pursued
in discourse. However, motivated arguments have to be cast
in words that point beyond individual interest. In discourse, a
balance can be sought between conflicting objectives, demands and
interest.

Those who subscribe to the 'new public management' outlook
place their emphasis on setting objectives. The focus on setting
objectives can distort, because the problem of the balance between
them is neglected. It is not the setting of objectives that creates
problems in the public domain, but the balancing of them, for
objectives both complement and conflict with each other. For
example, in transport policy, there will be conflicting demands from
economic, social and environmental considerations; in economic
policy, employment objectives vie with inflation objectives; in social
services, the need for support is balanced with the need for control;
in the private sector, different organizational interests compete with
each other as in the internal conflict between production and marketing, but these will be determined by the interests of the firm,
expressed in overriding financial objectives.

In the public domain there are organizational interests, but the
objectives, demands and interests that have to be balanced lie in
society, not in the organization. There is no overriding objective
that can determine the 'right balance'. The public interest can never
be finally defined but has to be sought through a discourse of
reconciliation and balance.

Vickers has described policy-making as:

the setting of governing relations or norms rather than in the more usual terms as the settings of goals, objectives, or ends. The difference is not merely verbal; I regard it as fundamental. I believe that great confusion results from a common assumption that all course holding can be reduced to the pursuit of an endless succession of goals. (1995: 46)

The setting of norms expresses the search for balance and necessarily involves the art of judgement.

The necessity of judgement

The exercise of judgement has been neglected in management studies, but it cannot be neglected in the public domain. As Walsh puts it:

The public realm is one where values must be balanced one against the other. In order to do so we need to develop the power of judgement, which involves the ability to weigh values against each other in order to reach acceptable conclusions. Judgement is difficult, but the public realm deals with the sort of services that cannot be delivered without discretion at the point of implementation and delivery, and choice at the political level, both of which demand good judgement. (1995: 256)

Vickers highlighted the multi-valued choice:

Multiple criteria of success are inherent in the government of any political or social unit, however small. For the multiple needs and diverse standards of expectation of people living together in a place, interact with and limit each other in ways that cannot be ignored. . . . General organisations, . . . must decide not only what to do but what to want – more exactly, what to value most in the concrete situation of every decision. They must define and redefine the unacceptable, not in one dimension alone but in many. (1972: 134)

The multi–valued choice depends upon political judgement, which cannot be predetermined although it can be informed. Management processes often limit the range of information given to those called upon to make political judgement, because they are not based on an understanding of political processes. Political judgement involves balancing values and interests and that, in turn, requires understanding those values and interests. Political judgement requires that assumptions that are made and constraints that are asserted be tested. The plotting of interests, the testing of values, the challenge to assumptions and the querying of constraints can all aid political judgement. The development of management in the public domain has to encompass the requirement of political judgement.

Beiner has argued that political judgements 'are implicitly about the form of collective life that it is desirable for us to pursue within a given concept of possibilities' (1983: 138). He suggested that these judgements should be formed through discourse because they 'concern not merely what I want or the way of life I desire, but rather, entail inter-subjective deliberation about a common life (or how we should be together)' (ibid. 141). Public discourse is the condition of political judgement, and management should enable the development of discourse.

Ensuring equity

Equity is realized in the public domain, for it is only in the public domain that resources can be allocated by need. The meaning of equity is contested, but there are few who do not see the need for a degree of redistribution of resources, even if at one extreme it is only to provide a safety net below which people are not allowed to fall. Others argue for a more egalitarian society. Management in the public domain should support discourse on equity as well as its achievement. Both require an understanding of the impact of public action on different groups in society. Yet whereas data are collected on economy, efficiency and, more rarely, on effectiveness of services, data on equity are rarely collected.

Many services are rationed and distributed unevenly between different groups. Rationing may take place consciously according to defined criteria, through the exercise of professional judgement or by waiting times. It may, however, take place in ways unplanned by the organization. The means of access, the location of premises, the forms used and the language can all deter or attract. Management in the public domain requires an understanding of how services are being rationed in practice, as a means of ensuring that it is in accordance with public purposes set for equity.

Osborne and Goebler (1992) argue that 'what gets measured gets done', but what is not measured does not get done, and many of the most important aspects of public action are not easily measured. The pursuit of performance measures can be a distortion of public

effort, if it limits understanding to the measurable. Many performance measures are, in any event, not 'dials' that can simply be read
off as if they were an instruction for action, but instead resemble
'tin-openers' (Carter, 1991) which draw attention to issues that
require exploration before their significance can be understood. To
treat a tin-opener as a dial can distort action because its significance
has not been fully understood. In the public domain there can be
disagreement about what amounts to good performance. There are
different stakeholders with different aspirations. There are different
criteria to be applied, not least in consideration of equity. It is not
sufficient that public action is efficient or even effective. It must be
equitable.

Conclusion

Management in the public domain is an issue for any progressive
movement if its aims are to be translated into action. In building
the welfare state, bureaucratic professionalism was seen as a neutral
instrument that, in reality, built an enclosed process of government.
The emergence of 'new public management' was a response that
gave expression to market values. Third Way exponents in the
American and British governments have, through *Reinventing
Government* and *Modernising Government*, sought to correct some
of the weaknesses of 'new public management', while accepting
much else. They have failed to ground their approach to management in a consideration of the distinctive purposes, conditions and
tasks of the public domain in a period of rapid change. This chapter
has tried to do just that. It has led to a series of ideas about
approaches that move into unfamiliar territory for management,
such as the search for the public interest, for citizenship and for
public learning. It has seen discourse as a key instrument of management in the public domain and in so doing poses a critique of
sound-bite politics. The test of effective management in the public
domain must be whether it builds understanding, discourse and
reflection. Without these, the purposes of the public domain cannot
be achieved, nor can the requirements of a learning society be
realized.

References

Beiner, R. (1983) *Political Judgement* (London: Methuen).

Carter, N. (1991) 'Learning to measure performance: the use of indicators in organisations', *Public Administration*, 69: 85–101.

CM 4310 (1999) *Modernising Government* (London: HMSO).

Dalton, T. and Dalton, L. (1988) 'The Politics of Measuring Public Service Performance', in R. Kelly (ed.), *Promoting Productivity in the Public Service* (London: Macmillan).

De Leon, L. and Denhardt, R. (2000) 'The Political Theory of Reinvention', *Public Administration Review*, 60(2): 89–97.

Kettl, D. (1994) *Reinventing Government?* (Washington, DC: The Brookings Institution).

National Performance Review (1993) *From Red Tape to Results: Creating a Government that Works Better and Costs Less* (Washington, DC: Government Printing Office).

Osborne, D. and Gaebler, T. (1992) *Reinventing Government* (Reading, MA: Addison Wesley).

Ranson, S. and Stewart, J. (1994) *Management for the Public Domain* (London: Macmillan).

Rittel, H, and Webber, M. (1973) 'Dilemmas in a General Theory of Planning', *Policy Sciences*, 4(3): 155–69.

Stewart, J. and Walsh, K. (1990) 'Change in the Management of Public Services', *Public Administration*, 70.

Vickers, Sir G. (1972) *Freedom in a Rocking Boat* (Harmondsworth: Penguin).

Vickers, Sir G. (1995) *The Art of Judgement* (London: Sage Publications).

Walsh, K. (1995) *Public Services and Market Mechanisms* (London: Macmillan).

12

Corporate Power in the New Gilded Age

Charles Derber

Under President Clinton, the New Democrats in America rejected the New Deal welfare state that had defined the Democratic Party for fifty years in favour of a new progressive vision tailored to the new millennium. Initially, Clinton described himself as a communitarian, later as a follower of the Third Way and, ultimately, as a leader of a new movement for Progressive Governance. All were efforts to lead the centre-left Democratic Party coalition in US politics towards a viable majority for the new century. The Republican success in recapturing the White House in 2000, however much the electoral victory was contested, cast doubt over the strength of the Third Way as a political strategy.

However, irrespective of their electoral successes or failures, the New Democrats have not really advanced the cause of progressive politics significantly. Nor, indeed, have they come up with a truly 'new' approach to governance. A few historical reflections will show that forerunners of New Democrats emerged in a prior period resembling our own, that their core economic agenda is far from progressive and that they are not likely to achieve any profound improvement for either the Democratic Party or the health of democracy itself. While New Democrats have put forward incremental social policies that are welcome, they have failed to pioneer the new vision for the party and nation that could guide progressives in the global age. I offer here historical parallels that shed light on what the politics of the New Democrats means, discuss its fundamental flaws and limits, and suggest what alternatives those on the Democratic Left might entertain, especially in the face of the rapid growth of corporate power.

The first 'new' Democrat was not Bill Clinton but Grover Cleveland, also a two-term Democratic President who stands out as a lonely figure in a sea of Republican Presidents after the Civil War. Elected first in 1884, Cleveland was re-elected in 1892, exactly a century before Bill Clinton. While Cleveland's principles anticipated some of the clean government reforms of the Progressive Era, his core values and vision proved to be anything but progressive. Although Cleveland's re-election in 1892 created uncertainty among some business tycoons of the Gilded Age, the President quickly reassured corporate leaders that 'no harm shall come to any business interest as the result of administrative policy so long as I am President'. Cleveland lived up to his promises. In his most famous action, he sent federal troops to help crush strikers in the legendary Pullman strike of 1894. Said the President to those who pleaded on behalf of the workers: 'You might as well ask me to dissolve the government of the United States.'

Railroad baron Jay Gould telegraphed Cleveland to say that he felt 'that the vast business interests of the country will be entirely safe in your hands'. Cleveland repeatedly used the 1890 Sherman anti-trust act to outlaw labour strikes, which were at the time virtually the only way workers could hope to achieve a living wage. The President's anti-labour principles, also linked to conservative fiscal and monetary policies, were part of a broader embrace of business in an age of financial crisis, widespread labour and farmer unrest, and overwhelming corporate concentration and power. Cleveland's 'New Democratic' politics put both major political parties squarely in the camp of business. A Gilded Age business leader wrote: 'It matters not one iota what political party is in power or what president holds reins of office.' The robber barons had no sentimental attachment to either Democrats or Republicans because both had become parties of business.

At Bill Clinton's second inaugural, in 1996, a protestor carried a sign saying: 'The best government business can buy.' This was a sad testimonial to the parallel between Bill Clinton and Grover Cleveland. While Clinton had campaigned against George Bush Senr. as a leader of a 'people's party', he would soon show that his administration would re-invent the business philosophy of the Cleveland Administration and repudiate the populism of the 1892 People's Party. Clinton ended the last vestiges of the New Deal that defined the Democratic Party as a countervailing power to big business.

It did not start this way. Clinton originally proposed an earned income tax credit programme that redistributed income to the poor, a modest public investment agenda to rebuild the social infrastructure and a major national health initiative, put together by his wife Hillary, that could have taken him in a genuinely progressive direction. But the bond markets sabotaged his public investment programme and the Clintons botched their healthcare initiative, leading to major Republican gains in the 1994 Congressional elections. Always a quick learner, Clinton shifted gear and unfolded his New Democratic agenda, which would embrace key economic issues and policy positions long advanced by the Republican Party.

Like Cleveland, Clinton explicitly redefined the Democratic Party as a party of business, free market and free trade. Working with Wall Street financier Robert Rubin, his first-term Secretary of the Treasury, as well as Chief of the Federal Bank Alan Greenspan, Clinton rejected public investment and Keynesian approaches to growth, shifting towards a policy of zero deficits, debt reduction and reduced government spending. While rejecting the radical deregulation of the Gingrich Republicans, he embraced a new era of Democratic-led fiscal conservatism and 'small government'. He championed an aggressive policy of free trade and globalization. While ending welfare for the poor, he ratcheted up government subsidies for business – dubbed 'corporate welfare' by critics. As mass mergers created corporate empires dwarfing anything that the robber barons imagined, Clinton took a narrowly economistic view of anti-trust which ignored the social and political implications of the new monopolies. Despite its high-profile anti-trust case against Microsoft, the Clinton Administration readily gave its seal of approval to more than 95 per cent of the huge corporate mergers – from Exxon/Mobil to Disney/ABC to Chase/Chemical and Citibank/ Travelers (Citigroup) – which would redefine the global economic landscape. At the same time, despite some campaign finance reform rhetoric, Clinton became the biggest corporate fundraiser in US Democratic history, and helped institutionalize the flooding of big business money into politics – a move that subverts democracy.

Clinton's rerun of Cleveland is part of a larger parallel between our times and the Gilded Age. The mass mergers, huge inequality between rich and poor, attack on labour and government, speculative financial trading, and building of corporate alliances into a networked capitalism of formidable power all mark our era as a second Gilded Age. The worship of the market and rise of the corporation as the dominant social institution are signatures of both periods. Countervailing power wanes, leading to the subordination of society as a whole – including government and both major US political parties – to business (see Derber, 2000: 23ff).

Gilded Age abuses by unchecked business gave rise to the Progressive Era. Theodore Roosevelt, or TR as he came to be known, founded the Progressive Party in 1912 after governing as a reformist Republican for almost two terms. He is remembered not only as a flamboyant imperialist and ardent conservationist, but as a 'trust buster'. Most historians have tended to see Progressivism and TR as part of a middle-class reform movement that sought to end the blatant corruption of Gilded Age government and to renew democracy by placing limits on rising corporate power.

Historian Gabriel Kolko has argued that Progressivism actually served to institutionalize corporate capitalism rather than make it accountable to the people. Kolko (1963) argues that Progressives and TR created a regulatory state that underwrote and legitimated the new corporate system. It gave the appearance of accountability while actually providing business with the national planning and rationalization of the market necessary for corporations to thrive. Kolko's argument has merit. The most powerful business leaders, such as J. P. Morgan, aggressively promoted and benefited from Progressive state planning. TR worked closely with Morgan and Rockefeller's trusted partners, such as Nelson Aldrich. Nonetheless, many manufacturing leaders were far more hostile to TR and Progressivism than financial leaders such as Morgan and Rockefeller, and Kolko's argument should not cloud the fact that TR sought limits on corporate power and monopoly. He was hardly an enemy of corporations, but he built a federal Corporation Bureau that imposed a measure of corporate public accountability. TR was not a populist but he was willing to contemplate a level of national corporate regulation that would today be seen as socialist (see Sklar, 1991).

This helps to distinguish Clinton and the New Democrats from Progressivism. While Clinton refers to TR as one of his heroes, and embraced the label 'Progressive Governance', he never developed a remotely progressive political discourse about the corporation or the larger economy. Unlike TR, he did not view the question of systemic corporate power – and its threat to democracy – as a legitimate political issue of the day. Instead, he argued that the government's role is to enhance US business's capacity to compete in the global market, implicitly suggesting that the problem is not corporate power but corporate vulnerability.

While Clinton's repudiation of Franklin Roosevelt and his New Deal legacy is widely discussed, his differences with TR have been largely ignored. The *Washington Post*'s E. J. Dionne has argued, in fact, that Clinton's New Democrats resurrected TR's Progressivism, by reviving faith in limited but efficient government and by aiding both business and labour in a new form of economic nationalism.

But the differences are more compelling than the similarities. The problem of corporate power never inspired Clinton's political passions after a modestly populist first term as Arkansas governor led to his political career's one and only electoral defeat. This is not to say that he viewed corporations as entirely benevolent. He denounced the cigarette corporations, the gun companies and Hollywood for eroding public welfare. But nobody could call Clinton a trust-buster and, unlike the Progressives, he did not see corporate accountability as a viable Democratic issue. The years that TR spent contemplating the trusts and seeking new public regulation had no parallel in the Clinton years.

Clinton and the New Democrats argued for an entirely different tack to protect the public interest. Accepting the 'free market' as sacrosanct, they proposed incremental social policy designed to remedy market-generated inequities. Clinton and Gore argued that well-designed and targeted social programmes can be fruitfully linked to a neo-liberal economic orthodoxy for progressive ends. This integration of fiscal and monetary conservatism – and pro-business economic policy more generally – with liberal social policy can be viewed as the essence of Clinton/Gore-ism. There are merits to this approach. Clinton and Gore proposed and enacted a wide array of modest, targeted programmes for elderly people, mothers, poor children, low-income workers and others in need. They continued to pursue an activist government, even as they argued for paring it down and making it more efficient (on this point, see John Stewart's 'Modernizing Government', ch. 11 this volume). Their approach succeeded in bringing important benefits for vulnerable groups, and they may well have persuaded new groups that a 'reinvented' government has an indispensable if limited role to play in our lives.

Moreover, by embracing fiscal conservatism and free market economic policies, Clinton and Gore stole much of the Republican agenda, which helps to account for why conservatives seem to hate Clinton so passionately. He remained very popular – much more so than the Republican Congressional leadership – for most of his presidency, despite the scandals surrounding him and the relentless assault against him by right-wing conservatives. In a deeply conservative era, Clinton succeeded in turning the Democratic Party into one that could hold the White House for at least eight years. Yet the Administration's melding of pro-business economics and liberal social policy remains deeply flawed, finally derailing the Democratic Party and the country from the vision that they need. By embracing the corporate agenda on matters of core economic philosophy and policy, Clinton has sterilized mainstream politics, robbing the country of the transforming debate that could have captured the public imagination. He has prevented the Democrats from doing what some Progressives tried: to arouse the public about the power of corporations and markets and harness the corporate system to the public interest. He repudiated the 1890s populist aim: to mobilize a popular movement that denounced the amoral foundation of corporate capitalism, show its incompatibility with democracy and advance notions of cooperativism, public ownership and egalitarianism.

The belief that social policy can correct or compensate for the harsh social impact of neo-liberal orthodoxy is deeply misguided. This is not only because the social policy of the New Democrats is so incremental and thus can touch only a small number of those injured by the market. Nor is it simply because the social policy itself is often punitive and regressive, as in the case of welfare reform which pulls the props out from under the poor without providing them with the means to work their way out of poverty. The flaw lies in the concept itself. Even a less incremental and consistently progressive social policy would constitute 'band-aid politics' within the New Democratic framework. Since the party has been unwilling to tackle structural market change, it tacitly signed into an economic model that by its nature can only spawn endless social problems – from chronic inequality and poverty to the erosion of democracy and community. The New Democrats are tunnel-visioned, making no challenge to unfettered global financial markets and hyper-mobile corporations driven by short-term profit imperatives. No social policy agenda that embraces such finance-dominated capitalism can do anything but patch up the agonizing stream of human problems that follow inexorably from the system itself. Nor can it address the central issue of our times: the corporate subversion of democracy.

That the New Democratic agenda is a politics that addresses symptoms rather than causes is hardly surprising. As in the Gilded Age, government and the larger public sphere are harnessed inexorably to wealth. Clintonism represents a willing adaptation by the Democratic Party to an age of giant business and market theology. Corporate exit power, along with the escalating grip of corporate money over elections, dictates that government will increasingly serve property rather than people.

Pragmatists argue that Clintonism was the best that could be expected. Only a new depression or other seismic decline in people's fortunes might have allowed the majority of Americans to be interested in systemic change. In the meantime, the New Democrats prevented right-wing conservatives from using even harsher means to abuse the poor at home and abroad. This is an understandable sentiment, particularly as mass media that shape public opinion concentrate under the ownership of a small number of global companies such as Disney, GE and AOL-Time Warner. These media close off avenues for the expression of what may be termed 'constitutional politics'.

But the historical accomplishments of the populists and the Progressives a century ago suggest that the New Democrats may have squandered opportunities. While the 1890s populist movement had many flaws, including jingoism, racism and oversimplified economic solutions, it succeeded in mobilizing millions of Americans against a new finance-dominated oligarchic capitalism and creating an alternative vision for the nation. The new Gilded Age, like the first, has politically explosive contradictions. It has broadened the gap between rich and poor, left millions of working Americans in or near poverty, and subverted the stability and community that cemented agrarian society in the nineteenth century and helped create an American middle class in the twentieth. Most importantly, it has supplanted democracy with corporate sovereignty (see Derber, 2000: chs 1–4).

In the Gilded Age, unregulated and oligarchic corporate capitalism was born from a locally based pre-corporate economy to exploit a newly created national market. Both the populist and Progressive movements emerged to help make the new finance-driven corporate system more responsive to the needs of the majority. Today, the birth of an unfettered global finance capitalism exploiting new worldwide markets calls out for a new populist and progressive politics to promote global democracy and protect the world's billions of vulnerable and disenfranchised new workers. Despite relative prosperity and the apparent appeal of the New Democrats' politics of accommodation and incrementalism, we live in a 'constitutional moment' that offers the possibility of a more visionary and system-altering politics. The world got a glimpse of these possibilities in the Seattle protests of 1999: an unprecedented global populist coalition rallied in Seattle against the new 'corporate globalism' being crafted by the World Trade Organization (WTO). The protestors saw the WTO meetings as a constitutional convention for the new world economy, and recognized that the drafters of the new constitution represented mainly the rich within rich nations who are unaccountable to the planetary public. They understood the WTO as the forerunner of a new world government.

'Constitutional moments' are periods in history when the underlying rules of the social order are up for grabs. They reflect unusual eras where qualitative shifts in power and markets dislocate existing norms and subvert the routines of politics and everyday life. A century ago, in the Gilded Age, the rise of a nationally integrated corporate market necessitated dramatic shifts in the US constitutional order, with the Supreme Court using the Fourteenth Amendment to vest rights in corporations hitherto vested only in people. The restructuring of the state and legal order to serve corporations at the expense of the rights of workers and farmers catalysed the 'constitutional politics' of the populist movement. The populists were concerned with the underlying values and rules of the new corporate system and refused to accept the palliatives offered by either of the major political parties. They were among America's greatest historic practitioners of constitutional politics who should inspire us today (see Goodwyn, 1978).

Despite their many flaws, the nineteenth-century populists challenged the constitutional compatibility between the new corporate order and democracy. They saw their politics as a last-ditch effort to save the popular sovereignty Jefferson had struggled to enshrine in the Constitution and the Bill of Rights. Like Jefferson, they believed that vast concentrated wealth in monopoly trusts, unbridgeable gaps between rich and poor and the bending of the Constitution to ensure the existence and legal personhood of the corporate entity would destroy the republic. They called for constitutional and charter reforms which would democratize the entire corporate order, and they turned politics into a national conversation about corporate power and the values that the Constitution sought to protect (see Derber, 2000: ch. 9).

President Lincoln foresaw the 'constitutional moment' at hand and the urgent tasks of preserving democracy from the corporate assault. In 1864 he wrote:

> I see in the near future a crisis emerging that unnerves me and causes me to tremble for the future of my country. Corporations have been enthroned and an era of corruption in high places will follow, and the money power of the country will endeavor to prolong its reign by working upon the prejudices of the people until all wealth is aggregated in a few hands and the Republic is destroyed.

Seattle signalled the inevitable rise of a constitutional politics in our own Gilded Age, which again arises from the contradiction between corporate power and democracy. The outcome of this new struggle will shape the fundamental rules of the emerging global economy – and the individual nations within it – for the century to come. As in the first Gilded Age, a new populism is developing outside the two main political parties in the USA, midwifing itself through new political vehicles and coalitions. The agenda of this movement – which bursts periodically into public view at each successive meeting of the world's financial architects – parallels that of the nineteenth-century populists but is fundamentally internationalist. It seeks to draft a global constitutional order grounded in human rights rather than property, and to ensure that global and national governance become genuinely democratic.

The new constitutional politics is the authentic progressive politics of our times. It must – as its core agenda – craft a democratic governance system for the world economy. The Iron Triangle of the emerging global government – the WTO, the IMF and the World Bank – is deeply flawed. The three monoliths are constitutionally mandated to protect property and contract rights over social rights. They have no constitutional mandate to enforce global human rights and are driven by a neo-liberal economic orthodoxy that subverts national regulatory regimes and social development. This is a serious departure from the vision of the founders of the IMF at Bretton Woods in 1944, who sought a trade system that would enhance social development and a global governance system ultimately rooted in the UN and its Declaration of Human Rights.

The emerging global market ensures that the rise of global governance will become the central political revolution of our times. Global constitutional rules rooted in a deformed Bretton Woods system are already subverting the human rights foundation for global trade, while threatening to undermine labour and environmental standards around the world. This reflects the disenfranchisement of poor nations and the dominance of rich nations and corporations in the WTO and IMF. Change will require the eventual replacement of these institutions with more broadly representative and accountable governance. Ultimately, this will require putting limits on US global hegemony and building support for a new collective security system, probably based in a revitalized United Nations (see Wallach and Storza, 1999).

US-led corporate globalization jeopardizes the constitutional social protections that have been built by progressive movements within most Western countries over the last century. Inside the USA, constitutional politics will require numerous changes governing the role of money and corporations in politics – including reinterpretations of the First Amendment and the legal personhood of the corporation established first in 1886. It will also require fundamental change in corporate charters. The charter is the constitution of the corporation, and the challenge to current systems of corporate governance – that will involve shifts from stockholder to stakeholder forms of electoral representation within the corporation – is a central arena to today's progressive agenda (see Derber, 2999: esp. chs 13 and 14).

The unfolding relation between constitutional politics and Clinton/Gore-ism will shape the future of both the Democratic Party and national progressivism. In the 1890s, the populists formed a People's Party led by William Jennings Bryan, and by 1896 the populists had mobilized enough strength to get Bryan nominated as the Democratic Party candidate. Bryan's absorption within the Democratic Party before populism had fully crystallized its message – as well as his crushing defeat by William McKinley – spelled the end of the populist movement. Nader's Green Party in the USA will face similar dilemmas in relating to Democratic Party politics. As in the 1890s, the grip of the New Democratic agenda ensures that the Democratic Party is not currently an inviting venue for constitutional politics. But the building of a new 'People's Party' or grass-roots movement outside the Democratic Party could change this equation over the long term, either by creating a strong third political force outside the party or gaining enough public support to capture control of the party itself.

The novelty of the current situation is the connection between the political struggle over the soul of progressivism within the USA and similar struggles in other parts of the world. Clintonism finds its counterpart in most European nations, in British Blairism and German Schröderism most notably. Labour and social democratic parties of Western Europe have increasingly embraced the neo-liberal thinking and social policy incrementalism at the heart of the New Democratic agenda. And in Europe, as in the USA, grass-roots movements are rising to challenge this corporate turn and raise the systemic issues of our 'constitutional moment'. The prospect of close relations between the new movements not only in the USA and Europe but in the global South as well, where the new political economy wreaks its most devastating effects, will impact on what have formerly been largely insular national political struggles in unpredictable ways. This is likely to be a century-long struggle, but grass-roots struggles and new parties and coalitions that are surfacing in the post-Seattle era offer hope that we will see movement towards an authentically democratic politics. The hope is that this movement will consolidate power early in the new century and that today's constitutional politics will become the common sense of the twenty-first century.

References

Derber, C. (2000) *Corporation Nation* (New York: St Martin's Press).
Kolko, G. (1963) *The Triumph of Conservatism* (New York: Free Press).
Sklar, M. (1991) *The Corporate Reconstruction of American Capitalism, 1890–1916* (Cambridge: Cambridge University Press).
Goodwyn, L. (1978) *The Populist Moment* (New York: Oxford University Press).
Wallach, L. and Storza, M. (1999) *Whose Trade Organization?* (Washington, DC: Public Citizen).

13

The Need for More Democracy

Benjamin R. Barber

For all its undeniable prosperity, in part precisely because of its undeniable prosperity, there are many things amiss in America today. For each thing that is right, something has gone wrong. For all the prosperity, there is far too much inequality; for all the practised tolerance, there is too much incivility; for all the push to the centre, there is too much recrimination, too much polarization; for all the productivity, there is too much unemployment, too much meanness, too much commercialism; for all the rollback of bureaucracy and welfare-statism, there is too much anti-government paranoia, too much distrust of democracy. In a word, for all the democracy, there is not enough democracy.

Yet the Left appears to have neither an obvious constituency nor a persuasive political programme to deal with these ills. The old coalition that created the New Deal and the Great Society represents an ever-tinier minority of voters. The old programmes embody living ideas but dead policy options too wedded to vanished notions of nineteenth-century capitalism. Are there new 'first principles' that can make a difference? Or will old first principles do? Although we progressives often make sport of our historical legacy, America's most promising progressive principles have in fact always been its first principles; for America's first principles (if not its practices) have always been fundamentally progressive. Foremost among those principles is Jefferson's bold claim that the remedy for all the defects of democracy is simply more democracy.

More Democracy

'More democracy!' has from the outset been the American battle cry – the cry of colonialists against the British, of tenants against landowners, of farmers against bankers, of disfranchised women against men, of slaves against slaveowners and of workers against those who would expropriate their labour. Radical proponents of democracy have historically made war not on American ideals but on hypocrisy – the distance that power elites have put between those ideals and the nation's actual practices. Where Europeans have seen in politics the rationalization of class hegemony and called for a revolution against the political, Americans have seen in politics the means of their emancipation and have used political means to forge revolutions of inclusion. Revolution has taken the form of 'Let me in!' 'More democracy', and has been the American ticket to emancipation, inclusion, equality and social justice. For more democracy means institutions and attitudes that are more democratic, which itself means a more democratic democracy and thus a better democracy.

In the years before the Civil War when the women at Seneca Falls sought a place in the American sun, they refused to assail the rights language that had empowered men. Instead, they held that language up to the test of its own entailments, asserting that the 'self-evident truths' of the Declaration made all men *and women* equal. William Lloyd Garrison proclaimed he would 'strenuously contend for the immediate enfranchisement of our slave population' precisely on the basis of those 'inalienable rights' vouchsafed by America's founding documents. To abolish slavery required – more democracy. Martin Luther King assailed the American nightmare of racism by embracing the American dream: more democracy.

What does such a broad formula mean today? More democracy, yes, but how? Where? The answer, as Walt Whitman would say, is 'everywhere!'

> Did you suppose [he queried in his *Democratic Vistas* (1994)] democracy was only for elections, for politics and for a party name? I say democracy is only of use there that it may pass on and come to its flower and fruit in manners, in the highest form of interaction between men, and their beliefs – in religion, literature, colleges, and schools – democracy in all public and private life.

If democracy is, as John Dewey insisted, less a form of government than a way of life, then more democracy means specifically more democracy not only in the domain of government but in the domain of business and the domain of civil society. More democracy in each of these domains could engender three small revolutions and compel significant progress toward more equality, more justice and more security for all.

More Democracy in Politics

To make our politics more democratic is the easiest (and, because we refuse or are unable to do it, apparently the hardest) of the tasks we face. For all the influence of money, special interests and transnational markets, our politics remains formally and legally democratic – which is to say, generically democratic. One person, one vote. That half of the eligible electorate does not vote and that those who do not vote are those who would benefit most by more political democracy (the young, people of colour, the poor) is ironic and fateful. Ironic because non-voters compose a significant proportion of the missing Left constituency and, if they voted, their numbers would crucially alter the composition of our representative bodies. Fateful because by not voting they surrender the very power that could break the cycle of despair that paralyses them politically.

The conservative cynic says to the homeless person soliciting a handout, 'Get a job!'. The progressive says, 'Vote!'. We know from Richard Cloward and Frances Fox Piven (1979) that non-voting is about far more than apathy or complacency, that – disempowered economically and socially by a system that seems closed – the marginalized find it hard to feel that an occasional vote for mostly indistinguishable candidates will be very empowering. But they are in error: what they feel is truly false consciousness. For politics remains the sovereign domain, which means its rules are universally regulative. The law creates corporations and the marketplace and can contain and moderate them as legislators and their constituents please. Legislators are first chosen in primaries, and if they lack excellence or ideological variety, participation in the political process can change that.

However useful as an explanation for the failures of the Left, there is something disingenuous about a sociology that claims the referendum and the ballot box are somehow irrelevant to the challenges of social and economic injustice; that those very injustices destroy the viability of the processes by which they might be remedied. A vote *is* a vote, and the majority still carries the day. Our problem is winning the majority.

If we were to do no more than use the democratic means (federal, state, local) in front of our very noses, we could bring a great deal 'more democracy' to the political domain. The Christian Right figured this out a long time ago and made inroads first into local and then into national politics. The Rainbow Coalition registered a lot of people, but too few of them ever actually voted. Getting out *its* vote apparently remains the Left's greatest challenge.

Changing demographics compound the difficulties. As the natural constituents of the New Deal and the Great Society grow old and disappear from the voting rolls, as organized labour becomes a fraction of what it once was, as suburbanites become more numerous than city-dwellers and successful minority groups become more politically variegated, and as people without kids at home are increasingly asked to support children's programmes, progressives need to rethink how to advance an agenda of inclusion, social equality and justice.

The key to meeting each of these challenges is cultivating citizens – through programmes of civic education, voluntarism, community service and social responsibility that teach the young and old alike the arts of liberty and the competencies and responsibilities of self-government. The Corporation for National Service has been a vital tool of civic education, as have the dozens of campus-based programmes of community service. The fight for public schools and against vouchers is in part a struggle for civic education, a battle to preserve the civic role of schools as creators of citizenship and social responsibility.

More Democracy in the Economy

Among the reasons for the failures of political democracy is the changing nature of the deeply undemocratic commercial sector, which today controls not only the production and distribution of durable goods but the production and distribution of ideas, information, knowledge, pictures, news and entertainment, as well as the means by which they are transmitted. It is time to recognize that the true tutors of our children are not schoolteachers or university professors but film-makers, advertising executives and pop-culture purveyors. Disney does more than Duke, Spielberg outweighs Stanford, MTV trumps MIT.

As tutor to our commercialized civilization, consumerist culture has been teaching antipathy to government and a misplaced faith in privatization and markets. Rather than serving personal needs in the name of social goods, the market has turned to the manufacture of human needs at the expense of social goods in an economy of endless consumption. It replaces citizens with consumers, urging us to regard ourselves, even in civic clothes, as 'customers' of state bureaucracies and clients of government. But as consumers we get choice without power: individual selections from an agenda we do not control and with social consequences we cannot deal with.

Corporations have nurtured an ideology of privatization that has diminished the power of the democratic institutions by which public agendas are forged and common decisions taken. The marketplace must then be democratized: not deregulated but decentralized; not rendered safe and secure by corporate welfare but rendered competitive and self-sufficient; not made merely profitable but made more fair. This means corporations must now themselves become more democratic. Ideally, this entails workplace democratization – minimally via employee stock-ownership plans, cooperatives and stronger (and more internationalized) unions. Democracy is about obligations as well as rights, however. And as the government sector is diminished, corporations will be obliged to assume some of the responsibilities of citizens. Corporate responsibility can no longer be a discretionary policy of those occasional companies headed by civic-minded CEOs. It becomes the price of privatization, an obligation incurred by the private sector's complicity in curtailing democracy in the political domain. As governing institutions (prisons, schools, telecommunications) are privatized, private corporate institutions, willy-nilly, will become more public.

Rapacious capitalism that brutalizes workers and rides roughshod over the common goods of civil society in the long run befouls its own nest. Capitalism needs competition, democracy and civility, which means it needs to democratize its practices and civilize its executives – especially if it pursues a politics of privatization and government delegitimation.

But I am not so naive as to think that corporations will take to civic responsibility merely because it is a good thing, or because they have a long-term interest in doing so even where it unbalances quarterly profit sheets. Government can act here as a jawboning partner – as it did in the Apparel Industry Partnership against child labour in foreign plants; as a provider of inducements, through tax breaks for corporations that agree to responsible work practices (now they get tax breaks in return for nothing at all); and as an enforcer, by negotiating effective workplace standards, meaningful protection for labour organization and citizen-friendly policies for international institutions such as the WTO and the IMF that depend on US cooperation.

More Democracy in Civil Society

The disillusionment with politics makes political democratization difficult. The private character of the commercial sector makes economic democratization voluntary and thus improbable. The civic domain is, however, democratic by its very nature. It is local, composed of voluntary members committed to association and common goods, and it is by definition not for profit. It contains those 'free spaces' where we learn to be citizens. It is in the arena of civic education. In these spaces, democracy does not depend on the reputation of leaders, only on the competence and civic responsibility of citizens.

Strong democratic civil society shares with government a sense of publicity and a regard for the general good and the common weal, yet it also partakes in that liberty that is the special virtue of the private sector. It is a voluntary and thus private realm devoted to public goods – the realm of church, family, education, culture, recreation, art and voluntary association.

Without civil society, citizens are suspended between big bureaucratic governments they no longer trust and private markets they cannot depend on for moral and civic values. Where the public square once stood there are only shopping malls and theme parks. In the absence of a vibrant and pluralistic civil society, formal democratic institutions atrophy. What is central democratic government but civil society organized for common action? Government is civil society's common arm, just as civil society is government's restraining hand. Civil society calls for decentralization rather than privatization, sharing rather than abdicating common power. At the same time, it can dissipate the atmosphere of solitariness and greed that surrounds markets. Both government and the private sector can be humbled by the expansion of civil society, for it absorbs some of the public aspirations of government (its commitment to public work) without being coercive, and it maintains liberty without yielding to the anarchy of commercial markets. A reinvigorated civil society can rehabilitate democratic government, now in such low repute. Indeed, to a considerable degree, democratization of civil society is the so-called Third Way being touted by politicians like Tony Blair and Bill Clinton – a condition for democratization of both politics and commerce.

For this to happen, however, programmatic action must take place by citizens and by government. Civic space is at a premium in a commercial culture that privileges theme parks, malls and suburban developments. In response, the Walt Whitman Center, for example, has been working with architects, developers and urban planners to create a model of multi-use public space in consumption-dominated commercial malls. The centre has also designed a civic website that features a moderated civic chatroom for political deliberation that is both serious and entertaining. Why should the new technologies profit only the private sector and become the medium exclusively of commerce and entertainment? Why should civil society not have its own educational, cultural and political sites supported, if necessary, by an independent government-sponsored organization? Arts education is also an important way to nurture civil society, for the arts are its very soul and the source of that creative imagination indispensable to both culture and democracy.

More Democracy, More Revolution!

In old, well-entrenched democratic states, it is easy to forget that democracy is a radical principle, perhaps the most radical of all principles. It derives from the root claims that people have a right to govern themselves and that no one has the right to govern another. Together, these claims legitimize revolution: a people's right to seize the power necessary to govern themselves. Liberty is rarely a gift of the powerful. It must be wrested from them in democratic revolutions that are just because they are democratic and effective because they are revolutionary.

Jefferson summed up the inherently revolutionary spirit of democracy when he insisted that each generation repossess its first principles anew, observing that the tree of liberty had to be nurtured from time to time with the blood of patriots. You cannot inherit freedom. You may be 'born free' in the abstract, but to possess your birthright, you must fight for and earn it. Yet as prudent democrats from Hannah Arendt to Bruce Ackerman have noticed, the revolutionary democratic moment in America has had to contend with an equally potent establishmentarian moment averse to change and popular empowerment. Our real problem may be that we are immersed on the Left in one of America's cyclic establishmentarian moments. Feeling swamped by a placid popular culture and its obsession with sex and money, dazzled by a wildly productive if ethically indifferent economy and frightened by a globalization process that seems to remove choice not only from individuals but from democratic nations, we have lost touch with democracy's revolutionary American core. This moment of stasis and uncertainty is the moment to reclaim our radicalism – our *radice*, or root, principles – and bring the fervour of democratic rebels back to our cause: Jefferson writing the Declaration, John Brown at Harpers Ferry, America's disfranchised women at Seneca Falls, Martin Luther King at the Lincoln Memorial. These Americans did not wait for America to give them the liberty they claimed as a birthright. In the name of America, and with the collaboration of coalitions of citizens, they mobilized and took it.

At the end of the last century, a fearful Frenchman cried, '*Trop de zèle!*' (Too much zeal!). Our plea at the close of this century must be '*Plus de zèle!*' More zeal! More democracy! More ardour, more rebelliousness, more gumption in the struggle for more votes, more corporate responsibility and more civil society.

Just a few yesterdays ago, Marxist revolution failed because it refused to take democracy seriously, thinking it had first to establish revolutionary economic and social justice by hook or by crook. It would be a perverse irony if democracy were to fail a few tomorrows from now because it refused to take revolution seriously – refused to enlist America's great revolutionary ideals in the ongoing and neverending struggle for more democracy.

Note

The above is based on the article 'More Democracy! More Revolution' by Benjamin R. Barber, published in the 26 October 1998 issue of *The Nation*. Materials reprinted with permission. Portions of each week's *Nation* can be accessed at http://www.thenation.com

References

Fox Piven, F. and Cloward, R. (1979) *Poor People Movements* (New York: Vintage).

Whitman, W. (1994) *Leaves of Grass and Democratic Vistas* (London: Everyman).

PART IV

GLOBALIZATION AND NEW CHALLENGES

14

The Threat of Globalization to Democracy and the Environment

Mark S. Cladis

Danger and Hope

Recently, we have heard much about the promise of globalization. Improved economies, higher standards of living, greater cultural exchange, enhanced environmental awareness and practice, even world peace – these are some of the benefits, in the minds of many, that globalization will bring to the planet. There may be disagreement about the origin of globalization, whether it has emerged organically, as a complex phenomenon from diverse, impersonal social forces, or, in contrast, as a planned, managed development by particular individuals representing Western democracies and businesses. But most assume that globalization, like progress, is both inevitable and beneficial. There would seem to be little reason, then, to contest that which is propitious and which, in any case, cannot be arrested. Yet celebrated developments in the past have brought disappointment, and this should caution us to be especially circumspect when confronted with current global developments that promise to revolutionize our lives. In this chapter, then, I offer reasons why globalization should give us pause to think. In particular, I explore lines of thought that suggest that the current trend of globalization is jeopardizing democracy, local communities and the natural environment. I cannot provide a systematic treatment of globalization, addressing, for example, its purported benefits; I focus, rather, on its alarming characteristics.

By globalization, I refer to developments, roughly since the Bretton

Woods sessions in 1944, that have contributed to the global expansion of free market capitalism. This expansion has entailed the deregulation and privatization of economies, the removal of protective tariffs, foreign investment regulations and any other obstacles to the flow of goods and currency. North and South, East and West, governments are adopting unrestricted market policies to compete in global markets and attract foreign investment.

There is another and more recent feature of globalization. With the fall of the Soviet Union and the rise of digital technology, an unprecedented global integration has taken place among nations, markets, corporations and individuals. The information revolution – connecting the world inexpensively and instantly by way of computers, faxes and telephones – has surmounted the confines of the local, putting within reach the expanse of the international. Never before in history have humans been able to reach and be reached by so many, so far away.

The expansion, integration and free flow of information and capital that mark globalization have, in some cases, enhanced democracy, local communities and the protection of the natural environment. These cases, however, are not extensive or impressive. At this point, globalization should cause at least as much alarm as celebration. Instead, however, it has been eagerly greeted or promoted by European and North American liberal democracies. Some of the governments in these countries have claimed that they want to adapt progressive and social democratic ideas to the global age. Their aim is to forge a 'Third Way' that runs between and beyond laissez-faire liberalism and authoritarian socialism. However, in so far as this political agenda has embraced globalization, it has endorsed questionable aspects of the very historical models that it supposedly sought to avoid. It emulates laissez-faire liberalism in so far as it has granted unprecedented autonomy to transnational corporations, disassembling national, state and local regulations. These transnational corporations, in turn, resemble authoritarian socialism in terms of vast concentrations of power that are not publicly accountable – except to private shareholders. Earlier in US history, during eras of laissez-faire policy, corporations and individuals accrued much power via wealth. Yet such power pales when compared to the current concentrations of power of those transnational corporations whose financial holdings are greater than the GNP of many countries. Given this immense and unregulated concentration of power, I am suggesting that support of corporate globalization by governments, supposedly wedded to Third Way politics, in fact promotes troubling aspects of the old two-way politics – laissez-faire capitalism and authoritarian socialism. This, in turn, has posed serious threats to democracy, community and the natural environment.

Unregulated concentration of power subverts the sovereignty of citizens and the autonomy of local communities. Moreover, it drives a non-sustainable, extractive, polluting economic engine designed to maximize shareholder earnings. Increased profits require an ever-expanding global economy, and global development has required the misuse of renewable and non-renewable resources, the runaway extinction rate of animals and plants, the catastrophic loss of soil, fisheries and forests, and unparalleled pollution of the planet's land, water and air. The earth's self-renewing ecosystems, on which we and our children's children depend, are now being quickly traded in global markets by shareholders who, for the time being, live in areas relatively sheltered from the environmental havoc that their proxies accomplish. In the meantime, governments are pleased with the economic growth, shareholders with the increased earnings and corporations with expanded autonomy, wealth and power.

Any genuine attempt to renew progressive politics for the global age would promote public policies that sought to enhance democracy, community and the ecosystems that ultimately sustain human freedom, creativity and civic-mindedness. It would aim to foster within the nation-state a social order that properly arranges and regards the domains of local community, the wider civic community, government and markets – both local and global. Of special importance would be the support and maintenance of the local and civic community. The local community is where democracy and economies have a human face – in our daily activities, close to home. The civic community is where we come together, as a people, and deliberate about common hopes and projects, and about such developments as globalization. Without strong local communities, our wider civic existence risks becoming abstract and hollow; without a strong civic community, our local existence risks becoming parochial and escapist. Government can promote institutions that foster a democratic culture, protecting individuals and their communities, and encouraging a robust civic life. And, together, government and local communities can favour markets that fortify, rather than devastate, the relation among good work, strong community and human flourishing.

A Life as well as a Living

As a counterpoint to the so-called Third Way approach to politics, I would like to refer to *The Maple Sugar Book* by Helen and Scott Nearing (1950).[1] The final chapter of that book, not including the maple sugar recipes at the end, is titled, 'A Life as well as a Living'. It identifies seven principles, in three short pages, that contribute to a good 'life as well as a living'. I believe that some of today's most pressing problems spring from thinking that we can sever livelihood, that is, how we make a living, from life – the art of living well. The Nearings' principles provide me with an opportunity – a springboard of sorts – to offer my own reflections on the threat of globalization to democracy and the environment, and the promise of community and civic renewal.

The Nearings' first principle presents a stark alternative to the direction of globalization. '*First*,' they write, '*we wanted to control our own sources of livelihood*.' The implications of this are vast. First, however, I must qualify it, and state what this principle is not advocating. It is not advocating going it alone, in isolation, divorced from friends, neighbours, community, nation and nations. It has more to do with Emerson's notion of self-reliance – the capacity to forge a life from one's own convictions – than with self-sufficiency – living without the help of others. To control the sources of one's livelihood is, first of all, to know the sources. And to know the sources is to be intimate with those sources – usually a particular place or community close to home. Close to home, one is familiar with the land, the people, the community, the local enterprises. With knowledge of, and affection for, these local resources, one can belong to local economies that are subject to the will and convictions of those who are most affected by, and hence care about, their outcomes. Local economies responsive to local will and affections, I believe, is what the Nearings had in mind. Listen to their concluding statement on the first principle: 'We were looking for a source of livelihood that was beyond the reach of the privateers who were operating big business.'

'Big business' has become bigger since the publication of *The Maple Sugar Book* in 1950. Of the one hundred largest economies in the world, fifty-one are corporations. Transnational corporations hold 90 per cent of product and technology patents and control 70 per cent of world trade, and 1 per cent of the transnational corporations own half the total stock in direct foreign investment (Karliner,

1997: 5; Clarke, 1996: 298). These stateless corporations have little affection for local resources or communities except in so far as they can control and convert them into earnings for remote – and detached – shareholders. The Nearings' first purpose is about human freedom, the freedom of individuals and communities to fashion their lives and their social environment, and to care for their natural resources. Global corporations, in contrast, understand freedom as being free from the will of local – and even national – agents. And the cause for corporate freedom has powerful allies.

The Uruguay Round of the General Agreement on Tariffs and Trade (GATT), the World Trade Organization (WTO), the North American Free Trade Agreement (NAFTA) and even the International Monetary Fund (IMF) – these are the institutional allies that support, protect and extend the freedom of global corporations and financial institutions. Freedom, here, is understood as operating in a free market, a market that is not restrained by local or national interests. The WTO, the enforcer of GATT rules, and NAFTA are the most recent developments in this challenge to democratic rule. In the USA, for example, GATT and NAFTA regulations have the status of federal law and hence have precedence over state and local laws. Moreover, federal laws can be struck down by the WTO, that is, by a panel of unelected WTO trade experts. Specific initiatives are not allowed, such as sizeable subsidies for the development of alternative energy or sustainable agriculture, or safety and health regulations deemed to exceed international standards. These and other such initiatives can be ruled as obstructing the freedom of corporate activity. Nation-states, eager to capitalize on the economic rewards brought by transnational corporations operating in a free market, have traded national sovereignty – often, democratic sovereignty – for corporate favours. The choice facing nations often seems categorical: join the new global economy by agreeing to dismantle regulations designed to protect workers, consumers and the environment, or else flounder in isolation. Nations, then, have 'voluntarily' placed their citizens increasingly under the control of the global financial and corporate enterprises.

Control over one's source of livelihood stands as a radical alternative to having one's livelihood controlled by removed corporations and financial institutions. It demands the protection of the autonomy of citizens and of their right to shape the communities in which they live. It challenges what we might call economic liberalism – the protection of the autonomy of corporations and of their rights to the resources on which they live. It would hardly be unfair to say that it is in the nature of corporate interests to place commitment to profits over such social goods as community, social justice and the natural environment. Wendell Berry is justified to claim that 'the ideal of the modern corporation is to be (in terms of its own advantage) any-where and (in terms of local accountability) nowhere' (1995: 12).

This, then, brings us to the Nearings' second principle: they wanted to escape those social arrangements (cities, in this case) that impose *'upon its victims a life pattern based upon superficialities and upon an endless grind of routine that had as its chief purpose the fleecing of the poor and weak for the profit of the rich and powerful'*. Although I do not share the Nearings' implicit anti-urban sentiment, I am convinced that this second principle is less about escaping the city than it is about discovering an 'alternative to the wealth-power pattern'. Big business has immense power – political, social and economic – due to its capital and provision of employment. This power is wielded in a variety of ways – overt and covert pressure on government policy-makers and community leaders, financial gifts to candidates and elected officials, funding of think tanks that justify its strategic interests, and billions of dollars spent on media campaigns to capture the hearts, or numb the minds, of a nation's citizenry.

To reflect on such unaccountable power is not to demonize powerful transnational corporations. To reflect on the 'wealth–power pattern' is to call for governments to be more vigilant – not less – in the supervision of global corporate activity. It is also a call for citizens of all nations to be more circumspect about participation in the 'wealth–power pattern'. The moral dimension of this global pattern is not just a matter of increasing dependency on transnational corporations, as expressed in the first principle, but increasing social inequity, as expressed in the second principle. The creation of corporate wealth and the creation of global poverty are perversely connected. Ankie Hoogvelt, the noted political economist, recently reported that 'today there are over 1.2 billion people in the world living in absolute poverty and misery, and their number is grow-ing. . . . Furthermore, the gap between the richest and the poorest quintile of the world's population is twice as big today than it was 30 years ago' (1997: xi). The figures are truly astounding: 20 per cent of the world's population collects 82.7 per cent of the world's income, while the poorest 20 per cent receive a mere 1.4 percent of total income; the combined incomes of the top 20 per cent are nearly sixty times greater than the incomes of the bottom 20 per cent (Korten, 1996: 20). Moreover, there is consensus that the gap is growing. Many factors contribute to this ever-growing disparity between the rich and poor. Chief among them, however, is the global appropriation of social and natural resources by transnational corporations eager to satisfy the consumer demands that they themselves have inculcated. There is a close correlation between income and consumption gaps between the affluent and poor: 20 per cent of the world's population consumes 80 per cent of the world's resources – roughly the same as the income ratio.

As social inequity increases, public services are declining. Many have observed the connection between the growth of global corporations and the dismantling of social welfare. Hoogvelt has noted:

> The speed with which money can move across borders removes the need to anchor it firmly in (national) social relationships. Globalization makes national social solidarity (as expressed in transfer payments to the old, the sick, the unemployed and the lower income groups) *dysfunctional* from the point of view of the rational economic interests of those who participate in the global economy. (1997: 130)

In order to court and placate transnational corporations, governments are reverting to laissez-faire social models which shun programmes that achieve a transfer of wealth – unless, of course, the transfer is to transnationals in the form of corporate welfare, or paving roads for their trucks, providing water for their crops or paying the military to protect the flow of their freight and oil. In the United States and the United Kingdom, for example, even left-of-centre governments have cut social provisions, while at the same time they have expanded such corporate benefits as reduced taxes and eased regulations. The globalized economy, then, while augmenting the disparity between rich and poor, is contributing to government cutbacks in social provision. And these same global forces that have brought social impoverishment are also bringing environmental impoverishment. This brings us to the Nearings' third principle.

'*We wanted to get our feet on the earth and to get our hands into it – to make and keep that incomparably important contact with nature which balances life at the same time that it cleanses it, rejuvenates it, and keeps it sane.*' A pragmatic yet loving (non-exploitative) contact with nature can bring something like healing, or well-being, to one's life. If we become absent-minded and forget that food and warmth do not originate from the grocery and radiator, but from soil and sun, we risk becoming detached and indifferent to that which ultimately sustains human life. This danger is grave.

Consider the following state of affairs: calculated conservatively, the extinction rate of mammals is now a thousand times greater than during the last great age of extinction, the ice ages of the Pleistocene epoch (Ehrenfeld, 1993: 180); between 1900 and 1965, one half of the forests in developing countries was cleared for log export and for cattle grazing to supply the US hamburger industry, and such logging is not slowing down (Khor, 1996: 52); tropical forests are being destroyed at the rate of 168,000 square kilometres per year (Goodland, 1996: 214). Although there is disagreement on the exact numbers, few fail to concede that, due to contemporary economic and industrial practices, we are witnessing an unprecedented loss of wetlands, crop diversity, top soil and fisheries. Such catastrophic losses are matched by the inordinate pollution of the air, water and land from the massive use of fossil fuels, ozone depleting gases, herbicides, pesticides, industrial chemicals and heavy metals, among other toxicities. This is a short list of the material and tangible dangers that threaten those who, having forgotten about the basic sources of life, are cutting, polluting and despoiling the frail ecological systems that sustain human existence.

There is a clear correlation between accelerated environmental degradation and the increased power and wealth of transnational corporations. With little or no concern for the health of local areas but, rather, concerned only with maximizing profits, transnational corporations are usually indifferent to, and sometimes contemptuous of, environmental considerations.

The agricultural industrial food complex, for example, as conceived and run by global corporations, devours fossil fuels, exhausts soils and utilizes massive amounts of pesticides, herbicides, and fertilizers. The major corporate players – such as Monsanto, Cargill and Pepsico – control much of the world's food supply from beginning to end: from the genetic material in the seed to the chemicals dumped on the crops, to the transport of the final product. The stakes are high for these corporations. In the USA, for example, over 95 per cent of the food is produced by corporate agribusiness, with Philip Morris, for example, receiving 10 cents on every dollar spent on food. Cargill and Continental alone control 50 per cent of US grain exports (Lehman and Krebs, 1996: 122–3, 125). Transnational corporations have a vested interest in promoting chemical intensive, monocrop production, and also in discouraging local, sustainable agricultural practices. Monocrop production benefits, for instance, the twenty chemical companies that provide more than 90 per cent of the world's pesticides (Bruno, 1992: 9). And the production of synthetic chemicals, which are used to make pesticides, has increased from 1 million tons in 1930 to 63 million tons in 1970 to 500 million tons in 1990. We are now approaching a billion tons per year (Karliner, 1997: 15–16). Discouraging multicrop production in a single region, agribusiness promotes monocrop production that can be grown cheaply and then exported internationally. Environmentally, such international transportation incurs a heavy toll. In the USA, food travels on average 2,000 miles before being consumed. Transnational corporations consume vast amounts of fossil fuels to bring to dispersed consumers food and other products such as wood, minerals and manufactured goods. By 1991, 4 billion tons of freight were exported by ship alone (Goldsmith, 1996: 84). Not only does such international transportation squander our finite supply of fossil fuels – ancient, condensed, stored solar energy – it contributes greatly to deadly CO_2 emissions.

In sum, the entire food production and distribution system has become dependent on heavy usage of fossil fuels and agricultural chemicals – pesticides, herbicides and fertilizers – and such usage is devastating the planet's ecosystems. Few believe these practices are sustainable. Yet the global agri-food industrial complex is increasingly operating without government supervision, without citizen consent, without assurances to protect the environment. Indeed, the WTO has ruled illegal various environmental laws, maintaining that they create trade barriers and place shackles on the free market.

Thomas Friedman, in his bestselling book, *The Lexus and the Olive Tree: Understanding Globalization,* is convinced that 'we need to demonstrate to the herd [those caught up in economic globalization] that being green, being global, and being greedy can go hand in hand' (2000: 282–3). This optimistic position is expressed by Friedman in an anecdote about his sister. Each summer she had frequented a farmers' market to buy delicious South Jersey beefsteak tomatoes. Yet by the summer of 1998 she could no longer find the tomatoes: 'They were gone. Instead, the farmers' markets had these tomatoes that were all the exact same size, with a sort of pink color and waxy taste.' One of the farmers explained to her: 'This new variety could be stockpiled longer and shipped farther.' The sister was quite disappointed. Yet Thomas Friedman was hopeful:

> If there is still a market for them, and the seeds are still around, some farmer using the Internet, a Website – www.tomatoes. Jerseybeefsteaks.com – a Federal Express account and a Visa account will surely set up a virtual farmers' market where it will be possible to order original Jersey beefsteak tomatoes from your home PC, charge them on Visa and have them delivered by FedEx the next day – at least I hope so. (ibid. 432)

Friedman's belief – that green, global and greed can harmoniously coalesce – depends on much. In this modest case of the beefsteak tomatoes, for example, it depends on the availability of seeds (although we are losing crop diversity at an alarming rate); it depends on a wealthy middle and upper class that remembers what a good tomato tastes like and is willing to pay extra for it; and it depends on the abundance of cheap fossil fuels that would allow for the special delivery of a few tomatoes to a single household. Friedman's optimistic scenario of the beefsteak tomatoes also neglects much. It fails to address whether the beefsteak tomatoes were raised with chemicals that polluted the soil and water, or if their cultivation contributed to soil loss; it fails to address the CO_2 emissions from a fleet of FedEx trucks delivering the tomatoes; it fails to address the disconnection – except via Visa – between the farmer and the consumer; and it does not even consider the larger social problem of the affluent alone being in a position to purchase healthy, delicious produce.

Friedman's optimistic belief and example fail to address what may be the most pressing environmental and social problem that confronts us: how to ensure that economic markets are guided by practices that promote sound ecology and human dignity and fulfilment, rather than markets directing our social and ecological practices. Friedman's optimism would have us trust and work within the global economic system, rather than work to transform it. Hence, he writes approvingly: 'in the globalization system' where you are, and who you were, do not matter; 'what matters is *what* you *are*, and that depends on whether you make the choices for prosperity available in this system' (ibid. 246). In this view, your relation to a place or to a history and tradition are insignificant when compared to the potential prosperity made by working within the global system which ignores place and tradition. In contrast, the Nearings' first three principles – highlighting the importance of place, the connection to nature and the suspicion of power – would suggest that some of our deepest woes spring from a separation from the natural world and from social traditions and community. This separation increases as the global, free market converts lives and resources into spreadsheets and earnings.

The Challenge of Simplicity to Globalization

The Nearings' fourth principle is: '*We wanted to live simply, doing as much good as possible to our fellow humans and fellow beings, and at the same time doing them as little harm as possible.*' Citizens are not helpless in the face of powerful corporations. If we refuse to buy their products, watch their commercials, or become dependent on their wages, we circumvent 'the wealth-power pattern' – weakening it by dodging it. Escapism, however, is not the answer.

However much the Nearings were tempted 'to withdraw to the inaccessible mountains of Guatemala', they resisted and remained socially engaged. 'We play our part in setting up a good town, state, nation and world. We are not isolated in any but a very limited sense of that word.' They seemed to understand that alone, as solitaries, although they might avoid corruption and live protected from much pain, they could be neither truly happy nor moral. The Nearings, then, were not satisfied by being dedicated simply to doing minimal harm. They wanted more. They wanted a robust life that took duty to self to mean more than self-preservation, and duty to others to mean more than doing no harm. They wanted more because they knew that flourishing public and private lives take root not in isolated gardens, but in individuals and communities willing to embrace cooperation and risk.

Their fifth principle is this: '*We wanted to live solvently. That is, we did not want to beg or borrow or steal. . . . This meant an annual budget that would cover a simple but adequate livelihood.*' To live without debt is another radical act. Those societies providing most of the funding for transnational corporations are also borrowing the most. I am not referring here to the staggering third world debt owed to the first world – its admission ticket to the global economy. I am referring to members of affluent societies who borrow to participate in a relentless consumer culture, while simultaneously investing disposable income in the stock market. The economist Wynne Godley has noted that in the USA, for example:

[the economic] expansion has been driven to an unusual extent by falling personal savings and rising borrowing by the private sector. . . . The level of debt has risen in a spectacular way, reaching a record 165 percent of disposable income in the first quarter of 2000. Household debt . . . reached nearly 100 percent of personal disposable income – an all-time high. And corporate debt reached 74 percent of corporate GDP – another record. (2000: 1)

As consumers borrow to buy more and invest more, corporations themselves borrow to expand and eclipse, or take over, other firms.

Celebrating the benefits of advanced technology, Thomas Friedman tells of a farmer, Mr Wagner, who linked his tractor to a global positioning satellite (GPS) in order to better determine the water and fertilizer needs for his 4,200-acre farm. Friedman asserts that 'armed with more knowledge, Wagner can now delegate more things to his workers so he can concentrate on the key strategy, which is making his farm bigger so it will be the one that eats others and is not eaten itself' (2000: 91). Apparently, farmer Wagner is in agreement: 'If I can show my bankers these kinds of improvements [the GPS system], they will be more willing to lend me the money I need to grow.' More growth, more competition, more debt and hence the need for more growth – this is the vicious circle that maintains the big agri-food business. And this loop accompanies it: more chemicals, bigger equipment, more delegation, less contact with the earth, less care for the earth, still more chemicals.

Borrowing is sustaining the over-consumption of that 20 per cent of the world's population which is devouring 80 per cent of the world's resources. Economically, given the level of debt, it is uncertain whether such consumption can be sustained; environmentally, it is impossible. Yet the global economy is now working to turn segments of third world populations into debt-ridden consumers, thus escalating an already alarming pace of environmental degradation. These global trends are the logical procession of short-term, narrow economic rationality. Turn the global workforce into competitive, hard-working, materialistic consumers, turn frivolous wants into basic needs and anomic desires into increased debt. Populations that cannot be converted into consumers can still be exploited for their labour and natural resources.

The Nearings' sixth principle, deeply humane, perhaps presents the greatest challenge to the current global economy: '*We wanted, in one sense most important of all, to make a living in about half of our working time – say four or five hours a day – so that we would be freed from the livelihood problem and enabled to devote the other half of our time to study, teaching, writing, music, travel.*' By making do with less – by escaping the quagmire of consumer culture – the Nearings lived without debt, worked less and enjoyed more. Indeed, they possessed more. They possessed time: time for quiet contemplation, social engagement, education, art and travel. They adopted what they called the daily 4-4-4 formula: 'four hours for bread labor, four hours for one's vocation [i.e., reading and writing], and four hours for social intercourse'. I say this is perhaps the greatest challenge to economic globalization, because to work less entails buying and borrowing less. It is, in effect, to put a break on those global engines that would have us produce, consume and pollute more.

The Nearings' sixth principle, while not a substantive political response to the globalized economy, is a subversive one and, as I said, a humane one. Humane, because it advocates a way of life that grants time for good, satisfying work (as opposed to frantic work that produces shoddy results); time for community and civic partici- pation (as opposed to hectic schedules that require intense, individu- alized recreation, usually in front of a television or computer monitor); and time for reading and writing, arts and crafts. This principle does not suggest to me that we should all seek part-time employment – although that suggestion is worth exploring. Rather, it reaffirms what we probably already know but fail to live up to: time is more valuable than wealth; the life of the mind and of social engagement – with family, friends, community and civic projects – bring more satisfaction than the newest consumer product. And, happily, the Nearings' sixth principle contributes not only to human fulfilment, but to ecological health.

To some, I realize, these principles, especially this sixth one, may sound unrealistic or utopian. But how realistic is the prevailing tacit belief that current consumption and production – not to mention further expansion – is sustainable? We need alternatives. Although we cannot all head to Vermont and practise sugaring, listening to alternative patterns of life can help us imagine and take concrete steps in our own lives and spheres of being. Engagement in this creative process is open to us all, and is even incumbent on us. The Nearings have offered us their pattern of life, and this offering, as it turns out, was required by their seventh and final principle:

> *Last, we wanted to demonstrate a pattern that might be followed by those who felt with us that self-respect could properly be maintained only at arms' length from the centers of exploitation and only under conditions where the able-bodied individual was doing his share of the necessary social labor at the same time that he was satisfying his own creative urges in his chosen fields of the sciences, the arts, and social intercourse.*

Committed to Hope: Human Flourishing in the Local, Civic, Global and Natural World

Many of us long for a public life that is rich, diverse and meaningful. A satisfying public life includes such civic activities as involvement in elections as well as such informal activities as lunch at the local coffee shop. Public space includes not only the courthouse but also the public park; not only City Hall but also the neighbourhood bar or grocery.

A vibrant, meaningful public life, however, is becoming scarce. Increasingly, our public existence is marked not by civic or community activities, but by the impersonal transactions of the marketplace, the bureaucratic labyrinths of work and government offices, the programmed greetings from uninspired McDonald's employees and AT&T solicitors. There are fewer and fewer local establishments, groups and events in which community members can gather informally to share observations, work on common ventures and note the changes that have improved or disfigured their communities. As a shared history becomes forgotten – few care to hear it, fewer still can tell it – a shared future is neglected as well.

As the public life becomes cold, impersonal and bureaucratic, the private life becomes self-absorbed. As the public and private become increasingly differentiated, each becomes more extreme: the public becomes more impersonal, the private more cloistered. Between these two polarized, extreme modes of existence, there is little space for democratic reflection and participation. Without a robust civic life, we cannot hope to achieve a sensible economic and social existence that is both satisfying and ecologically sustainable. Simply calling for government regulation is not enough; a citizenry needs to be actively involved in the democratic practices that inform government. Hence the need for a renewed public, civic space in which diverse points of views can contribute to common projects. Such a civic space promises the best of liberalism (individual rights and autonomous reflection) and the best of communitarianism (commitment to shared goals and a common good). Unfettered economic globalization, in contrast, promises the worst of individualism (self-absorbed individuals committed to consumerism) and the worst of unity (a homogenized global culture that watches the same superficial television programming, reads the same facile news, and eats and drinks and wears the same corporate products). Such atomistic individualism and insipid homogeneity sabotage any prospect for a vibrant civic life.

The local community is probably the most promising place for democratic and civic renewal. When we are intimate with a place, we work with others to care for that place. I have in mind involvement in such local groups as business associations, guilds, community organizations, consumer cooperatives, and churches, synagogues and mosques. Of course, in order to care about a place – and to have knowledge of its history, its social fabric and its natural resources – we need to dwell there. We need to stay put.

Thomas Friedman asks us to imagine a 'visionary geo-architect' –
an omnipotent being who can design entire countries:

> Our geo-architect certainly would have designed a country with the
> most flexible labor market in the world – one that enables workers to
> move easily from one economic zone to another, and one that enables
> employers to hire and fire workers with relative ease. . . . In America,
> lose your job in Maine one day and you can get a new one in San
> Diego the next, if you're prepared to move. (2000: 372)

Yet to care about a local community, and the land that surrounds it,
is to be prepared not to move. Staying home requires staying power.
'It may just be that the most radical act we can commit is to stay
home. Otherwise, who will be there to chart the changes?' These
words, from Terry Tempest Williams (1994: 134), stand in stark
contrast to Friedman's global visionary. The visionary creates
employers who disrupt lives 'with relative ease' and workers who,
unattached to a community and its land, move at a moment's notice.
Who will remain, then, to 'chart the changes'? Who will care about
the decay of a community, or the degradation of its ecosystems?

In spite of Friedman's visionary and the increasingly mobile workforce in post-industrial countries, most people still have roots in a
particular place. These roots, I am suggesting, are the likely source
of democratic revival. As more and more people experience power-
lessness in the face of reigning transnational corporations and non-
responsive government, many will seek to regain freedom and
sovereignty.

We can imagine a people committed to a place, a people that
possesses knowledge of and affection for the young, the old, and the
vulnerable. We can imagine a people committed to a land, a people
that loves – and understands how to consult and manage – such local
natural resources as water and soil, plants and animals. From this
vision, other features would follow – for example, an emphasis on
local production and agriculture for local needs. Rooted in the
community, community-based enterprises – staffed by those who
know and care about the community and the land – could be more
responsive and accountable to local democratic reflection, and less
accountable to absentee shareholders. Such enterprises would have a
vested interest in, and desire for, contributing to community-building
and sound management of natural resources. Capital would not
principally flow in from, and out to, distant regions. Rather, valuing
local autonomy, most capital would be local, perhaps even in the

form of local currency, recycled many times throughout the community.

I am inviting us here to imagine alternatives to the corporate globalism of Friedman's visionary geo-architect. I have stressed the importance of the local, and one reason is because I believe this is the most likely place to recreate a public space – and culture – for democratic participation. From this arena of daily life, from what we are already familiar with and can learn to care about, could emerge a democracy with a human face. I have in mind a complex, often conflictual but ultimately satisfying democracy, not the inert, corporate projection of democracy displayed on television screens. Of course, attention to the local per se is not a solution. We cannot afford to neglect other spheres of being, such as the national. Democratic activities and projects take place in various overlapping spheres, from the neighbourhood to the nation. Moreover, the nation-state remains the only entity powerful enough to subject large corporations to the judgement of democratic processes. When democratic states relinquish control over corporate concentrations of unaccountable power, it is no longer clear in what sense they remain democracies, that is, nations whose social arrangements and natural resources are governed by the people, for the people.

A democratic governance and culture, which maintains commitment to the rights of the individual, whether rich or poor, will inevitably generate tension between public and private, between duty to the common good and the rights of the individual – including the right to acquire wealth. Yet such tension is a commendable hallmark of liberal, democratic societies. Political attempts to eliminate this tension – laissez-faire liberalism or authoritarian socialism – exact unacceptable heavy tolls. The goal should not be to eliminate the tension, but to cope with it, balancing the complex values and goods that are associated with both liberalism and communitarianism. Democratic liberalism would cease to be genuinely human if the rights of the individual were to become not a primary but the sole goal. Conversely, it would cease to be liberal if it put society first, in every case. For liberalism to continue as a promising social order, it must hazard the risks of commitment to such common goods as social justice and ecological sustainability. It must remain awkwardly wed to something like progressive communitarianism (Tam, 1998). My fear is that the promise of civic-minded liberalism is increasingly being traded for the bareness of laissez-faire liberalism – liberalism without a human face, liberalism without a soul.

In addition to strong democratic nation-states, global organizations need to be envisioned that can monitor the activities of transnational corporations. Trade is an ancient human institution, and even with a shift to local production for local needs, global trade would continue as a necessary and useful enterprise. However, we need international agencies, such as a strong United Nations, that serve and protect cultures and natural resources from exploitation by global corporations.

To envision alternatives to current global trends is not an exercise in quixotic thought. Quixotic is the view that there are no ecological limits to an extractive economy that fuels exorbitant production and anomic consumption. Fatalism, the belief that the worst aspects of globalization are inevitable, is not an especially reasonable position. Hope is more sensible, if only because it is more likely to bring the needful changes that are becoming increasingly conspicuous. More and more people are recognizing the social and ecological dangers that reside in unaccountable, global, corporate power. Those who care about a place will do much to protect it, and in the process they will experience the joy of working together with others, and their love of place and fellows will grow still more. My hope is that such affections are contagious.

Note

I am grateful to Jeff and Kathy Walker for bringing my attention to the Nearings' book. Moreover, I have learned more about ecological sustainability from Jeff and Kathy and their children than any book.
1   I do not individually cite the page of each principle, for they can easily be located on pp. 236–9 of Nearing and Nearing (1950). Each principle is developed in one paragraph, and each paragraph is numbered. Italics are mine.

References

Berry, W. (1995) 'Conserving Communities', in *Another Turn of the Crank* (Washington, DC: Counterpoint).
Bruno, K. (1992) *The Greenpeace Book on Greenwash* (Washington, DC: Greenpeace International).
Clarke, T. (1996) 'Mechanisms of Corporate Rule', in *The Case Against the Global Economy* (San Francisco: Sierra Club).
Ehrenfeld, D. (1993) *Beginning Again: People and Nature in the New Millennium* (Oxford: Oxford University Press).
Friedman, T. L. (2000) *The Lexus and the Olive Tree: Understanding Globalization* (New York: Anchor Books).

Godley, W. (2000) 'Drowning in Debt', *Levy Institute Policy Note*, 6 (also, *London Review of Books*, 6 July 2000).

Goldsmith, E. (1996) 'Global Trade and the Environment', in *The Case Against the Global Economy* (San Francisco: Sierra Club).

Goodland, R. (1996) 'Growth Has Reached its Limit', in *The Case Against the Global Economy* (San Francisco: Sierra Club).

Hoogvelt, A. (1997) *Globalization and the Postcolonial World* (Baltimore: Johns Hopkins Press).

Karliner, J. (1997) *The Corporate Planet* (San Francisco: Sierra Club).

Khor, M. (1996) 'Global Economy and the Third World', in *The Case Against the Global Economy* (San Francisco: Sierra Club).

Korten, D. C. (1996) 'The Failures of Bretton Woods', in *The Case Against the Global Economy* (San Francisco: Sierra Club).

Lehman, K. and Krebs, A. (1996) 'Control of the World's Food Supply', in *The Case Against the Global Economy* (San Francisco: Sierra Club).

Nearing, H. and Nearing, S. (1950) *The Maple Sugar Book* (New York: John Day Company).

Tam, H. (1998) *Communitarianism: A New Agenda for Politics and Citizenship* (Basingstoke: Macmillan).

Williams, T. T. (1994) *An Unspoken Hunger* (New York: Vintage Books).

15

Rhetoric and Reality of a New Politics for the Global Age

David Donnison

Christians can't [be socialist?]

Introduction

Communitarians, Christian Socialists and Third Way advocates all seek to map out a new politics for the global age. They all want to fashion a better future than those offered by oppressive bureaucracies or exploitative markets. The former gave people too little freedom and responsibility; the latter gave these things only to those who prospered in the marketplace. Gurus of the middle way, they might be called. Their doctrines deal not only with social priorities but also with forms of governance, for many of them recognize that the rapidly changing, knowledge-based economies we are creating, and the increasingly well-informed, global society we live in, call for new power structures.

With the global economy, human beings are gaining greater capacity to create – and destroy – their own communities, along with the values that govern their development and the environment in which they have to survive. Previous governments set the ship of state on a new course, if only to keep afloat on a boundless sea. Today, we need a new kind of ship, and – for better or worse – are creating a new kind of sea too. This has led people to argue that some decisions should be devolved to more local, collective groups, better equipped to set their own standards and develop their own projects; others should be taken at a larger, international scale by authorities more accountable than present supranational institutions are to the people of the nations they serve. Standing between these levels, state governments should be more concerned to establish priorities and standards and less burdened with day-by-day production of goods and services: 'steering not rowing' is the phrase often used. Stated so broadly, hopes of this kind are shared by most humane and intelligent people.

Those who have been first into print with ideas of this kind work mainly in the world of the library, the seminar, the conference hall, the television studio and the think tank: an intellectual, metropolitan, widely travelled world. That is not a bad place to start: it has enabled the best of them to draw on ideas from different disciplines and different countries. But to give these ideas a cutting edge – to get beyond rhetoric to realities – calls for closer involvement with the people who experience the harsher problems to be tackled; people who must gain a voice which cannot be disregarded in debates about their future. No one should write about social justice or the good society without trying to base the discussion firmly in the experience of people who are excluded from these things, and feeling comfortable with the thought that such people might be looking over their shoulders as they write. Nick Davies's work (1997) is a model for such writing.

Those who have tried to work in this way usually focus on the places where things have gone badly wrong – the neighbourhoods where there is widespread unemployment, poverty, crime and trouble of every sort. We may be more helpful to them if we look also at communities that seem to be doing pretty well – particularly those that have achieved this despite handicaps of various kinds. We can often learn more from success than from failure. These thoughts suggest a way of exploring the issues I want to discuss.

First, I will describe a small and remote community, chosen partly because it has been well researched in a recent study (Ringblom, 1998), and because I happen to know it and have been able to check my story with people who live there. This community is particularly interesting because many of its members would be described as living in poverty, as defined by the European Union: that is to say, they have incomes that are less than half their country's average for households of their size and type. Yet most people would not regard them – nor would they regard themselves – as being poor or excluded from the wider society. Thanks to links they have forged among themselves and with the wider world, this is in many ways a communitarian society. If we can explain how that has been achieved, we shall be better equipped to understand the needs of less fortunate places.

Next I shall outline what is happening in urban communities not far away. Many of their people would describe themselves as poor, and would be so described by others elsewhere, and there are many outward signs showing that they would be right. These are the kinds of neighbourhood on which the UK government's Social Exclusion Unit and its Scottish counterpart are focusing their efforts, following the trail blazed by many similar programmes since the 1970s. I hope to explain why these programmes have generally been less successful than governments hoped they would be.

Finally, I will very briefly bring together the lessons to be learnt from both kinds of community to show the main things that must be done in the face of rapid globalization if we are to achieve social justice and create a good society. The prescription is a daunting one, but nothing less will do.

A Small Island and its People

Let us begin with a small community of about sixty people, including a dozen children, living on a Scottish island small enough to walk round in half an hour. About sixty more go there fairly often to their holiday cottages. Most are Scots, but a large minority is English. There is no division between 'locals' and 'incomers', for all are incomers. The island is approached from another that is larger and more accessible. Its inhabitants live in a cluster of little white houses that crouch together against the wind around irregular green squares. Most of them are owner-occupied, a few rented. There are no cars and no roads; just pathways along which people wheel their shopping home in barrows. Outside the village there is a rather desolate landscape of brambles, rock and broken slate, interspersed with deep lagoons – flooded quarries from which slate was for three centuries hacked out, cut to shape and exported to put on roofs all over the world.

Quarrying stopped when the slate ran out, ninety years ago, and then two world wars took many people off the island, never to return. By the early 1960s there were only a few elderly residents left amidst the ruins of a decaying village. But in recent years there has been a revival. This growth comes about in four mutually supportive ways – from tourists, week-enders, footloose workers and pensioners. Many arrive first as tourists, to walk round, admire the views, the birds and wild flowers, and perhaps to take a swim in one of the quarries; they might visit the excellent little museum, a small shop selling ice-creams and postcards, and the attractive restaurant and pub. They may stay in bed-and-breakfast for a night or two or rent a self-catering cottage. Others arrive in yachts – there is a small, fair-weather anchorage in the sound – in canoes and as scuba divers.

A few of these visitors return to buy a holiday house. Others decide to settle full time. Some of these commute to neighbouring towns – the nearest is fifteen miles away – and others have jobs that may take them anywhere in the world – a consultant engineer, a technician working on oil rigs, for example. Some work at home: there is a writer of popular novels as well as various kinds of electronic cottager. A number of residents and week-enders are retired people or people with disabilities, which make full-time work difficult. This is a world in which transitions from work to retirement or from sickness to recovery do not have to be sharply defined. To these four sources of growth should be added a fifth which responds to them – the work of builders, mainly done by one small firm based on the island, who repair and rebuild existing houses and add a few new ones.

Wages are low by the standards of the city: the economy of a remote island cannot support high pay. Those who choose to live and work there are not primarily interested in money. But everyone who wants to work is employed, at least for most of the year. Some depend on pensions or disability benefits, but no one depends for long periods on income support or job-seeker's allowance. So what is special about this community? This is not the garden of Eden. Here, as elsewhere, people quarrel, become mentally ill, break up painfully from their partners, depend too heavily on alcohol – and struggle out of that dependency. But it is a good place to be if things go wrong for you. When a man, recently arrived, became severely depressed and was unable to work or even to cope with his own housework, neighbours noticed and helped him several times to clean up his home. They then got him to the doctor on the neighbouring island and took him to the mental ward of a hospital thirty miles off, where they visited him regularly. They arranged a rota to feed his dog and take it for walks, and did their best to support him when he came home. When a visiting tourist fell and damaged her leg badly, locals telephoned the doctor and helped to care for her until a helicopter arrived to lift her away to hospital.

The small primary school in the village across the sound does well. It is one of a group that feeds pupils into the high school in the nearest town. Four of the last six 'duxes' in this high school (an annual award for top academic performer) came from the island school. The head invites parents to come in and help: a one-time merchant seaman taught the children to tie knots, a talented guitarist got some of them started on this instrument. When a parent took his son, who has Down's syndrome, to start at the school, he explained that although the boy cannot speak he uses within his family one of the sign languages of deaf people. 'That's fine', said the head; 'I and my staff will learn his signs and so will all the children in this school. Then we can all talk to him.' And they did.

Politically, the islanders are a formidable bunch. With the support of local planners, a developer acquired from the owner of the island, who lives in London, a lease of one third of it, which he proposed to fence off and use for fish-farming. The islanders mobilized through their residents' association and the local community council, arguing that the whole island had long been a conservation area within a regional scenic area where such intrusions should be prohibited. The fish farm, they said, would introduce dangerous wheeled traffic, damage pathways, pollute land and sea and destroy the shellfish on which local fishermen depend. Fish-farming, they demonstrated, creates few local jobs and would set back the sustainable but fragile growth of the island's economy. Together, they raised funds to pay for the help of a first-rate planning lawyer and fielded a dozen witnesses at a three-day public local inquiry, which conclusively rejected the proposal. Few of them had heard of Local Agenda 21, but their campaign was a classic assertion of its principles.

The ruined houses, which had been sold at modest prices to people who turned them into attractive homes, are now running out. Sooner or later, the islanders recognized, someone would find another way of making money out of their island, and fish-farming is by no means the worst thing that could happen there. So they had better set about shaping their own future in collaboration with the island's owner, or even buy him out. To this end, they set up a charitable trust which organizes musical and drama events and which aims to rebuild the leaky hall, provide new sewage and refuse disposal plant and rebuild the decaying harbour. Many of the celebrations which go on throughout the year are designed to raise money for these projects. To develop this strategy they have gained much useful advice from a community worker, expert in helping remote communities, who goes to the island from time to time.

Much more could be said, but this account is sufficient to show the character of a small society. Many other small communities in the Scottish highlands and islands could tell similar stories. Amitai Etzioni would recognize them as models for communitarians, show-ing the 'thick' or 'substantial' 'core values', the processes of 'reconcil-iation' and many other features of his moral democracy (1997: ch. 7). Michael Young and Chelly Halsey (1995) would admire their confident, thriving, well-behaved children, who are, in a sense, brought up by the whole village – running free but constantly under the friendly eye of people who know them. Daniel A. Bell (1993) would find here all three of his 'constitutive communities' – of 'place', 'memory' and 'psychology'. Anthony Giddens (1994) would note that these are 'dialogic', 'reflexive' and 'energetic' people, plugged in to the global society through their websites and in many other ways, and determined to shape their own future – creating for themselves a tradition, 'but not in the traditional way'. The language of these scholars makes it clear that when it comes to practical politics they are unlikely to lead anything more formidable than a seminar. But seminars, too, may ultimately be influential.

What are the distinctive features of this island community, which, despite the disruptive forces of globalization, have made this achievement possible? One that should not be forgotten is the high quality of most public services. People would not have settled there if there had not been a reasonably reliable supply of water and electricity piped across the sound. (And when a force ten gale blew away the water supply recently, a helicopter arrived as soon as the wind dropped with tanks of water and canisters to be carried around to every household.) People are more likely to give voluntary help to a good school than a bad one, and more likely to help a mentally sick neighbour if they know there are good doctors and a hospital ready to take over if they get out of their depth. Community action does not replace public services; it complements and depends on them.

The size of the community is important too. It is small enough to mobilize in unity when that is most needed – as when resisting the fish farm – but large and varied enough to give people a choice of social circles – games of bridge for some, darts or music for others. People fall out from time to time, but cannot altogether avoid each other, and that helps them to learn how to manage conflict constructively. It is difficult for two people to nurse their wrath convincingly as they both try to keep their feet, in driving rain and spray, in a bouncing little ferry boat, or refill each other's glasses at a Christmas party in a crowded cottage room.

Housing is much the same for everyone, and all those who are not retired or sick work for most of the year and are respected for what they do. There is work on the island, low paid though it may be, for nearly everyone who wants it. Strong young men find opportunities in the island's labour-intensive building and repairs industries, which would be harder to find in a city. Those with professional skills earn more per hour but may only work intermittently, so their incomes are not much greater. The elite, if there is one, consists of those who can repair your plumbing, your roof, your computer or your outboard motor.

The range of activities and the social mix of those involved in them sustain each other. If the islanders did not include enough young men, accustomed to heavy manual labour, they would no longer be able to import their own coal and logs each year. The skills required for acting, making music, dancing and playing football are not confined to any one class, age group or gender. The presence of several extended families on the island is also a community-building influence. If children run freely in and out of the pub, adults are more likely to stay sober. If everyone knows and respects the children's parents, they are most unlikely to be abused or harassed. But if all the housing on the island is eventually tarted up and sold to middle-class or retired people, leaving no room for many of those now living there, these community-building strengths will be lost.

Important, too, is the fact that people have chosen to live there and could go elsewhere if they preferred to do so. Indeed, each year some do go. Those who stay find they are treated with respect and have opportunities for trying out new identities and new ways of making a living. In how many pubs could a young man walk in, clad in a dress, knowing that he would be as welcome as ever to all in the bar?

To sum up: this is a small, socially mixed and pretty equal society with good public services, where people have choices, work, self-respect, hope, friends and a well-founded conviction that, collectively, they can exert some influence on external forces that may threaten their community.

Social Exclusion in the City

I turn next to urban Scotland. The main fact underlying every social problem in the towns is the disaster that has occurred in their traditional industries. Investment and employment opportunites have been shifted to other parts of the world because they offer better financial returns for the businesses concerned. It is an experience that is replicated on a worldwide basis. In the former coal fields, in Dundee, on Clydeside and, above all, in Glasgow, there has been a devastating loss of jobs in manufacturing and mining. Greater Glasgow lost two-thirds of its manufacturing jobs between 1971 and 1997.[1] These have never been replaced by jobs of the kind that can readily be done by those thrown out of work. Of the most deprived tenth of the postcode districts in urban Scotland, 58 per cent – nearly three-fifths – are in this one city, which contains only 13 per cent of Scotland's population (Gibb et al., 1998). This has devastating social effects. In Glasgow, 37 per cent of households with dependent children have no one in paid work and 27 per cent include only one adult. Many other signs of stress follow: high rates of family break-up and lone parenthood, poor educational attainment, poor health, rising homelessness among young people, high rates of crime and drug addiction. Glasgow is still Scotland's biggest city. Its decline, and the problems that flow from it, affect the whole country. Scotland's falling population can be accounted for entirely by the loss of people from Clydeside. The Barnett formula, which is used to allocate central government funds to different parts of the UK, means that Scotland will get a steadily declining share of these funds as its population falls. Glasgow's plight is one of the most extreme examples of similar conditions which are to be found in the core cities of many of Britain's old industrial conurbations.

What has gone wrong? The people of Clydeside and other urban areas that are having a hard time are not idle or incompetent. Unemployed people in Glasgow are, on average, better qualified than unemployed people elsewhere in Britain, and they try as hard to find jobs. The city's most poverty-stricken housing estates are full of tenants' associations, community-based housing associations, credit unions, food co-ops, voluntary play groups and youth clubs, church groups and other signs of active citizenship.

To understand the factors at work, we have to unravel a story. Due to worldwide economic factors, which I do not have space to discuss here, many industrial sectors have ceased to be viable. The decline in job opportunities for men was exacerbated by the growth of opportunities for women who have moved into the labour market in growing numbers over the past generation. They have not driven men out of work, because they have generally taken the growing number of jobs in clerical and service industries – more traditional female employment. But they have blocked opportunities for men who might have transferred into these industries.[2]

The main response of workers to this disaster has been to move to other places. Throughout the 1980s Greater Glasgow's population was falling at a rate of more than ten thousand a year – faster in earlier years, more slowly since then. The people who leave the stricken cities tend to be the younger, better-qualified, two-parent families. Such selective emigration leaves behind it increasingly impoverished communities, inhabited by an ageing population, by the less skilled and lone parents. As populations of stricken areas decline, housing space is freed and it becomes easier for those left behind to move. Families that used to wait twenty years for a transfer to a better council house find they can quickly move out of the least popular places. They are replaced by those who have nowhere else to go. Some are squatters and others only use their addresses as 'giro drops'. Some blocks of housing become 'transit camps', where people no longer know their neighbours or care about them. Social capital – central to which are hope for the future and relationships of trust and mutual respect – unravels.

Thus urban neighbourhoods are sifted and stratified: some becoming increasingly affluent, while others become increasingly poor. Heavy selling of public housing under right-to-buy provisions hastens that process. There are council estates where more than half the households with children have only one adult in them, and other neighbourhoods where nearly every household has at least one car. Business withers in the poorer areas; banks, building societies and the better shops move out. The local secondary school – which may have been one of the few remaining centres of order and courtesy outside people's homes – also closes, and youngsters have to take long bus journeys to schools in distant neighbourhoods where they are regarded with hostility by local children. Truancy increases. Attainment suffers. Concentrations of deprivation grow larger.

In places where the legitimate economy collapses, other economies develop. Some of these activities – unpaid voluntary work of various kinds – would be welcome in richer neighbourhoods, but they may be criminalized in poorer places by social security regulations which require people living on job seeker's allowance to be available for full-time work. Other activities that flourish would be criminal anywhere: burglary, extortionate money-lending, drug-dealing, protection rackets and their operators' battles for territory. These criminalize young people and reinforce social polarization by hastening the outflow of those who are able to escape to safer streets.

Declining populations lead to reductions in municipal income from central grants and from local council tax-payers. The growing costs imposed on central government – particularly for social benefits – compel it, too, to search for ways of saving money. Cuts follow in housing expenditure, social benefits and many branches of local government. Cities trying to get their unemployed people into work find that the reductions they have to make in their own staff are among the main causes of unemployment. Further cuts in local spending have to be deducted from the services which local authorities are not compelled by law to provide, closing down preventive family and youth services, reducing support for teachers in hard-pressed schools and adding a further twist to the vicious spiral. Many of Scotland's poorest places have suffered further from the abolition of regional authorities and the loss of resources that used to be transferred to areas selected for priority treatment.

Meanwhile, legislation protecting workers has been dismantled and, thanks to the high unemployment of the 1980s and early 1990s, wages and working conditions at the bottom of the labour market have deteriorated. Twenty years ago it was exceedingly rare for anyone to get more money from social security benefits than they could earn from work. But the decline in wages and the growing insecurity of jobs at the bottom of the labour market, the increase in rents and the spread of means-tested benefits – housing benefit in particular – all combine to make this kind of poverty trap much more common today. They help to explain why a huge proportion of our middle-aged and older workers have opted out of the labour market into early retirement, sickness and disability. Inactivity rates, showing the proportion of people of working age who are neither employed nor unemployed, behave more and more like unemployment rates, suggesting that they mean much the same thing. Real unemployment rates in stricken places are clearly much higher than the numbers officially recorded as out of work (Webster, 2000c).

Thus poverty, originating from the loss of jobs, sets off side-effects which concentrate vulnerable families in places where it is hardest to survive. There, too often, the morale of public service workers decays: bins are not reliably emptied, letters take days to arrive, house repairs are neglected, the better teachers move out. The growing hardships experienced by families living in such conditions cause more of them to break up. Through the 1980s female lone parenthood became increasingly closely correlated with male unemployment: the maps of these signs of stress are now difficult to distinguish (ibid.). No one should preach sermons about 'family values' who does not also offer practical proposals for ensuring that families are able to support themselves decently.

All the plagues of Egypt follow the break-up of families: poorer health, poorer performance in schools, more rent arrears, more trouble between neighbours, more domestic violence, more teenage pregnancies, more homeless youngsters, more addiction, more crime, more suicides ... I am not suggesting that in a prosperous, equal society there would be no problems of this kind, but it is clear that all of them are strongly linked to unemployment and the growth of poverty, inequality and the breakdown of communities and families. We shall not make much progress in solving any of them unless we first achieve a decisive reversal of these destructive trends.

The UK has a higher proportion of its children in poverty than any other country in Europe, East or West. The best estimates suggest that while current policies may lift a million of them out of poverty by 2002, we shall still have one of the highest child poverty rates in the West (Piachand and Sutherland, 2000). Unemployment has been falling – but in Glasgow male inactivity rates are still rising. Low-paid workers with children should soon be getting significant increases in their incomes; childcare should be a bit easier to find and pay for. But for unemployed or disabled people who are unable to get a job, little has changed. Indeed, the government's policy of reducing benefit rights for unemployed people while increasing subsidies for low-paid working families is transferring millions of pounds from cities where unemployment remains high to more prosperous places where it has been falling.

In areas where unemployment often stands at less than 2 per cent, the government's assumption that the problem lies mainly on the supply side of the labour market – in lack of training, self-confidence and motivation – will often be true. But in Scotland's areas of heaviest unemployment, as in similar areas elsewhere in the UK, the problem lies on the demand side: jobs of the kind that unemployed people could get are still declining in numbers. We can of course get unemployed people into work if we try hard enough, but only by excluding others who will take their places in the dole queues. It may be argued that training schemes should lift unemployed people into more skilled work, but in Glasgow the next layer of less-skilled non-manual jobs is also declining. Growth is concentrated further up the ladder in professional, technical and managerial jobs which are unlikely to be open to those who have been out of work for a long time.

Conclusions

What should political thinkers and policy-makers learn from this comparison between two worlds? The UK, let us remember, is still one of the world's richest societies. Taken as a whole, Scotland's economy is doing well. Even on Clydeside we can find some of the richest local authorities in Britain – commuter suburbs whose council taxes make no contribution to the central city on which they all depend. The problem is essentially political, not economic.

Governments naturally want to show that they can quickly do something to help the poorest communities. They focus on homelessness, children excluded from school, drug addiction and so on. No harm in that. But trust, hope and purposeful ambition are the best preventers of addiction, school failure, teenage pregnancy and many other problems. We have to start by ensuring that everyone of working age and capacity has the opportunity to earn an honest living in a decent job. We have to rebuild communities which have a richer mixture of age groups, family types and social classes. That will be a slow job, for we cannot attract those who can choose where they live to neighbourhoods where there are no banks, no decent shops, no good schools and many hazards on the street; and it takes time to change those things.

Yet there is much that can be done. There are plenty of vacant industrial sites in our stricken cities – 9 per cent of Glasgow's land is vacant or derelict, much of it superbly located (Webster, 2000b), but investors looking for a place to build a new plant will get more generous subsidies in the new towns. We have yet to establish that companies attracted by big public grants have an obligation to help the more deprived communities in the country providing this money. There are cities in Britain where people are working with some success to build a tradition of that kind.[3]

In some places the state will have to intervene to create the jobs required. A great deal of work needs to be done to make poverty-stricken neighbourhoods safe and decent places in which to rear families, to care properly for their frailer people, to give their youngsters a good education and more challenging things to do out of school, to insulate and heat homes more effectively, to supervise parks and other public spaces and so on. Civic leaders usually know best what needs to be done, who could do the work, what training they will need and who could provide it, but they are not given encouragement to mobilize for this task. Meanwhile, for those unable to get into regular, full-time, paid work, it should be easier to take on voluntary work and part-time, temporary jobs without falling foul of the social security system.

Globalization fuels the economic drivers of the destructive changes I have described. They produce, in turn, all sorts of side-effects with feed-back loops which make things even worse. The state, central and local, and the private sector play important parts in these loops, exacerbating exclusion and the hardships suffered by our most vulnerable families. Strong and imaginative civic leadership, involving private and corporate enterprises as well as the state, will be needed if these influences are to be unscrambled and reversed. The Americans have been much more successful at gaining the help of private sector employers in urban renewal. They involve them from the start instead of seeking their help later in schemes already under way (McGregor et al., 1999). However, there are enlightened investors in Britain who do recognize that they have an interest in building social as well as financial capital. In Scotland the Cooperative Wholesale Society is helping credit unions in deprived areas, and the Bank of Scotland has made special arrangements through *The Big Issue* (the weekly publication sold by homeless people) to help homeless people open bank accounts and make down-payments for rented flats.

If civic leadership is to be effective and consistent, it has to be rooted in close consultation with the people who experience the problems to be solved. That is not only to treat them with the respect they deserve; they are also an essential source of the evidence we need to tackle these problems. I have repeatedly been told by Whitehall's government advisers to whom I have put the arguments in this chapter that 'every unemployed person lives within one hour's [sometimes it is half-an-hour's] journey by public transport from a major centre of employment' (HM Treasury, 2000). That is roughly true; but far short of the whole truth. If the government's advisers had talked frequently with people who live in our more impoverished housing estates and rural areas, they would question whether these people are likely to hear of the jobs – which are rarely advertised in job centres or newspapers – whether they could afford to travel two hours a day by public transport, and whether the total number of jobs in these centres, of the kinds accessible to unemployed people, is growing or declining.

I have focused particularly on problems of employment. The government itself starts from there, and it is right to do so. Its welcome, new-found commitment to recreate something close to full employment will compel it to recognize that there are large areas where the main problems lie on the demand, not the supply, side of the labour market. Sufficient jobs of the right kinds are not available. Governments that are no longer prepared to act as guarantors of income of last resort must instead be prepared to become guarantors of employment of last resort.

There are signs that this lesson is being learnt. The National Strategy for Neighbourhood Renewal, published by the government in April 2000, puts the reduction of 'worklessness' – an encouraging change of language – at the top of its priorities. It calls for close consultation with local communities, recognizes that their needs will vary and says there must be flexibility of policy at local levels.[4] But it will not be easy to turn around the lumbering tanker of long-established policy-thinking on these matters.

Meanwhile, we must remember that in places that have steadily lost their more employable citizens there are large numbers of elderly, disabled and sick people who cannot expect any increase in income unless social benefits are improved. Since much of their money is spent in nearby shops, pubs and other local services, their poverty impoverishes the neighbourhoods in which they live. Any government that is seriously concerned about its credibility among these people has to explain why their social benefits are so much lower than those of many neighbouring countries, and set about putting that imbalance right.

Looking back to the people of the island with whom this discussion began, it is clear that we cannot make every community as small as theirs; and we may not be able to assemble in every neighbourhood so rich a mix of skills and creativity. But we can try to ensure that everywhere people have opportunities for earning a decent living; we can improve public services in deprived neighbourhoods, and bring back to these places more of the people who have a choice about where they live. To achieve that, we shall have to go back to the origins of the destructive processes which have for so long been dividing our society and set about unravelling the mess we have created. Globalization is not simply to be welcomed as an opportunity for macro-economic growth to be supported with more deregulation for corporations with money to invest. It is also a process to be harnessed and managed so that the damages, which can so easily be made by private investment decisions, can be anticipated, avoided or at least remedied by public investment support to sustain the conditions for vibrant community life.

What conclusion should we offer the gurus? Those who call for a revival of 'community spirit' and 'family values' without considering how to recreate the economy which makes these things possible – those who call for 'layered loyalties' within a 'community of communities' (Etzioni, 1997: ch. 7) without considering whether people can find those things in a violent transit camp of the most deprived – are not listening to those who have to survive in such places. Those who write a whole book about the 'Third Way' and conclude that 'the objective of full employment, so closely tied to the welfare state, makes little sense any more' (Giddens, 1994: 177) are accepting, whether they recognize it or not, that the good society they hope to create is unattainable on their terms. Politicians who think they can transform schools by demanding more of their teachers without changing the circumstances in which their pupils are growing up will fail. So will those who think they can reduce drug abuse by 'cracking down' on the dealers. While the demand for drugs remains buoyant, competitors waiting for a chance to take over the dealers' territory are only being helped. Such policies start at the wrong end of the problem.

Meanwhile, those who talk about social exclusion of those at the bottom without considering how we may reduce the self-exclusion of those at the top are blind to fundamental factors that divide our society. Take, for example, the banking executive who embarked on closing many branches of his bank and sacking thousands of his staff. He earns £6 million a year and stands to collect a further bonus of £30 million. No doubt he will enter the House of Lords in due course and be very welcome there. A hospital cleaner who leads her tenants' association and sets up a rape crisis centre for her neigh-bourhood would be more use to them. In the global age, if exponents of 'new' politics think they can make the world a better place without upsetting powerful people, they will achieve very little.

Notes

1 This and much of the subsequent data here quoted come from Webster (2000a, 2000b) and Bailey et al. (1999).
2 Few people have explored this conflict between the interests of working women and unemployed men: Robin Marris (1996) is one of them.
3 Webster (2000b) cites Leeds and Liverpool as good examples.
4 For a useful discussion of this neighbourhood strategy, see Polly Toyn-bee's article in the *Guardian* (12 April 2000): 'Blair is now going all out to tackle the concrete jungle'.

References

Bailey, N., Turok, I. and Docherty, I. (1999) *Edinburgh and Glasgow. Contrasts in Competitiveness and Cohesion* (University of Glasgow: Department of Urban Studies).

Bell, D. A. (1993) *Communitarianism and its Critics* (Oxford: Clarendon Press).

Davies, N. (1997) *Dark Heart* (London: Chatto and Windus).

Etzioni, A. (1997) *The New Golden Rule: Community and Morality in a Democratic Society* (London: Profile Books).

Gibb, K., Kearns, A., Keoghan, M., Mackay, D. and Turok, I. (1998) *Revising the Scottish Area Deprivation Index* (Edinburgh: Scottish Office).

Giddens, A. (1994) *Beyond Left and Right. The Future of Radical Politics* (Cambridge: Polity).

HM Treasury (2000) *The Goal of Full Employment: Employment Opportunity for all Throughout Britain*, February. Cited in Webster (2000a).

Marris, R. (1996) *How to Save the Underclass* (London: Macmillan).

McGregor, A.,Glass, A., Richmond, K., Ferguson, Z. and Higgins, K. (1999) *Employer Involvement in Area Regeneration* (Bristol: Policy Press).

Piachaud, D. and Sutherland, H. (2000) *How Effective is the British Government's Attempt to Reduce Child Poverty?* CASE paper 38 (London: London School of Economics).

Ringblom, M. (1998) Dissertation for Master in Environmental Studies, University of Strathclyde.

Webster, D. (2000a) 'The Geographical Concentration of Labour-Market Disadvantage', *Oxford Review of Economic Policy*, 16(1).

Webster, D. (2000b) 'The Political Economy of Scotland's Population Decline', *Fraser of Allander Quarterly Economic Commentary*, 25(2).

Webster, D. (2000c), 'Scottish Social Inclusion Policy: A Critical Assessment', *Scottish Affairs*, 30: 32–54.

Young, M. and Halsey, A. H. (1995) *Family and Community Socialism* (London: Institute of Public Policy Research).

16

Beyond Growth: New Progressive Economic Thinking

David Dyssegaard Kallick

Since the 1990s, the debate inside the Democratic Party in the USA and the Labour Party in Britain has been old politics versus new politics – and 'new' always wins: in the UK, New Labour, and in the USA, New Democrat. But the new generation of political leadership has not been as unified as it might seem. There has been a split between, on the one side, the Clinton/Blair formula, which might be called a New Centrism, and on the other, a more grassroots-oriented, movement- and community-based politics, which could perhaps be called New Progressivism.[1]

The traditional centralized, big-government model has indeed reached the end of its road. But the path forward has a fork in it – and it may be that the 'New Democrats' of the Gore/Clinton Democratic Leadership Council and New Labour under Tony Blair's early years have not been leading us down the right path towards political modernization.

The old model of the Democratic and the Labour Party alike was built on extensive faith in the power of the national state and big business. Massive (though not yet multinational) corporations created the wealth; government smoothed out the edges by redistributing the wealth. Keynesian economic policies, protectionist trade policies and a modest social welfare state were all readily embraced.

New Centrism relies on even bigger companies, now multinational in scope, to create the country's wealth by operating in a more starkly competitive context. New Centrism's economic policies are globalization and unrestrained markets. It is worried about the inequalities being created by these 'free' markets, but not too worried as long as the GDP is growing. What's good for General Motors is good for the country, according to New Centrists and Old Democratic/Labour Parties alike.

From the perspective of New Progressivism, the extraordinary growth over the past decade of countries such as the USA and the UK must be seen together with a staggering degree of income polarization, a commercialization of culture and public spaces, a decrease in free time and a very weak sense of how to protect the environment or prevent urban sprawl. While growth, as George Burns might quip, is better than the alternative, growth in itself is not enough; it has to be growth of the kind we want – good jobs, safe and appealing products, and businesses we would welcome into our communities.

New Progressivism envisions a robust economy that allows us to consume better, not to consume more. An economy that embraces markets – but structured markets, not free markets. New Progressivism stresses a richly mixed economy; it entails some big state enterprises (postal service, railroads, utilities), and some big companies (with corresponding large unions and a government role to balance their power). But it also entails a vital ecology of community economics – a much larger portion than we have now of small businesses, locally owned farms and socially oriented enterprises, as well as a lively and healthy sector of non-profit, non-governmental organizations.

In a New Progressive economy, a good salary is important – especially at the bottom of the pay scale. But important, too, are job satisfaction, control, opportunities to advance, ability to balance work with family and a sense of contributing positively to society. New Progressivism is (or should be) attentive to issues of racial, ethnic, class, gender and regional inequalities. And it is focused on the level of the community, not just the nation. Achieving this economic vision – to use language that is becoming increasingly widespread – requires both cutting off the 'low road' and paving the 'high road' (see, for example, Chen, 2000; Krant et al., 2000; Rogers and Luria, 1999; Swinney, 1998). Macro-economic policy will not be enough – it requires reaching down into micro-economics to shut down some economic options (the low road) and to restructure the rules to benefit others (the high road).

The Role of Government

A New Progressive approach to taxation would support a vital mixed economy. The real-world limits of taxation and spending are by now fairly well established. The options do not range from 0 per cent taxation to 100 per cent taxation, as conservatives seem eager to suggest. They run from roughly 35 per cent of GDP for government expenditures (the level of the USA) to 65 per cent of GDP (the level of Sweden). Only extremists pose alternatives outside those bounds. That leaves about one-third of a nation's economy 'on the table'. A huge amount, to be sure. But it is not a choice, as conservatives like to frame it, between 'free' markets and non-free markets. It is a debate in which the options range between a mixed economy with one-third of GDP government expenditure and a mixed economy with two-thirds of GDP government expenditure.

In the USA, two big items that a New Progressive agenda might add to government's responsibilities would be healthcare and higher education. Privatization in the USA and the UK would generally be halted, and in some cases (such as the disastrous privatization of California electric utilities or Britain's railways) reversed. It is not inconceivable that some currently public responsibilities would be made private – although the role of privatization has gone so far in recent years that it is hard to see at the moment what they might be.

Where New Progressives begin to diverge more significantly from the New Centrists is around what this money is used for. In relation to an economic programme, New Progressives are not satisfied just with growth; it must be high-road growth. Investment in infrastructure or research and development, for example, would be central to a New Progressive economic agenda. Just as government investments in railroads and spaceship technology paved the way for economic development in the past, government investment in the Internet and computers are spurring economic development at the present.

New Progressives, too, stress the need to be far more conscious of getting a social return on public investment. We must make sure, for example, that the economic growth resulting from government research funds entails *good* jobs, not just more jobs. And we need to be much more strategic in thinking about what local economic development activists call a 'sectoral' strategy. Which types of research and investment will create good work and liveable communities? A research and infrastructure agenda needs to be shaped not around fear of Sputnik, as it was in the 1960s, but around concern about environmental degradation, a polarized economy and suburban sprawl – as it should be today.

A New Progressive regulatory policy would also be necessary, to put in place – and in some cases to put back – strong and decent minimum standards for salaries, worker safety and environmental protection. In the USA, as perhaps elsewhere, this entails not just higher standards, but also stricter penalties for violations, and full funding to regulatory agencies to allow them to do real monitoring. In too many instances companies violate standards knowing that they probably will not get caught, and that even if they do, the fine may be less than the cost of complying with regulations from the beginning. But a New Progressive agenda would not try to use regulations to accomplish something they cannot in practice achieve. Regulatory policy is good for establishing minimum levels of compliance. It is not good at providing an incentive for innovation for maximum levels of social benefit.

Creative Solutions: Engaging the Private Sector

Not all of a New Progressive economic programme would be about direct government action. A significant part should be about stimulating creativity in the private sector. Perhaps this sounds like archetypal conservative policy: 'freeing the power of the markets'. Not exactly. New Progressive politics will not be aimed at 'freeing' the private sector, but, rather, at structuring markets and providing support to benefit enterprises that combine making a profit with achieving social ends. Ideologically, the difference is between allowing markets to do what they will (conservative), regulating markets so they do not do too much harm (centrist and Old Democrat/ Labour) and fostering the creative enterprises that are socially responsible (New Progressive).[2] The juxtaposition is of unregulated support for multinational corporations, regulated support for multinational corporations, and support to develop an enhanced sector of community enterprise.

A New Progressive economic agenda for engaging the creative forces of entrepreneurs has not been tested at the national level, at least not in generations. But there have been substantial tests at the level of local government. Two well-known examples come to mind as the kind of government programme that could be expanded to the level of national policy. From one side of the Atlantic is the economic development policy of Chicago during the administration of that city's first black mayor, Harold Washington, in the 1980s – looked upon by many as a 'golden age' in that city. From the other side of the ocean, one might look to the Greater London Enterprise Board in the mid-1980s.

Neither London nor Chicago proposed large-scale creation of government jobs, nor did they focus on attracting big business. Instead, each undertook a serious effort to create a climate in which small businesses could start and grow, with special attention to making sure they grew in all parts of their cities, not just in the centre, and among all city populations, not just the dominant socio-economic groups. They gave support to socially beneficial industry without 'picking winners'. They fostered an expansion of a pluralistic group of businesses that broadened ownership of business in the city. And they asserted that government assistance must be linked with social obligations.

The tools tested in Chicago and London included the following:

- investing in firms, and using an ownership share as leverage over issues of social concern (environment, social exclusion, community needs), as well as supporting positive new enterprises (e.g. women- and minority-owned businesses, co-ops). These ranged from small firms of a few people to larger locally owned enterprises of 100–300 employees;
- providing aid to strategically chosen sectors of production (known among progressives as a 'sectoral strategy'). For example, in London the Greater London Enterprise Board helped set up a computer-aided design system, a showroom and training for textile industry workers – things no individual firm could afford to do (in the USA, Sustainable Milwaukee is well known for the success of its similar efforts);
- low-interest loans, and/or loans made available with smaller down payments based on sweat equity or other forms of security;
- technical support for investment in businesses owned by ethnic minorities (in tandem with support for jobs for ethnic minorities in large firms, which is where the most jobs can be found but where the owner is almost always white);
- developing property for use by small business, focused on where there was an unfilled market need (small industrial space), and requiring as a term of the lease compliance with higher than minimum standards on health and safety, wages, hours and conditions of work;
- using procurement procedures – what the government purchases

for its own use – as leverage not only to achieve cost savings but also to leverage compliance with social standards in firms;

- orienting training for workers to take into greater account the needs of workers and the social good of jobs rather than simply the stated needs of industry;
- making grants to labour groups and community organizations to provide resource centres and technical support to job-seekers and entrepreneurs.

In both cities, issues of race and ethnicity (and, in London, also gender and class) played a central role in thinking about an economic development strategy that is also designed to foster social cohesion.

At a national level, a New Progressive economic agenda would want to engage on a larger scale this type of creative entrepreneurship to expand the sector of small businesses, minority-owned enterprises and alternatives to big-box stores and multinational companies. But a national progressive programme would include action not just by the national government, but also by local governments.

Today, the problem is not just that some people do not share the benefits of our growing economy. It is that even for those doing fine, a society that is overly dominated by big corporations winds up atomizing and commodifying society and individuals, leaving even the middle classes feeling alienated.

Moving Upstream and Affecting the Context:
Civil Society

Labour unions

Polarization of income and wealth is one of the clearest economic problems of our time. There has not been a social revolution, one could argue, because over time even poor people are a little better off than they were before. But, meanwhile, income polarization is eating away at the fabric of our society.

Solutions to the problem today are generally proposed as either market solutions or state solutions. A New Progressive solution would add to these a strong role for civil society – in this case, in particular, labour unions. In order to address income polarization in countries like the USA and UK, we are going to have to move 'upstream'. No realistic amount of taxing and spending would achieve in the USA or UK the income distribution of the less polarized countries. What is needed is a way to make salaries more equal *before* taxes. And the biggest factor here will be organized labour.

Let us look at just one quick indicator. In the UK, the ratio of the top 10 per cent to the bottom 10 per cent of incomes is 4.57:1. In the USA it is 5.57:1 – the only country except Russia in the 25-nation Luxembourg Income Study to break the 5:1 ratio. In economically thriving Denmark, by contrast, it is 2.85:1 (Luxembourg Income Study, 2001). How does Denmark achieve such a low ratio of top to bottom income brackets? It's not redistribution. The most central factor is that unionization density in Denmark is upwards of 85 per cent. Wages – for all industries, and for managers as well as line workers – are all negotiated simultaneously. There is significant pressure among unions to keep the gap between top and bottom salaries relatively small. The bottom is, by international standards, quite high, and the top is relatively modest.

Unions are not without their problems – they can be bureaucratic, and they can resist needed change. But consider, too, that a big part of the problem with unions in countries such as the USA and the UK comes not from being too strong but from not being strong enough. In an archetypal instance, a labour union will oppose modernization in a factory because it will result in laying off workers. Yet, in a context of very broad unionization (and corollary government support), capital investments that modernize a workplace will in a great many instances be embraced. Unions would enthusiastically support investments in technology that can be used to improve work conditions, and to increase productivity (thus allowing for high-wage jobs). The reason unions often end up opposing – or dragging their heels on – new technology investments is that some of their members will lose good jobs paying decent wages. In a country with high union density, it is likely that they will move on to other good jobs (and, between jobs, that they will get benefits from the unions and the government). This, certainly, is how it plays out in Denmark – where it is relatively easy for employers to lay off workers, but where workers are likely to find new jobs equivalent in pay terms to their previous one.

Unions should be democratized. They should be more inclusive and more participatory. But to move from the, roughly, 5:1 ratio of the USA or UK towards something more like a 3:1 ratio will require a substantially expanded union role. A New Progressive government cannot take the initiative for unions, of course. But there is plenty government can do to strengthen labour's hand. Just as President Reagan signalled his willingness to tolerate a very hostile anti-labour environment by firing the air traffic controllers, a New Progressive government that signals its eagerness to see a revitalized role for labour could usher in a new period of union growth by being ready to embrace union initiatives that arise.

Civil society employers

In addition to civil society action (in the form of unions) to make sure corporate jobs are good jobs, it is important to recognize that civil society organizations are themselves a substantial source of employment and economic production. In a New Progressive vision, the civil society 'sector' would expand as a portion of the overall economy, creating a substantial economic space in which people work in a diverse group of mission-driven (as opposed to profit-driven) organizations.

Envisioning a society with a substantial portion of non-profit employers does not require a huge leap of the imagination. In New York City, according to the Non-profit Coordinating Committee of New York, 12 per cent of the workforce is directly employed by non-profit organizations – including hospitals, churches, arts organizations, social justice advocates and many more. Add to this union staff members, journalists, people working in cooperatives and others often considered part of 'civil society' but not part of the non-profit sector, and the existing space for mission-driven work is already quite large in at least some geographical areas.

To call them 'mission-driven' is not to romanticize civil society organizations. This is not a bland do-good sector – some of society's most controversial ideas and policies are promulgated by not-for-profit groups, and for every organization on one side of an issue there is almost always one on the other side as well. Still, taken as a whole, non-governmental not-for-profit groups are important for all the reasons de Tocqueville outlined nearly two centuries ago. They are also a buffer against the relentless expansion of market thinking into all aspects of our lives.

The role of consumers

Finally, politicians on both the Right and the Left have traditionally thought about consumers the way academic economists do – as rational actors who make narrowly economic decisions on a purely individual basis. New Progressives, by contrast, see consumers also as citizens. Nothing affects the shape of our economies more than our collective decisions about what we purchase. If we as consumers like inexpensive, mass-produced bread, there are jobs in bread factories. If we develop a taste for and are willing to spend the money on bread baked in bakeries, we create jobs for skilled bakers.

The consumption path we are on today leads to an increasingly hollowed-out economy, with a few very good jobs at the top, and a large number of low-paying, alienating, short-term and dead-end jobs at the bottom. It leads to corner grocers and local stores being driven out by big-box development, and to open space and attractive environments being ravaged by toxic dumping and poor planning. But consumers can be drawn to products made by high-road production, even if it means greater cost to them. The rising popularity of organic produce is one example. Driven by social movements and increased public education (as well as by some genuine health panics), ecological produce today is a booming field – the fastest-growing sector of the agricultural industry. This is not just good for health; it is also good for land use, good for farm workers, good for family farms – and it is driven primarily by consumer choice (and sustained with a government regulatory role).

Part of the issue of persuading consumers to support high-road production is convincing them to trade short-term for long-term benefit. Many of the higher-ticket items are less expensive in the long run – efficient washing machines that save money on water bills, vacuum cleaners that last twenty years instead of two, fluorescent light bulbs that cost more than incandescent but over the course of their lives save many times their price in reduced electricity use. All the above are not only better for consumers, but also create better jobs producing the higher-quality goods and are at the same time better for the environment.

That is not to paint a rosy picture of a win–win world. For one thing, any consumer pressure assumes that people have money enough to make reasonable choices. If you're skipping breakfast so your children can eat lunch, it is absurd to imagine paying extra for bread with a crispier crust. In addition, socially beneficial purchases will not always be cheaper in the long run. And there is the important question of externalized costs – you may save money for someone else by creating less garbage. The main point, however, is that consumers can be mobilized and educated to their long-term interest – and their interest not just as consumers, but as citizens.

New Progressives must in this regard break with a leftist tradition of underestimating the power of consumer culture.[3] Instead of asking consumers to sacrifice, we should aim to wean ourselves off immediate gratification in favour of long-term fulfilment. Our consumption strategy should be to ask people not to consume less, but to consume better. And, of course, if enough people do it, consuming better also means good jobs instead of McJobs, family farms instead of agribusiness.

Conclusion

Where do we stand in relation to a New Progressive economic policy today? There is little altogether new that needs to be invented – virtually everything described above exists in some form, somewhere. Creating a New Progressive economy is not a matter of forging a new form of production and a 'New Man' to go along with it, as was once thought would be the case for a communist economy. Rather, creating a New Progressive economy entails the slow work of building on the pieces we have, fostering new types of businesses here, increasing government there, expanding civil society all around. It requires work from all three sectors – electing a New Progressive government would surely help, but even the best government will not be able to change the economy without corollary actors in the other sectors. For this reason, New Progressives should not hope for a leader to bring this vision to fruition – we also need to build a party and a movement.

All this seems a long way from the New Democrat/New Labour forces that dominate the major progressive parties of the USA and the UK. Corporations have a tight hold on the major political parties. Wresting it from them will not be easy. Still, there are grounds for optimism. Public opinion surveys, for example, seem to indicate support for a New Progressive agenda. A recent survey in *Business Week* (see Bernstein, 2000) reported that 72 per cent of Americans think 'business has gained too much power over too many aspects of their lives'. More than 80 per cent said popular culture is overwhelmed by corporations. And these results received an approving editorial nod from the magazine. Perhaps public opinion is at last up for grabs.

Notes

1   'New Progressive' groups are generally clustered around a rather broadly defined array of left-of-centre political perspectives. I do not here speak

for them, but at the same time I do not pretend to invent the ideas or perspectives represented. What I here call New Progressivism is a synthesis in which I draw from different groups, blended with my own individual interpretations.

2 Practically speaking, it should be noted, conservatives have rarely supported actual 'free' markets, instead supporting rules that favour their preferred industries – but that's another story.

3 That is, we need to break with an ideological tradition; few leftists I know are immune to consumer culture in their personal lives.

References

Bernstein, A. (2000) 'Too Much Corporate Power?: Amid the Good Times, Citizens Feel Uneasy about Big Business. The Growing Political Issue is one that Companies Ignore at their Peril', *Business Week* (cover story), 11 September.

Chen, L. C. (2000) *Taking The High Road: Our Journey in Health Research for Development* (New York: Rockefeller Foundation).

Kraut, K., Klinger, S. and Collins, C. (2000) *Choosing the High Road: Businesses that Pay a Living Wage and Prosper* (Boston, MA: United for a Fair Economy).

Luxembourg Income Study (2001) (www.lis.ceps.lu/).

Rogers, J. and Luria, D. L. (1999) *Metro Futures: Economic Solutions for Cities and their Suburbs* (Boston: Beacon Press).

Swinney, D. (1998) *Building the Bridge to the High Road* (Chicago, IL: Center for Labor and Community Research).

17

Globalization, Exclusion and Progressive Economic Policies

Bill Jordan

It is always risky to try to prescribe progressive policies at a time when long-term shifts in the balance of power between economic forces, or in the cycles of expansion and stagnation of the global economy, are just in the process of starting. One of the key premises of this chapter is that something like this *may* (just may) be occurring at this time. If so, it is important to spell out the assumptions on which strategies and programmes are recommended.

After all, it took twenty-five years from the first oil-price shocks (1972–3) for the Labour Party in the UK to adopt a set of policies that assumed the ascendancy of capital, based on its swifter mobility in an era of globalization – longer than it took the Swedish and Austrian Social Democrats to recognize the advantages of joining the European Union; longer than the Soviet Bloc's regime of central planning endured under intensified competitive pressures; but less time than the German social state has been able to hold out against all attempts to make it more 'flexible'. And perhaps the Labour Party has transformed itself just in time to be wrong again, and the German social state has survived as an anachronism just long enough to be once more in tune with the requirements of a new age.

In all the OECD (Organization for Economic Cooperation and Development) countries, programmes of reform and retrenchment have been forced on governments by the erosion of collective institutions for protecting employment, redistributing income and providing social services (Scharpf, 1999). It was possible to establish these institutions in the postwar period because national governments were able to control their economic boundaries; levels of transnational trade were low because of the war and capital movements were limited by law. According to today's prevailing wisdom, the rapid growth in trade and the breakdown of restrictions on the free movement of capital have brought about the integration of production and markets, which undermines nation-states' capacities to manage demand and employment, raise revenue and protect living standards.

However, the least plausible forecast for the next twenty-five years is that the global strategy that has served capital so well for the past twenty-five will remain successful in its present form. After all, economic development has always proceeded in long waves of about this duration (Kondratieff, 1926), in which labour's share of national income tended to increase during sustained periods of expansion, and sink during recession or stagnation. Globalization has been a recurrent tendency in the world economy (Polanyi, 1944) rather than a continuously dominant movement. The international corporation and the accelerated transnational movement of capital were responses to a particular set of institutional constraints, and to the strength of labour movements in the developed economies. If another period of sustained growth, as a result of technological change and the restructuring of production, is now feasible, then capital might be keen to reach a new set of accommodations with national governments, or with regional authorities like the European Union.

There are already straws in the wind to suggest that a fundamental change may be brewing. The most significant of these concern inflation and interest rates, falling in both the USA and Europe, and already extremely low in Japan. Some commentators argue that this signals a shift towards a deflationary economic environment, in which new technology and competition bear down upon the prices of manufactured goods, consumers delay purchasing in the expectation of improved quality and better value, and lower returns to annuity holders require changes in saving patterns (Potter, 2001). Such an environment would require a very different strategy by capital from the one that has prevailed during the great inflation, as well as an entirely new one from governments. It would also be a potentially benign environment for steady growth (like the second half of the nineteenth century), in which labour organizations would be well placed to gain through collective action.

Already in the UK there are some indications of a shift, with recent evidence that companies previously hostile to trade unions are now reaching agreements to recognize and bargain with them. However, membership of unions as a proportion of the workforce has not grown (BBC Radio 4, 18 January 2001). This suggests that, in the short term at least, a large part of the workforce will not benefit from the changed situation, especially those involved in the growing sector of private employment in social reproduction tasks – the modern equivalent of nineteenth-century domestic servants. This is one of the issues I shall address in this chapter.

Finally, there are clear indications that skills shortages and competition for particular competencies (especially in information technology) have shifted policies on immigration control. In the UK, for example, 'economic migration' was treated as synonymous with 'bogus asylum seeking' in New Labour's early policy documents (Home Office, 1998), and in the moral panic about rising asylum applications during the summer of 1999. But the following year a remarkable turn-around occurred, with the relevant minister proclaiming:

> As with other aspects of globalization, there are potentially huge economic benefits for Britain if it is able to adapt to the new environment. We are in competition for the brightest and best talents. . . . Britain has always been a nation of migrants. . . . Many immigrants, from all over the world, have been very successful here, bringing economic benefits to Britain as a whole. . . . The evidence shows that economically driven migration can bring substantial benefits both for growth and the economy. (Roche, 2000: 2–3)

The German government has announced similar measures for easing controls on the recruitment not only of high-tech workers, but also of unskilled seasonal labour, for instance in fruit and vegetable picking, another category mentioned by the British minister. At a time when Germany still has an unemployment rate of around 10 per cent, and spends DM45 billion annually on retraining citizens for the labour market, these developments were striking, and their implications will be another theme for this chapter.

In the postwar period, large-scale movements of populations across borders (as a result of wartime displacement, resettlement of minorities and flight from Communist camps) provided supplies of labour power for the reconstruction of the European economies. Kindleberger (1967) argued that this explained Europe's rapid rate of growth, because migration from refugees, from the poorer countries of Southern Europe, and from the agricultural sector, all allowed what he described as a 'delayed Industrial Revolution', with similar growth rates to those in the UK in the middle of the nineteenth century, and in the USA in its latter part. But labour movements have been able to bring about substantial gains in their share of national income only when they achieved representation of a major portion of the working class. This, too, has important implications for the prospects of progressive policy development.

Labour Movements and the Service Economy

In the first world, advanced countries, two aspects of the future trajectory of economic development complicate progressive policies, because they diverge from previous patterns. The first is the post-industrial nature of expansion – that growth in employment is likely to be in services rather than in manufacturing. The second is that labour movements are unlikely to be able to mobilize or include the whole working class. Both these will be reviewed in this section.

It was Adam Smith who first identified the dynamic of economic development that stemmed from growth of higher-wage and higher-productivity employment in industry, drawing workers from less-productive and lower-paid agricultural work (Smith, 1776). This dynamic was still at work in the postwar growth of the European, American and Japanese economies, and formed the basis of theories of development of that era (Lewis, 1954). It could be recognized in the expansion of 'catching up' of the Newly Industrializing Countries of South-East Asia, Central and South America and the Middle East in the 1970s and '80s, and more recently in China, India and Indonesia. In global terms, it can therefore be expected to continue to provide the driving force for the improvement in the living standards of the largest populations of the world during any future period of sustained growth in the first quarter of this century.

However, the past 30 years have seen a relative (and in most cases absolute) decline in industrial employment in the advanced economies, spectacularly mirrored in the post-communist countries during the 1990s. The shift has been towards service work – a mixed bag, which includes highly paid jobs in financial and business services, the professions and IT developments, but the great bulk of which takes the form of relatively low-skilled, low-productivity work in personal and social services, such as care of elderly people, catering, retailing, cleaning, etc. (Esping-Andersen, 1990, 1996). Characteristically, this involves increased labour-market participation by women, the formalization of work previously done in the household or informal economy, and a trend towards the 'flexible' use of labour power – part-time, irregular or sub-contract employment or self-employment

(Standing, 1999). It has also led to high rates of unemployment among redundant male industrial workers (especially in Europe and the former Soviet Union).

There have been three main economic strategies addressing these issues. In the continental European countries, most clearly in Germany, the institutions of the 'social state' – minimum wages and working standards, relatively high replacement values of unemployment and disability benefits – have been sustained, and paid for out of higher social insurance contributions (Scharpf, 1999); but the expansion of service employment, especially for women, has been slower, and long-term unemployment remains high. Successive German governments of each main political grouping have preferred high expenditure on craft-orientated retraining of redundant workers to the relaxation of these 'rigidities', or the subsidization of low-paid work. In the Scandinavian countries – though more clearly in Sweden than in Denmark (Cox, 1998) – mechanisms for sustaining high employment and wages in public services more or less survived a crisis in the early 1990s (Lindbeck, 1995), though the willingness of the public to continue to pay high taxes and contributions may be precarious. Finally, in the Anglo-Saxon countries, employment in services, especially in the private sector, has been boosted by the supplementation of low and part-time wages, mainly through tax credits; but this has contributed to growing inequality among wage-earners, and a large sector of 'working poor', in the USA and New Zealand, as well as the UK. Thus, as Iversen and Wren (1998) point out, no regime has been able to achieve all three goals of expanding employment, controlling wage differentials and budgetary restraint.

In principle, the labour movements in the former two types of regime might be in a better position to take advantage of a period of sustained economic growth than those of the last-named kind. Peak organizations of trade unions are still represented in corporatist negotiations about the distribution of national income, and indeed also at the European level (Falkner, 1998). Hence, collective action by organized labour, one of the most important instruments for progressive economic policies in the postwar period, appears merely to await the shift in the balance of power with capital that would occur with such an upswing in demand for labour.

However, it is not clear that either model can readily be adapted to emerging conditions. The continental European model (and especially in Germany) rests on a culture and tradition of trade-unionism that seems ill-fitted to a service economy, and especially one with high levels of female participation. It would take a major reorientation to steer it towards the adequate representation of this sector of workers and to prioritize their interests; on the contrary, the high wages and good working conditions enjoyed by German men have rested on the exclusion of women from the labour market, and on a substantial household and informal economy of care (Esping-Andersen, 1996). Conversely, the Scandinavian model has been so firmly rooted in public services, collectively organized and financed, that it must be questionable whether this can be sustained, especially in view of some of the global changes discussed in the next section.

But an even greater problem afflicts the Anglo-Saxon model. The supplementation of low wages, mainly in the service sector, by transfers through the tax-benefit system, creates a large sector of workers whose incomes are determined by government decision rather than by collective bargaining. Employers have a strong incentive to contract for these workers on a part-time basis, to maximize their subsidy from the government; and workers, in turn, are caught in poverty traps that give them little short-term incentives to improve their earnings (Jordan et al., 2000). In other words, the institutional system created to deal with the issues of unemployment and the transition to a service economy act as barriers to the re-inclusion of a large proportion of workers in the mainstream labour movement, and could prevent the kinds of solidarity and collective action necessary to improve their relative position.

The above analysis assumes that global capital will continue to follow a strategy of locating new heavy industrial plant in countries like China, India and Brazil, while focusing more high-tech and specialized production in the advanced economies. But scope for variations on this strategy will be provided by the potential of the post-communist countries of Central Europe, and eventually of the former Soviet Union, for reindustrialization. These countries therefore have the possibility of developing new institutional forms for progressive policies, though many political factors militate against such developments – especially the tendency to undervalue the importance of their relative equality of incomes as a starting point for such policies.

Another likely tendency will be the polarization of earnings between those branches of production involving firms linked with transnational companies, and those producing goods and services purely for local markets. Obviously, many service employers will be of the latter kind. However, as I shall argue in the next section, globalization could affect them in another way.

Mobility, Exclusion and Community

The retrenchment of welfare states in the final quarter of the last century reflected their perceived vulnerability in a period when capital was highly mobile and states were required to compete for investment from international enterprises (Rhodes, 1998). This in turn led to resistance from voters to bearing the high costs of protecting vulnerable fellow citizens, with 'tax competition' limiting the fiscal scope of governments, especially in relation to their property incomes (Genschell, 1999). However, this analysis was based on the assumption that capital is necessarily more mobile than labour power, and that governments must adapt to this asymmetry. In this section I shall argue that transnational mobility of people may become a much more important issue during a period of sustained growth, and that it poses difficult challenges both for labour movements and for governments attempting to adopt progressive economic policies.

Part of the shift in political culture that has occurred during that period has been the replacement of a notion of passive social citizenship by one of active self-responsibility (Lister, 2000). The idea that collective contributions, through taxation and social insurance levies, embodied a contract for mutual restraint and a collective guarantee of protection from the adverse impact of market forces, has been challenged by one of an individual contract between the citizen and the state. Each citizen is expected to demonstrate a willingness to support him- or herself through work, and to maintain their employability by retraining (Mulgan, 1991). These ideas have been pioneered in practice under welfare-to-work schemes in the Anglo-Saxon countries, but have influenced a general shift from principles of entitlement to benefits and services to ones of 'rights and responsibilities' (Cox, 1998, 1999).

But the other side of this emphasis on the citizen as an active and autonomous individual with obligations to sustain independence is that he or she has freedom to exercise choice over welfare goods, and to improve his or her relative position by effort and mobility. Thus, at the same time as the state takes stronger powers to enforce conditions around public benefits and services, and to require reciprocal obligations or evidence of incapacity, the citizen in turn gains leverage in requiring public agencies to achieve acceptable standards. This was recognized in a UK government policy document.

Society has become more demanding. . . . Three trends highlight the rise of the demanding, sceptical, citizen-consumer. First, confidence in the institutions of government and politics has tumbled. Second, expectations of service quality and convenience have risen – as with the growth of 24-hour banking – but public services have failed to keep up with these developments; their duplication, inefficiency and unnecessary complexity should not be tolerated. Third, as incomes rise, people prefer their own homes and investments. (DSS, 1998: 18)

In this view, welfare benefits and services are conceived as private goods, with the state required to reach the quality standards and performance measures set by the commercial sector, and the public sector to compete with the private over the supply of such goods. In other words, the state must submit itself to market disciplines, and please its 'citizen-consumers' – a tendency identifiable in all countries, including the Scandinavian ones (Erikson and Weigård, 2000).

The long-term implications of these changes are striking. Already – and especially in the Anglo-Saxon countries – mobility within states is following certain clear patterns. Citizens in pursuit of 'positional advantage' (Hirsch, 1977) move to more favoured residential districts, with better public facilities (parks, libraries, recreational resources), and cluster around the best schools, health clinics and hospitals (Jordan, 1996). Through residential polarization of this kind, 'communities of choice' make up the mainstream of society, with homogeneous populations, comprising residents of similar incomes and tastes, while those unable to move remain in inner-city ghettos (Wilson, 1996) or outer-city 'sink' estates (Power, 1997).

In economic terms, this opens up the possibility, first conceived by Wicksell (1896), of sovereign individuals with full control over the supply of collective goods in their territory, voluntarily consenting to taxes imposed to supply these goods. Simply by choosing where to live, and which bundle of collective goods to pay for, the citizen votes with his or her feet (Tiebout, 1956) for a particular contribution rate and level of public services. However, this mechanism rests on freedom of exit, and the capacity of the system automatically to exclude those who cannot afford to pay the necessary contributions – poor people, consigned to 'communities of fate', with concentrations of crime and other social problems (Jordan, 1996; 1998).

If these changes have occurred spontaneously during a period when capital was dominant, it is obvious that they will be strongly reinforced when labour is in demand, and individual workers are able to market their skills across national boundaries. Already skills shortages are causing a loosening-up of immigration controls, and governments like that of Ireland, for example, are seeking the return of citizens who have emigrated and advertising to recruit workers from Central Europe. Hence, there is the prospect that a shift in the balance of power favouring labour will also strengthen the autonomy of individuals in relation to states, and allow workers to increase their strategic options for positional advantage.

But this gain would be very differentially distributed. At the top end of earnings, individuals are already highly mobile across borders, and can have jobs and houses in several countries; these options are likely to widen, to embrace a broader range of skills and occupations. But at the bottom end, those with low earning power, or with extensive responsibilities to dependent family members, would be excluded from these strategic options, and become more reliant on state benefits and services. Above all, solidarity between those with such divergent life-chances and choices would be increasingly difficult to sustain.

Indeed, greater mobility would challenge the whole conception of progressive economic policies as concerned with the distribution of roles and resources between a settled population in a bounded territory. During the last century, the notions of social justice that found expression in welfare states assumed that national economies were systems of cooperation between members, whose interdependency related to their participation in production (Hobhouse, 1922); institutional systems formalized collective relations between capital and labour, as partners with the state in decisions aimed at both efficiency and equity. In this sense, national populations were taken as 'communities of fate' whose relationships were to be managed, rather in the manner of a benevolent factory-village, such as Robert Owen's New Lanark. Instead, the possibility now arises that individuals will have the option to decide which aspects of their lives they wish to share with others, on the basis of what contributions, and for how long – more like joining a club (Buchanan, 1965; Mueller, 1989; Starrett, 1998) than taking employment in an isolated factory community. But at the same time, this presupposes a weakening of compulsory solidarities and redistributions, in favour of more instrumental and consumerist socio-economic relations, narrower mutualities and the exclusion of the most vulnerable (Jordan, 1996).

However, this leaves at least three questions unanswered. The first is the role of government, both national and transnational, in a scenario which might be labelled 'the redundancy of politics'. The second is the relationship between formal and informal activities in communities – the extent to which interdependency and sharing might transcend the consumerist basis of communities-as-clubs. The third concerns the likely strategies of poor and marginal groups faced with exclusion, and their consequences for progressive policies.

Individual Autonomy and the Public Authority

The immediate difficulty facing governments wishing to pursue progressive economic agendas is the transition from an inflationary to a deflationary global environment (Potter, 2001). As can be seen in the USA at the time of writing, and as has been evident in Japan since the early 1990s, this involves a shift towards policies for stimulating demand and investment, and represents an opportunity to rebuild the public infrastructure. However, the latter goal is in some tension with the dynamic of individualism and self-interested strategic action analysed in the previous section.

During the final quarter of the twentieth century, the whole thrust of government rhetoric, and of policies for the gradual retrenchment of public services, was in the direction of lowering expectations of the state as a provider of security and well-being and raising the requirement on individuals to plan and control their own lives. It has therefore strongly reinforced the fragmentation of societies into narrower mutualities and interdependencies, to reliance on private accumulation and commercial sources of welfare, on cars rather than public transport, and so on. Political parties have competed with each other in their zeal to encourage individual autonomy and initiative, and reduce the role of the state in economy and society – nowhere more than in the post-communist countries (Bryant and Mokzycki, 1994).

Furthermore, there are obvious difficulties in trying to repackage compulsory collectivism and the political management of such significant aspects of individuals' lives at a time when state socialism has been so comprehensively discredited, when political corruption and neglect have been blamed for threats to the environment, and when the performance of public services has come under such heavy criticism. Here again, the European countries are in a somewhat better position than the Anglo-Saxon ones, because none of these tendencies has been taken so far, but even there much evidence of unwillingness to rely on political management and public services is available. It is simply implausible to argue that individuals have an interest in surrendering some of their autonomy to a public authority that has been at such pains to emphasize the benefits of self-reliance, and when most have experienced the stimulation, as well as the anxiety, associated with a more self-directing life-style. The notion of restoring the image of society as factory, and citizen as passive beneficiary of political benevolence, carries few attractions.

Hence, what is at stake is much more likely to be a trade-off involving individual autonomy and political authority, with simul-taneous gains in both, than a simple restoration of collective prin-ciples (Jordan, 1985, 1998). Individuals are unlikely to subscribe to an extensive and costly refurbishment of the public infrastructure (including education, health and social services) unless their control over their own decisions and their choices over how to use such services are simultaneously enhanced. It is easy to see how the Third Way policies in the USA and the UK attempt such a combination, which emphasizes individual freedom and responsibility but tries at the same time to promote community and public services as political priorities (Lister, 2000). However, these examples also illustrate the pitfalls of this political strategy, as in Bill Clinton's failure to create a national health insurance scheme, and Tony Blair's travails over transport, health and education policies.

Above all, there is a danger that this political balancing act can topple over into forms of populism that merely reinforce the fragmen-tary tendencies in economy and society, rather than countering them. In the UK, the New Labour administration has been far more successful with those policies (such as welfare-to-work) in which it has followed mainstream opinions (Hills and Lelkes, 1999) than in those that have tried to lead in the direction of a unified national purpose. This reflects the fact that there are larger short-term returns for the politics of tough enforcement against unpopular groups (like unemployed people and lone parents) than for long-term measures for redistribution or economic regeneration (Jordan and Jordan, 2000).

Hence the risk that governments will consolidate their powers over criminal justice and the surveillance of those dependent on welfare benefits, rather than challenge the inequitable and divisive consequences of polarization and exclusion. An example of this is immigration policies in the UK, where reforms in the 1990s focused on limiting asylum seeking, and especially on deterrent conditions for applicants (Home Office, 1998). However, little attention was given to the fact that significant numbers of people from over the world were coming to the UK (and especially to London) as tourists or students to take up positions in the shadow economy, especially in hotels and catering, construction and textile work (Jordan and

Vogel, 1997; Düvell and Jordan, 1999). The subsequent shift of policy in favour of 'economic migration' (Roche, 2000) allows greater flexibility for the recruitment of workers from abroad, but on a temporary and conditional basis. Hence, the government gains political capital from tough enforcement against asylum seekers, but allows immigrants to be recruited as 'club servants' (Breuer et al., 1995) to meet the needs of various communities of choice. Significantly, many of those treated as priority categories for recruitment – doctors, nurses, teachers, child protection and other social workers – are for public services in areas (such as London) with very high housing costs. In other words, policy colludes with the distortions caused by mobility and the self-interested strategies of mainstream actors, rather than pursuing the long-term reform of public services.

How then might the trade-off between individual autonomy and public authority be better pursued? The scope for progressive policies may well open up through the contradictions and unintended consequences of intensified competition for positional advantage among middle-income groups (Jordan et al., 1994). An example of this comes from the field of childcare. In the UK, policy has favoured increased formal labour-market participation of all kinds, and focused on lone parents (mostly mothers) as part of its welfare-to-work strategy. One consequence of this has been to drive up the cost of childcare facilities, including the employment of nannies, now reported to be £20,000 a year, plus keep, in London (*Evening Standard*, 25 January 2001). Another has been to create inequity between households in which both partners earn, and those in which only one does. This has led to the recommendation of a 'toddler tax credit', which would go to all parents of young children, to allow them to choose between staying at home to care for their children, working part time, or paying for formal childcare (*Guardian*, 30 January 2001). This principle of funding improvements in distributional equity and in the infrastructure of services (including public services), in such a way as to increase autonomy and choice, represents an attractive alternative approach.

There are, after all, logical limits to the extent to which social reproduction work can be efficiently formalized as jobs, and households gain qualitatively from increased earnings through employment. In the UK, the attempt to improve incentives for labour-market participation ('to make work pay') is already pushing against these limits. It is far more lucrative for lone parents to claim Working Families Tax Credit for looking after each other's children and doing each other's washing on an employed basis than to claim income support for doing their own. The idea that individuals should be able to determine their best combinations of formal and informal activities, and that public services should support and sustain these choices, is in line with progressive values, and especially those espoused by Third Way politicians.

However, the scope for adopting such policies is limited by the priority of enforcing work obligations upon poor people. The idea that parents of young children, or carers for people with disabilities, or volunteers in community initiatives might opt for informal activity rather than employment is already politically feasible; the notion of poor people receiving benefits unconditionally is not. This is a legacy of the 1980s and '90s, when large sectors of low-skilled workers became trapped in the benefits system, with few incentives to take the kinds of formal work available. Hence, their best strategy was to survive on income support, but do some undeclared work for cash, or other informal activities, 'on the side' (Evason and Woods, 1995; Jordan et al., 1992). It has been precisely to counter such a strategy that welfare-to-work measures have been adopted in the Anglo-Saxon countries (DSS, 1998).

Thus it seems more likely that governments will adopt a gradualist approach towards the kinds of policies envisaged in this section. Starting from either the tax credit principle of the Anglo-Saxon countries or the more traditional social security and public assistance traditions of Europe, these could move towards a form of 'participation income' (Atkinson, 1995) for supporting these kinds of 'deserving', socially valued activities, and creating new roles, such as 'social entrepreneur', now coming into vogue in the UK (HM Treasury press release, 18 December 2000). In this way, policy could 'stumble towards' the principle of an unconditional income guarantee, or Basic Income, rather than embrace it (Jordan et al., 2000), while at the same time developing programmes for investment in public services that were complementary to, and supportive of, the kinds of informal mutual support and community development that emerged spontaneously through the choices of individuals.

Conclusions

This chapter has argued that the scope for progressive economic policies is likely to increase in the first quarter of this century, as a result of a shift in the overall global economic environment, away from inflationary pressures and the ascendancy of transnational capital. I have not attempted to deal with several issues that have preoccupied other proponents of progressive goals in recent years, because their recommendations have often been derived from assumptions about the continuation of previous directions in globalization. For example, Giddens takes as one of his basic premises that international capitalism sets very stringent limits on the potential for national states to protect their citizens from market forces; yet he simultaneously asserts the feasibility of regulating the *international* operations of capital through existing 'global governance' and 'global civil society' (1998: 140). This suggests, as Carling points out, that 'what appeared to be an uncontrollable monster from the domestic perspective stands revealed as a pussy cat on the world stage' (1999: 239). It seems implausible to argue that institutions such as the World Bank, or a hypothetical 'Economic Security Council of the United Nations' (Giddens, 1998: 151) could be transformed into instruments of progressive policy, solely on the grounds that they alone deal in global issues. The same arguments apply to those who urge the case for global institutional restraints for the sake of ecological sustainability, without specifying which political forces might make such policies stick.

Instead, I have tried to argue that there are some grounds for believing that the collective actors who have previously countered the globalizing power of capital – labour movements and states – will again enjoy more scope for doing so, and that the factors which will limit this scope have more to do with the cultural resources and transformative ideologies at present available to these actors than with the irreversibility of the logic of globalization. I have also argued that the forms of collectivism developed in the past two centuries – compulsory restraints on individual autonomy, standardizing mass solidarity and the 'magic of averages' – are unlikely to remain effective in the present one. Gains in equity and security will have to be seen to enhance autonomy and choice, not sacrifice them.

My analysis has focused particularly on probability and exclusion, because they have provided the basis for a spontaneous polarization of life-chances in the past twenty-five years, which progressive economic policies would seek to reverse. Put simply, mobile individuals have been winners, and have increased their strategic options; immobile ones have been losers, and have been excluded from the mutualities that conferred positional advantage. For winners, community has been a means of sustaining their gains by privileged access to the exclusive public goods of their enclave; for losers, it has often been the only resource for the means of survival or resistance, but the price has been high in terms of violence or conformity to enforced cultural standards (Jordan, 1996) – the 'blood and guts code' (Jordan and Jordan, 2000) of populations with little option but to use the covert 'weapons of the weak' (Scott, 1985).

This dynamic has been particularly clearly played out in post-communist Central Europe in the 1990s. Educated young people who have acquired language skills have been among the most mobile in Europe, turning up in the capital cities of the West on various forms of student exchange, as au pairs, marriage partners or simply as shadow employees in bars, cafés and factories (Düvell and Jordan, 1999). Now they stand to benefit most from the relaxation of controls on immigrant workers, and from eventual freedom of movement with access to the European Union. By contrast, the Roma (gypsy) ethnic minority, the victims of the economic transition – with unemployment rates of 100 per cent in many districts, and confined to the worst housing, as well as suffering racist violence – have provoked a whole series of new immigration controls and deportation measures in West European countries when they tried to use the asylum system to improve their situation. Their plight, as a classic 'community of fate', has demonstrated that there is no exit for an excluded underclass. Denied mobility, they must turn to mutual support and a long, slow road to democratic citizenship and the recognition of their human rights (Van der Stoel, 2000).

Central Europe will also provide a laboratory for the other dynamic of economic development, the interplay between re-industrialization (drawing on plentiful reserve supplies of labour from the former Soviet Union) and the expansion of the service sector. On the face of it, Poland is ideally placed for rapid economic growth, because of its geo-political situation, but it remains to be seen whether its labour movement and political forces can devise ways of using these advantages for progressive purposes. Without an intelligent strategy and farsighted alliances between interest groups, the Polish economy could easily become stuck in a state of underdevelopment, reflecting the requirements of West European capital rather than those of its citizens (see Wesolowski and Gawkowska, ch. 4 this volume).

Finally, there seems to me to be no economic determinism about the emerging role of nation-states and regional institutions in this period. The records of contemporary left-of-centre political regimes suggest that they are strong on the values of equality, but ineffective in their implementation. Anglo-Saxon regimes have pioneered the expansion of the service economy, but their governments are left with a role mainly focused on enforcement of work obligations on the poor, and protection of the property rights of the mainstream. European states, in turn, and the European Union itself have yet to find new solutions to the problems of differential productivity in a period when employment is polarizing between high-tech production and low-tech reproduction. As the basis for new progressive economic policies, the idea of a universal, unconditional basic income has been widely canvassed (Van Parijs, 1995; Standing, 1999; Jordan, 1985, 1998) for its potential to combine freedom and security and to universalize the rights presently enjoyed only by property-holders. Whether this idea can unite progressive forces remains to be seen. If it could, the prospect of a guaranteed minimum, set according to the national income level of each state, would perhaps allow individuals to balance the competing claims of mobility and community commitments, as well as those of productivity, earning and care.

References

Atkinson, A. B. (1995) *Public Economics in Action: The Basic Income / Flat Tax Proposal* (Oxford: Oxford University Press).

Breuer, M., Faist, T. and Jordan, B. (1995) 'Collective Action, Migration and Welfare States', *International Sociology*, 10(4): 369–86.

Bryant, C. G. A. and Mokrzycki, E. (eds) (1994) *The New Great Transformation? Change and Continuity in East-Central Europe* (London: Routledge).

Buchanan, J. M. (1965), 'An Economic Theory of Clubs', *Economica*, 32: 1–14.

Carling, A. (1999) 'New Labour's Polity: Tony Giddens and the "Third Way"', *Imprints: Journal of Analytical Socialism*, 3(3): 214–42.

Cox, R. H. (1998) 'From Safety Nets to Trampolines: Labour-Market Activation in the Netherlands and Denmark', *Governance: An International Journal of Politics and Administration*, 11(4): 397–414.

Cox, R. H. (1999) *The Consequences of Welfare Reform: How Conceptions of Social Rights are Changing* (Norman, OK: Department of Political Science, Oklahoma University).

DSS (Department of Social Security) (1998) *A New Contract for Welfare*, Cm 3805 (London: Stationery Office).

Düvell, F. and Jordan, B. (1999) 'Immigration, Asylum and Citizenship: Social Justice in a Global Context', *Imprints*, 4(1): 15–36.

Erikson, E. O. and Weigård, J. (2000) 'The End of Citizenship? New Roles Challenging the Political Order', in I. Hampsher-Monk and C. McKinnon (eds), *The Demands of Citizenship* (London: Continuum), pp. 13–34.

Esping-Anderson, G. (1990) *The Three Worlds of Welfare Capitalism* (Cambridge: Polity).

Esping-Andersen, G. (1996) *Welfare States in Transition: National Adaptations in Global Economies* (London: Sage).

Evason, E. and Woods, R. (1995) 'Poverty, Deregulation of Labour Markets and Benefit Fraud', *Social Policy and Administration*, 29(1): 40–54.

Falkner, G. (1998) *European Social Policy in the 1990s. Towards a Corporatist Policy Community* (London: Routledge).

Genschell, P. (1999) *Tax Competition and Welfare States* (Cologne: Max-Planck Institute for the Study of Societies).

Giddens, A. (1998) *The Third Way: The Renewal of Social Democracy* (Cambridge: Polity).

Hills, J. and Lelkes, O. (1999) 'Social Security, Selective Universalism and Patchwork Redistribution', in R. Jowell et al., (eds), *British Social Attitudes: 16th Report* (Aldershot: Ashgate).

Hirsch, F. (1977) *Social Limits to Growth* (London: Routledge and Kegan Paul).

Hobhouse, L. T. (1922) *The Elements of Social Justice* (London: Allen and Unwin).

Home Office (1998) *Fairer, Faster and Firmer – A Modern Approach to Immigration and Asylum*, Cm 4018 (London: Stationery Office).

Iverson, T. and Wren, A. (1998) 'Equality, Employment and Budgetary Restraint: The Trilemma of the Service Economy', *World Politics*, 50: 507–46.

Jordan, B. (1985) *The State: Authority and Autonomy* (Oxford: Blackwell).

Jordan, B. (1996), *A Theory of Poverty and Social Exclusion* (Oxford: Blackwell).

Jordan, B. (1998) *The New Politics of Welfare: Social Justice in a Global Context* (London: Sage).

Jordan, B. and Jordan, C. (2000) *Social Work and the Third Way: Tough Love as Social Policy* (London: Sage).

Jordan, B. and Vogel, D. (1997) 'Which Policies Influence Migration Decisions? A Comparative Analysis of Qualitative Interviews with Undocumented Brazilian Immigrants in London and Berlin', ZeS Aubeitspapier 14/97, Centre for Social Political Research, University of Bremen.

Jordan, B., Agulnik, P., Burbidge, D. and Duffin, S. (2000) *Stumbling Towards Basic Income: The Prospects for Tax-Benefit Integration* (London: Citizen's Income Trust).

Jordan, B., James, S., Kay, H. and Redley, M. (1992) *Trapped in Poverty? Labour-Market Decisions in Low-Income Households* (London: Routledge).

Jordan, B., Redley, M. and James, S. (1994) *Putting the Family First: Identities, Decisions, Citizenship* (London: UCL Press).

Kindleberger, C. (1967) *Europe's Postwar Growth: The Role of Labour Supply* (Cambridge, MA: Harvard University Press).

Kondratieff, N. (1926) 'Die langen Wellen der Konjunktur', *Archiv für Sozialwissenschaft und Sozialpolitik*, 56(3): 599–642.

Lewis, W. A. (1954) 'Development with Unlimited Supply of Labour', *Manchester School*, XXII: 139–91.

Lindbeck, A. (1995) 'Objectives and Strategies in the Development of the

Swedish Welfare State', paper given to Workshop on Objectives and Strategies in the Development of European Welfare States, Centre for Social Policy Research, University of Bremen, 24–5 April.

Lister, R. (2000) 'To Rio via the Third Way: New Labour's "Welfare" Reform Agenda', *Renewal*, 4(3): 9–20.

Mueller, D. I. (1989) *Public Choice II* (Cambridge: Cambridge University Press).

Mulgan, G. (1991) 'Citizenship and Responsibilities', in G. Andrews (ed.), *Citizenship* (London: Lawrence and Wishart), pp. 30–51.

Polanyi, K. (1994) *The Great Transformation: The Political and Economic Origins of Our Time* (Boston: Beacon Press).

Potter, D. (2001) 'The Spectre of Deflation', *Guardian*, 16 January.

Power, A. (1997) *Estates on the Edge: The Social Consequences of Mass Housing in Europe since 1850* (London: Routledge).

Rhodes, M. (1998) 'Globalization, Labour Markets and Welfare States: A Future of "Competitive Corporatism"?', in M. Rhodes and Y. Mény (eds), *The Future of European Welfare: A New Social Contract?* (Basingstoke: Macmillan), pp. 178–203.

Roche, B. (2000) 'Migration in a Global Economy', Speech to Institute of Public Policy Research Conference, 8 September.

Scharpf, F. W. (1999) *The Viability of Advanced Welfare States in the International Economy: Vulnerabilities and Options*, Working Paper 99-9 (Cologne: Max-Planck Institute for the Study of Societies).

Scott, J. C. (1985) *Weapons of the Weak: Everyday Forms of Peasant Resistance* (Princeton, NJ: Princeton University Press).

Smith, A. (1776) *An Inquiry into the Nature and Causes of the Wealth of Nations*, ed., R. H. Campbell and A. S. Skinner (1976) (Oxford: Clarendon Press).

Standing, G. (1999) *Global Labour Flexibility: Seeking Distributive Justice* (Basingstoke: Macmillan).

Starrett, D. A. (1988) *Foundations of Public Economics* (Cambridge: Cambridge University Press).

Tiebout, C. (1956), 'A Pure Theory of Local Expenditures', *Journal of Political Economy*, 64: 416–24.

Van der Stoel, M. (2000) *Report on the Situation of Roma and Sinti in the OSCE Area* (High Commission on National Minorities, The Hague: Organization for Security and Co-operation in Europe).

Van Parijs, P. (1995) *Real Freedom for All: What (if Anything) is Wrong with Capitalism?* (Oxford: Oxford University Press).

Wilson, W. J. (1996) *When Work Disappears: The World of the Urban Poor* (London: Vintage).

Wicksell, K. (1896) 'A New Principle of Just Taxation', in R. A. Musgrave and A. T. Peacock (eds), *Classics in the Theory of Public Finance* (London: Macmillan), pp. 72–116.

18

Navigating Through Uncharted Waters

Wim van de Donk, Ernst Hirsch Ballin and Richard Steenvoorde

Introduction

The rise of sea levels might very well threaten the survival of a significant part of the world population. The reader will understand that the Dutch in particular are anxiously following the debates. The history of The Netherlands is, to a large extent, a history of water-management: the first forms of public administration were concerned almost exclusively with the development of dikes and polders in the 'Low Lands'. *Waterschappen* (waterboards) were formed out of a very Dutch logic of collective action: locally organized, decentralized responsibilities for those directly involved, and a focus on consensus. The famous 'poldermodel' of politics has dominated most of our political history and been transferred later on to nearly all the policy domains of the Dutch welfare state.

The management of water, and not only seawater, is now an important subject on the agenda of many international summits. Rising sea levels and floods all over the world are seen as a consequence of a new problem – global warming. This is a problem that does not respect existing territorial borders and institutions. But it is not about global warming and climate change that we want to write here (although there is an interesting relationship between physical geography and political life). The necessity to manage dikes and polders has radically influenced – and democratized – the Dutch political climate from the twelfth century on (Lendering, 1988).

This chapter is about the climate change in political life: the emergence of sustained efforts to renew progressive politics – to find an effective 'Third Way' between state-focused thinking and market-driven solutions. In many of the anthologies that have been published since the concept of a Third Way was reinvented in 1992 (Halpern, 1998), much attention has been paid to the way forms of Third Way policy-making could help policy-makers and politicians in facing the dilemmas and challenges that are represented by another concept that did so well during the last decade: globalization (e.g. Giddens, 1998: 64). Much less attention has been paid, however, to the question whether and how new progressive thinking could be applied to the way we administer the global polity itself. And this is what we seek to explore in this chapter.

In the next section, we will explore some of the sources of progressive Dutch thinking. We will highlight some of the most important historical, religious and socio-economic conditions that have formed it. We will see how Anglo-American Third Way thinking is very much related to the notion of the 'Poldermodel' that many progressive politicians are keen to show as an example of best practice in administering post-welfare state economies and societies. We will discover that the poldermodel represents, indeed, a very special logic of collective action that has effectively inspired the 'social market' kind of economy that characterized most of the Western European welfare states after the Second World War.

In the 1980s and 1990s these welfare states were confronted with a sharp change in the economic climate: state budgets were increasingly out of control, unemployment levels were rising high and effectively weakening and hollowing out the 'dikes' that had been built in social security and welfare arrangements. In the third section, we will see how these changing tides were, in hindsight, only the first waves of a more fundamental change in the position of nation-states. The nation-state can be described as a territorially defined 'scale of action' (the territorial or administrative dimension). But the state is also a legal and political institution, a 'pair of scales' (the democratic, legal and political dimension), in which values are deliberated and weighed in order to provide a basis for common action. States are now confronted with developments that hollow out one of the major pillars of their sovereignty: territory. The ever-stronger internationalization of economical activities, encouraged by the use of modern information and communication technologies (challenging existing economies of scale) are challenging the existing political institutions and the legal structures that were shaped to serve the national political communities. Collective and political action at the level of these communities is not likely to disappear, but it is clear that most of the political issues that emerge at the beginning of the third millennium go far beyond the abilities of national political communities. Most of the problems that are now threatening our ability to survive are doing so not just at a local, or at a national, but at a global level. 'Dikes' have to be thought of globally, not locally. Most of the key issues that shape the political agendas of the new millennium are, explicitly and unavoidably, of a borderless and global nature. These agendas demand innovations regarding both the territorial and administrative dimensions as well as democratic and political ones.

In the fourth section we will see how quickly the global community is developing various patterns of (largely informal and non-governmental) political behaviour which precede and provoke the formation and/or rearrangement of global political institutions that can perform the democratic functions that were earlier more or less exclusively located at the level of the nation-states. From now on, nation-states have to share this new global public space with a huge variety of citizens' movements and all kinds of more or less specialized non-profit organizations or non-governmental organizations (NGOs) which have discovered the global level as an important level for decision-making. In the fifth section, we will briefly explore the role of these social movements and NGOs with regard to the role of the World Trade Organization (WTO). We will see how these movements are broadening up the democratic polity, by explicitly claiming their role in processes of governance and accountability.

We conclude this chapter by stating that this situation must not be seen as an intermediate state of affairs, and that, in the end, we will only have one global government and one global market. We will have to navigate through the uncharted waters of the present and the future. We think that we can expect the development of a network model of global governance, in which third-sector organizations and social movements will remain as important as they have been in the Dutch polder. We explore some of the conditions that can explain why this has been the case until now, and investigate to what extent these conditions could also shape a kind of global polder: a safe and democratic polity that protects its inhabitants equally from external threats by means of involving them all as responsible citizens.

Polders, Dikes and a Third Way: Sources of Dutch Progressive Politics

In order to understand the origins of progressive Dutch politics, we have to look at the geo-physical and political history of The Netherlands. In the old days the common enemy was not the global warming of the oceans, but the descending soils and the force of the North Sea and some great interior lakes. In order to survive, land needed to be reclaimed from the water. These nether-lands ('nether' being cognate with the Dutch *neder*, meaning 'below', 'under') were formed by building a dike around a lake, descending soils or a part of the sea. On this dike windmills were placed to pump the water out.[1] The land emerging from that is called a 'polder'. Managing the joint effort required to carry out this enormous task thus became known as the 'poldermodel'. Polders were neither commercial, nor state-owned: they were initiated and managed by special boards, elected by all those who were involved and committed to work together in order to exploit and protect the land. *Wie het water deert, die het water keert* (all those threatened by the water are responsible for averting that threat): it was very clear that it was not only those who lived near the dikes who could be held responsible for maintaining them.

It is very interesting to see how, in administrative theory, the existence of these successful institutions has to be explained in relation to the background of theories that would have predicted 'institutional failure' and collective non-action. Polders are an example of a general interest for which, especially once it is realized, the 'rational' citizen would very much like to see others pay, opting themselves for the free-rider's position. Still, the tragedy of the commons did not arise, nor were the two ideal-type solutions to overcome such a tragedy (political centralization or an economic individualization by means of privatization of the interests involved) a viable option. Eleanor Ostrom has shown convincingly that there is a third way between state and market-oriented solutions to this dilemma, which also explains why the management of Dutch polders has not been another example of institutional failure. She mentions three conditions that effectively challenge the predictions of institutional failure (1990: 40–5; also see Raadschelders and Toonen, 1993). Such a failure can be diverted when three pre-institutional conditions are successfully met: there must be a consensus about the way in which people will work together, based on mutual understanding and trust; there must be a credible form of commitment; and there must be a reliable arrangement for mutual supervision. Raadschelders and Toonen (1993) talk about these waterboards as a 'third way' of organizing.

The poldermodel does not only have geographic origins. It originated in a predominantly Calvinistic society that favoured private initiative and a limited role of the state. Municipal waterboards and local polder councils, consisting of the inhabitants of a specific polder, shared the responsibility of maintaining the land. A commonly shared responsibility became the first form of local governance, and governmental institutions were prepared to uphold these boards. The dominant role of Calvinistic (and later, from 1900, also the Roman Catholic) tradition was important for a political system that has, most of the time, favoured pluralism and decentralization. The fact that this political culture was seen as an important incentive for a flourishing economy also has to be kept in mind. The first political coalitions in The Netherlands after World War II were formed between the Catholic and the Social Democratic Parties. They were mainly responsible for the introduction of the Dutch version of the welfare state. The principles of solidarity and (vertical) subsidiarity became very important in the legislation that shaped the welfare state. However, in the 1970s and 1980s, state bureaucracy overwhelmed many of the NGOs and other private initiatives in the field of welfare, healthcare, housing and education. Although The Netherlands have the biggest non-profit sector in the world, it is also clear that what were initially started as private initiatives have, for the greater part, become funded with government subsidies. This situation was harmful to private initiatives and to the responsibility of societal actors because of an excessive centralization and state regulation.

In 1990 The Netherlands again faced a tidal wave and 'descending soils': unemployment figures and the national debt were rising enormously. And again the Dutch flocked together – in this case the national government, the employers and the workers' unions – to discuss the best way jointly to counter this flood. It became the Wassenaar Agreement, in which drastic cuts in the national policy of disability allowances were made. This twentieth-century version of the poldermodel has become one of the favourite models of a progressive kind of Third Way politics. It could be sharply contrasted with the Thatcherite kind of policies that were mainly aimed at a reinforcement of markets; it was not so much about reinventing government but much more about rediscovering old principles of governance that had been so successful in Dutch society. The role of the state was reconsidered seriously and much was done to recover some of the conditions that were, in earlier times, important for societal responses to government and market failures.

The Ship of State in Heavy Waters: Progressive Politics beyond the State

In this section, we will address the question of how any Third Way approach to the renewal of progressive politics may relate to changes in the role of the state. Third Way politics is often positioned as a reinvention of social democracy, involving self-steering systems in an intelligent manner. But some critics have claimed that the Third Way is more akin to neo-liberalism with a human face: it accepts the primacy of a free market in the distribution of services, including many so-called public goods, while maintaining some basic guarantees for those citizens with less purchasing power. In our opinion, the strengths and weaknesses of Third Way ideas can best be analysed starting from the actual position of state and government.

The striking point is not so much that politicians can either promote or reduce the role of the state – the traditional difference between 'left' and 'right' (Giddens, 1994) – but that the 'sovereign' state has to compete with a variety of other forces. All politicians have to cope with the changed relations between state and economic realities across borders. Many observers have already noted the remarkable policy continuity in The Netherlands, Germany and Belgium since social democratic or liberal-led governments took over from their Christian democrat predecessors. The main reason why New Labour coming to power in Britain marked a sharper difference than the political changes on the continent was the radical style of modernization by the preceding government of Margaret Thatcher. The specific form of conservatism known as Thatcherism – certainly not typical for all conservatives – amounted to a capitulation rather than an adaptation to the changes in the role of the state. Contrary to common belief, she confronted the partners in the European Union (EU) not with an idle attempt to restore the United Kingdom's insuperable sovereign powers, but with a fundamentalist free-market approach to globalization (Giddens, 1998: 8). Her model for the EU was not a political union, but a NAFTA-style free-trade association.

The need to adapt the role of the state goes back to a change in the very concept of the national state: an entity that could be useful when territoriality was the primary framework, but not in our times of interconnectedness across borders. Social relations in the global era cannot be confined to distinct territories. In trade, culture, communications and crime, the significance of state borders is fading away, although the political and legal structures have not been abolished. No state on earth is at present in a position to secure complete control over some of the most important public functions, including combating crime, prevention of environmental pollution, poverty reduction and fair trade. The necessity of cross-border cooperation through international organizations dissolves the historic congruity of state, law and society.

At first sight, the EU substitutes the territoriality of the single nation-state for its own extensive territoriality. The legal and political form of cooperation in the framework of the EU however is not of the kind that will replace the statehood of the member states and reduce them to mere segments of a new state. Recent history has demonstrated the impossibility of a mere upgrading to a larger political unity, composed of merged states. The emerging constitutional structure of the EU does not show a hierarchical relation with the constitutions of the member states, but rather a network relation including hierarchical and cooperative elements. The EU is a part of an historically new kind of redistribution of sovereignty, on the basis of functional needs rather than territorial domination. Tilman Evers (1997, 1998) rightly argues that the EU differs from the multinational empires such as the Habsburg Monarchy and the Ottoman Empire. The profoundly democratic character of the European societies rests on the principles of shared powers, accountability and subsidiarity. Transnational forms of cooperation must have a bottom-up character. If the EU were able to overcome nationalistic remnants, it could serve as a model experiment for future political organization across borders. Within and beyond the territory, we can observe the usual degree of differentiation. Since the Treaty of Maastricht, it has been accepted that some member states engage in more far-reaching forms of cooperation (European Monetary Union, Social Chapter) than others.

The development of 'an ever closer union between the peoples of Europe' (the preamble of the Treaty establishing the European Community) responds to the need for public law and political frameworks. Notwithstanding the manifold state-like structures of the EU, many international institutions have a different decision-making procedure, primarily based on negotiated agreement. Normative political theories are biased towards democratic majority decisions, and often fail to respect the characteristic legitimacy of negotiated solutions in public law (Scharpf, 1998: 235). But even someone who accepts the legitimacy of negotiated transnational decision-making has to admit that the institutions of the EU and the WTO are unable to regulate the forces of globalization in economic life, e.g. the location factor competence or genetic modification in agriculture (ibid. 241). According to the Catholic bishops of England and Wales, democracy 'requires more than universal suffrage: it requires the presence of a system of common values' (Vallely, 1998: 14). The absence of such a system of common values appears to be the most relevant explanation for the aforesaid shortcomings.

The ongoing development of a body of substantive international law (Secretary-General UN, 1999) suggests that legal principles and political values are gaining in significance across borders and cultures. In as far as this development meets the growing practical need for transnational legal development, new centres of law-making may have the chance to grow. The work on a Charter of Fundamental Rights of the European Union is not only an attempt to contain the EU where its powers might affect the freedoms of European citizens, but will also guide the direction in which the EU should go forward.

James Goodman (1998: 331) concluded that where transnational networks, regulation systems and other forms of governance outside the scope of the state become more and more important, the nation-state can no longer exclusively incorporate democratic political life. The adaptation of national politics to the changed realities of a globalizing world has a negative and a positive side. The negative side is the need to take away inherited structures that have led to inflexibility in government expenditure and labour markets: phenomena that characterized the first debates about the role of the state in the 1980s and 1990s. The positive side is the desirability of support for non-governmental forms of solidarity and cohesion: phenomena that reveal the more fundamental challenges for the new century. Sometimes devolution of powers to regional and local levels can do better than the state-level structures, but the most important positive force results from the self-organizing capacities of societal initiatives (such as inter-governmental organizations). This seems also to be true at the transnational levels of decision-making that are now developed, and to which we will turn in the final section of this chapter. Before we prepare that section with a short exploration of the role that international NGOs play in these processes of 'horizontal subsidiarity' (Reinicke, 1998), we will take a look at the necessity of a fundamental reconsideration of normative democratic theories. It is striking to see that democratic theory lags behind the changes that have affected one of the major actors in the democratic arena: state bureaucracies. That does not only refer to the internal changes (see John Stewart, ch. 11 this volume), but also to the changes in its external and international position. When we are so busy reinventing governments, we cannot do so without reinventing democracies as well.

Reinventing Democracy

What strikes a participant in the public debate in The Netherlands is the similarity between the search for societal solidarity in Anglo-American Third Way politics and the so-called Dutch poldermodel, although the poldermodel goes back to the needs of society, where social democracy traditionally regarded the state as the steering point. Rendering to the state as the primary public framework is, however justified, not unproblematic. Political democracy offers a decision-making process that is essentially more than majority rule. The democratic procedure therefore does not 'exhaust' the democratic principle in view of the underlying political ethics. Democracy has a dimension of 'will' and of 'reason': the free will of the majority should express itself through majority decisions on the election or – at least indirectly – the appointment of representatives (and in some systems, to some extent through direct voting on major policy issues); once elected or appointed, officials are not entitled to express their will in a legally binding way 'at pleasure', but only after investigation, hearing and giving reasons. Doing so, democracy channels ethical discourse into law-making.

Different forms of democracy are needed in this era of border-crossing relationships and globalization. The relative weight of 'reason', i.e. reasonable ethical discourse, compared to that of (democratic) 'will', has to be increased. The EU, for example, has been hailed as a model of transnational decision-making (Schwengel, 1999), but the kind of democracy that operates in the EU cannot be identical to that at work in the national state.[2] In order to counterbalance shortfalls of democratic legitimacy at the European level, other forms of involvement of interest groups, as well as multiple ramifications with national politics, have been developed. In other alternatives to traditional democracy, we can also observe the understandable need to intensify the socio-ethical discourse in order to compensate the unavailability of democratically legitimate majority decision-making. In the idea of a new humanism, 'in the sense – primarily – that culture corresponds to the human person' (as Pope John Paul II termed it in his address to university teachers, Rome, 9

September 2000), one can discern an attempt to break ground for a worldwide moral dialogue concerning use and abuse of the potential set out by the developments in economy, science and technology on the threshold of a new century: following centuries of French, British and American predominance, the first century of the third millennium appears to be marked by global interdependence. Globalization and a renaissance of civil society and regional culture are two sides of the same coin. The 'civil society project' involves, for example in countries formerly under communist rule, 'the need (1) to decentralize the state so that there are more opportunities to take responsibility for (some of) its activities; (2) to socialize the economy so that there is a greater diversity of market agents, communal as well as private; and (3) to pluralize and domesticate nationalism, on the religious model, so that there can be different ways to realize and sustain historical identities' (Walzer, 1998: 25–6).

One of the virtues of the nation-state was its ability to establish the politicization of the social-ethical discourse on the solid foundation of shared culture and value systems. Decision-making after the decline of the national state will run into double trouble if the necessarily smaller role of majority 'will' cannot be compensated with growing legitimacy through intensification of the social-ethical discourse, i.e. the role of 'reason'. Progressive kinds of Third Way politics include a good deal of pragmatism. That may be helpful in building a consensus for institutional reforms in an outdated bureaucratic organization of public services and rigidity in the labour market. If politics for the twenty-first century proves unable to settle in the new forms of democracy, the withdrawal of old-fashioned social democracy could be in danger of setting free an ethos of 'anything goes'. In regard to the development of genetic engineering, New Labour takes the same free-market approach as former Prime Minister Thatcher once took towards aviation. The WTO for itself is unable to respond to such assignments. That is why politics, after the state-centred twentieth century, should establish an intense new relationship with regional entities, societal organizations, including those of ethnic minorities, and religious communities. New media offer formerly unknown vehicles for enhancing this social-ethical discourse, also at the level of the global community (Reinicke, 1998; Van de Donk and Foederer, 2000; *The Economist*, 2000).

Warming up Global Waters: Transnational Explorations of Progressive Politics

The city of Seattle, on the shores of Lake Washington, is named after an Indian Chief who advocated peace between the native Americans and the colonists. Even he could not have imagined that the town bearing his name would one day become famous for the 'Battle of Seattle', the clash between international NGOs and the negotiators for worldwide free trade during the early days of December 1999. While the delegates wondered what sin the WTO had committed, more than 100,000 protestors marched against the WTO in the streets of Seattle (Lamy, 1999). The protestors came from all walks of life and were united in their passionate belief that the ideology of free trade and consumerism had to be countered by an appeal for other values. In their perception, the WTO was an organization in which the multinationals had the final say and in which economics would always prevail over other concerns. The people in the streets were exponents of a broad spectrum of civil apprehension caused by the rapid and intangible changes that result from the process of globalization (Quaedvlieg, 2000: 69). It is understandable that the protestors did not applaud the statements of economists and WTO officials which said that the WTO was to become the role model of a world government. The protestors' call for more transparency should be understood as the wish that the delegates would take a broader look at the issues they were discussing because WTO decisions are exceeding the scope in which they are presented: as trade issues. The protesters were the representatives of an ever-growing concern that is brought to the fore by international NGOs that are working in the field of, for example, biotechnological developments, animals, food and nature.

Inside the heavily protected building the WTO delegates held to the position that they were an economic forum, a forum not suited to develop treaties on other issues. The delegates argued that free trade would be the best way to bring sustainable improvement. In their view, the WTO is a democratic institution, because the representatives are elected members of national parliaments or appointed by elected presidents. According to some delegates, consumer concerns were misused for ordinary protectionism (see also Reinicke, 1998). The delegates could not understand the double message the protestors were sending: on the one hand, they wanted to 'blow up' the WTO, and, on the other hand, to have the WTO establish a host of global rules to dictate social, economic, political and environmental conditions around the world (Zoellick, 1999: E16).

The WTO is right when it states that there is a strong argument that economic, social and political freedom is a basic prerequisite for development. But if the organization increasingly takes over tasks with worldwide consequences, it should also accept the fact that the world will want to be involved in the formation of its policies. This means a process of governance in which civil society will systematically be involved in the debate and its conclusions. This process has been called 'new governance'. New governance refers to the capability to realize societal values at a global level without legal pressure and without the law-enforcing institutions of the state. These round tables of reflection between governments, multinationals and NGOs will help to develop a broader understanding between the participants, and enable them to decide what they will have to do themselves in order to realize these values (Lubbers, 2000: 65). This does not mean that there will be no new protests. The protests are part of a Western demonstration of democracy, and their very existence prevents worse forms of uprising (Van Aelst, 2000: 77).

There are still some counter-reactions to the new kinds of involvement and participation that are sought by international NGOs. Especially in WTO circles, there is a longing for less civil society and stronger national governments. WTO Director General Mike Moore made this clear in a recent speech to the Committee on Development and Cooperation of the European Parliament in Brussels:

> Our agreements must be agreed by governments and ratified by Parliaments. We all need to be more accountable. Parliaments and Congresses sustain governments. Public opinion sustains governments. Elected representatives are the main expression of civil society. Their support is measured, they are accountable, they need to be more involved. (WTO, 2000)

This reaction against international civil society can also be found in the proposal by British Prime Minister Blair for the development of a doctrine of international community. In his speech to the Global Ethics Foundation at Tübingen University, Germany, he told his audience that the correct response to globalization could be found in the development of a doctrine 'based on the principle of enlightened self-interest. As within countries, so between countries. A community based on the equal worth of all, on the foundation of mutual rights and mutual responsibilities' (Blair, 2000). Again, countries and communities are mentioned, but there seems to be no place and role for independent civil society.

Navigating Through Uncharted Waters

Here we want to draw attention to a shortcoming of those who think that progressive agendas can only be pursued by progressing the role of the state. Adapting to more assertive roles of societal actors is not the same as recognizing and accepting their primary responsibility. Philip Selznick rightly stresses this principle of communitarianism and, more specifically, communal democracy: 'the primacy of the community over the state' (1998: 129; see also Selznick, ch. 5 this volume). It is here where we can identify a difference between contemporary Third Way politics and the moderate social reform policies of Christian democratic parties in postwar Western European politics, which, as a matter of fact, have so much in common (Giddens, 2000: 18). The latter were better at involving non-political organizations, but New Labour had more success – at least in its first years – in finding the right tone in a postmodern culture.

The Dutch poldermodel became successful because there was a consensus in society over the organization of cooperation: participants made credible commitments and were willing to work within a system of reciprocal community supervision. Today, we are faced with the fact that there is no consensus over the scale and organization of cooperation. It is not at all clear, as the NGOs point out, whether states and multinationals are making credible commitments. How can they, when there are thousands of people protesting in the streets of Seattle or Prague? And, finally, there is no consensus over a common system of reciprocal control. We do not favour the formation of a world government as the definitive scale of corporation. However, the active involvement of civil society at the global level should be nourished, rather than condemned. Civil society provides the necessary counterbalance to the global ambitions of nation-states and multinationals.

Amitai Etzioni (2000: 57) suggests that a moral dialogue and a 'counterculture' are needed in order to nourish globalization with the ideal of a 'good society'. The good society understands that ever-increasing levels of material goods are not a reliable source of human well-being and contentment, let alone of a morally sound society. Third Way politics has not yet fully taken into account that the democratic process of the national state cannot harbour the social-ethical discourse that is involved in transboundary legal development. Without the idealism of a new humanism, a mere shift from a state-centred politics would not help us navigate in a new world. Instead, we would run the risk of being stranded on an uncharted sandbank before reaching the open seas. Transnational infrastructures and networks in both the intergovernmental and business communities have to accommodate and integrate the democratic role played by NGOs. Reinicke rightfully sets out a strategy of horizontal subsidiarity, a kind of democratic innovation that seeks the same improvements as the vertical variant by 'delegating, or "outsourcing", part, but not all, of public policy-making to non-state actors: for example, to businesses and their associations, labor groups, nongovernmental and nonprofit organizations, consumer groups, foundations, and other interested parties of a combination thereof' (1998: 89). He sees an important role for these actors and arrangements in the challenge that lies ahead of us: the matching of economic and political geographies. To follow this line, we are very much navigating in uncharted waters. The Dutch experiences with dikes and water-management go back as far as the beginning of the second millennium. We think, however, that some of these experiences might very well be serving as a kind of compass that could help us to set sail for a global community that is more than a global market.

As Ostrom has set out for the locally operating waterboards, institutional failure of arrangements that go beyond statist or market-like solutions for administering the global polity might very well be diverted when we succeed in the design of arrangements that respect some of the conditions that formulate the ambitions in terms of governance more than in terms of government. When we succeed in defining the 'democratic deficit' of the global arena in a way that goes beyond the concepts of democracy that were developed to democratize the nation-state, we might very well be able to see the important role NGOs and others can play in administering the global community. We should talk more in terms of infrastructures than of structures, then, and try to foster and respect the conditions that were so important for the success of the Dutch waterboards: (i) a consensus about how to design and maintain the arrangements for administering the common good; (ii) a genuine commitment of the actors involved on the basis of an enlightened and mutually trusted belief to belong to a community that shares a common destiny; and (iii) a reliable kind of mutual inspection and transparent form of control that prevents individual actors from choosing the free-rider or 'exit' option. It is especially important to note that these forms of inspection and control are not left in the hands of statist actors only.

This is a demanding course, not only for governments, but also for NGOs and the international business community, which have to accept that their involvement will go far beyond the agenda-setting arenas and negotiation stage of global public policies.

Notes

1   The first windmill was erected in 1408 in Alkmaar, a private initiative by Jan Grietenzoon and Lord Floris van Alkemade. The idea of a windmill (already used for corn) was an Arabic one, imported into medieval cities by crusaders. See Lendering, 1998.
2   'The clearest example of the coming new order is the European Union. This is neither a union of nation-states nor an embryonic superstate. It can only be understood as a new species of governance' (Mulgan, 1997: 228).

References

Beck, U. (ed.) (1998) *Politik der Globalisierung* (Frankfurt am Main: Suhrkamp).
Blair, T. (2000) 'Values and the Power of Community', Prime Minister's Speech to the Global Ethics Foundation, Tubingen University, Germany. (http://www.number-10.gov.uk/news) under speeches 30 June 2000.
Etzioni, A. (2000) *The Third Way to a Good Society* (London: Demos).
Evers, T. (1997) 'Auf dem Weg zum postmodernen Imperium, Im Zeitalter der Globalisierung löst sich das Prinzip der Souveränität auf, und vergangenes kehrt zurück', *Frankfurter Allgemeine Zeitung*, 1 October: 12.
Evers, T. (1998) 'Wiederkehr der Reiche oder transnationale Demokratie?', in Hans-Lilje Stiftung (reissued), *Zeitenwende – Wendezeiten, Auf dem Weg in das 21. Jahrhundert* (Hanover: Lutherisches Verlagshaus).
Giddens, A. (1994) *Beyond Left and Right. The Future of Radical Politics* (Cambridge: Polity).
Giddens, A. (1998) *The Third Way. The Renewal of Social Democracy* (Cambridge: Polity).
Giddens, A. (2000) *The Third Way and its Critics* (Cambridge: Polity).
Goodman, J. (1998) 'Die Europäische Union: Neue Demokratieformen jenseits des Nationalstaates', in U. Beck, *Politik der Globalisierung* (Frankfurt am Main: Suhrkamp).
Halpern, D. (1998) *The Third Way. Summary of the Nexus On-line Discussion* (London: Nexus).
Lamy, P. (1999) Speech at the third session of the ministerial conference: WT/MIN/(99)/ST/3.
Lendering, J. (1998) *Hollands Glorie. De wortels van onze overlegcultuur*

(Holland's Glory. The roots of our consensus-culture) (Den Haag: Bureau Interim).

Lubbers, R. F. M. (2000) 'Seattle, tussen economisering en burgersamenleving', *International Spectator*, 54(2).

Mulgan, G. (1997) *Connexity, How to Live in a Connected World* (Boston: Harvard Business School Press).

Ostrom, E. (1990) *Governing the Commons. The Evolution of Institutions for Collective Action* (Cambridge: Cambridge University Press).

Quaedvlieg, W. L. E. (2000) 'Wat te doen met de scherven van Seattle?' *International Spectator*, 54(2).

Raadschelders, J. C. N. and Toonen, A. J. (eds) (1993) *Waterschappen in Nederland: een bestuurskundige verkenning van de institutionele ontwikkeling* (Hilversum: Verloren).

Reinicke, W. H. (1998) *Global Public Policy. Governing without Goverment?* (Washington, DC: Brookings Institution Press).

Scharpf, F. W. (1998) 'Demokratie in der transnationalen Politik', in U. Beck, *Politik der Globalisierung* (Frankfurt am Main: Suhrkamp).

Schwengel, H. (1999) *Globalisierung mit europäischem Gesicht, Der Kampf um die politische Form der Zukunft* (Berlin: Aufbau-Verlag).

Secretary General UN (1999) The Report of the Secretary-General of the United Nations on the United Nations Decade of International Law, 21 September(A/54/362).

Selznick, P. (1998) 'From Socialism to Communitarianism', in M. Walzer (ed.), *Toward a Global Civil Society* (Providence, RI, and Oxford: Berghahn Books).

The Economist (2000) 'Anti-Capitalist Protests, Angry and Effective', 23 September.

Vallely, P. (ed.) (1998) *The New Politics. Catholic Social Teaching for the Twenty-First Century* (London: SCM Press).

Van de Donk, W. B. H. J. and Foederer, B. (2000) 'E-movements or Emotions? ICTs and Social Movements: Blocking the Electronic Highway?' Paper presented to the XIVth meeting of the permanent study group on informatization in Public Administration of the European Group for Public Administration, Glasgow, August.

Van Aelst, P. (2000) 'The Battle of Seattle. Over de (internationale) democratie op straat', *International Spectator*, 54(2).

Van Creveld, M. (1999) *The Rise and Decline of the State* (Cambridge: Cambridge University Press).

Walzer, M. (ed.) (1998) *Toward a Global Civil Society* (Providence, RI, and Oxford: Berghahn Books).

WTO (2000) 'DG Calls for Closer Parliamentary Involvement in WTO Matters', press release 169, 21 February.

Zoellick, R. B. (1999) 'Clinton's Seattle Straddle', *Washington Post*, 14 December.

Further Reading

Hirsch Ballin, E. and Steenvoorde, R. A. J. (2000) 'Catholic Social Thought on Citizenship: No Place for Exclusion', in W. Derkse, J. van der Lans and S. Waanders (eds), *In Quest for Humanity in a Globalising World. Dutch Contributions to the Jubilee of Universities in Rome 2000* (Leende: Uitgeverij DAMON).

Van Creveld, M. (1999) *The Rise and Decline of the State* (Cambridge: Cambridge University Press).

Veneziani, M. (1999) *Comunitari o liberal, La prossima alternativa?* (Roma and Bari: Laterza).

Index